Praise for *Whitey on Trial*

"For a quarter century, Whitey Bulger terrorized the city of Boston and corrupted even the FBI agents charged with bringing him down. In this meticulous, day-by-day account of Whitey's final reckoning, Margaret McLean and Jon Leiberman vividly capture the drama of a major criminal trial and the downfall of one of America's most notorious gangsters. Like the best true-crime writing, it reads like fiction. Utterly riveting." —William Landay, *New York Times* bestselling author of *Defending Jacob*

"Fans of the Law & Order programs should turn off their television sets and unsheathe this book. . . . Like a good suspense novel, this real-life drama will dazzle you with its ability to make you feel for all the characters in it." —*Bookreporter*

"*Whitey on Trial,* cinematic in scope and presentation, brings to life the intense and complex experiences of the 'stage and battleground' of criminal prosecution. I was hooked from the opening paragraphs. If you read the headlines and think you understood this case, think again. This is a must-read." —Dr. Drew Pinsky, host of *Dr. Drew on Call, Loveline,* and *Celebrity Rehab*

"Leiberman helped me hunt Whitey for years with passion for all of his victims. This book is truly an inside and compelling view of a legendary trial. McLean and Leiberman have written a must-read for true crime lovers." —John Walsh, creator and host of *America's Most Wanted*

"Jon Leiberman is one of America's top investigative journalists. He and Margaret McLean have formed an incredible team—relentlessly searching for the truth in this case. You will be stunned by what they've learned. A can't-put-it-down, real-life thriller." —Jane Velez-Mitchell, HLN host

Whitey on Trial

SECRETS, CORRUPTION, AND THE SEARCH FOR TRUTH

MARGARET McLEAN
AND JON LEIBERMAN

A Tom Doherty Associates Book
New York

WHITEY ON TRIAL: SECRETS, CORRUPTION, AND THE SEARCH FOR TRUTH

Copyright © 2014 by Margaret McLean and Jon Leiberman

A Forge Book
Published by Tom Doherty Associates, LLC
175 Fifth Avenue
New York, NY 10010

www.tor-forge.com

Forge® is a registered trademark of Tom Doherty Associates, LLC.

The Library of Congress has cataloged the hardcover edition as follows:

McLean, Margaret, 1966–
    Whitey on trial : secrets, corruption, and the search for truth / Margaret McLean and
Jon Leiberman.—1st ed.
        p. cm.
    "A Tom Doherty Associates book."
    Includes bibliographical references.
    ISBN 978-0-7653-3776-4 (hardcover)
    ISBN 978-1-4668-3575-7 (e-book)
    1. Bulger, Whitey, 1929– —Trials, litigation, etc.   2. Gangsters—Massachusetts—Boston.
3. Organized crime—Massachusetts—Boston.   4. Racketeering—Massachusetts—Boston.
5. Trials (Murder)—Massachusetts—Boston.   I. Title.   II. Leiberman, Jon.
    KF225.B85 M35 2014
    345'.07

                                                                            2013417772

ISBN 978-0-7653-3777-1 (trade paperback)

Forge books may be purchased for educational, business, or promotional use.
For information on bulk purchases, please contact the Macmillan Corporate and
Premium Sales Department at 1-800-221-7945, extension 5442, or write to
specialmarkets@macmillan.com.

First Edition: February 2014
First Trade Paperback Edition: April 2015

Printed in the United States of America

0   9   8   7   6   5   4   3   2   1

For the victims' families: We hope you find peace.

Margaret's dedications:
To my mother, Carol O'Brien McLean, the best mom
anyone could ever have.
I miss you.

Jon's dedications:
To Bryce—You inspire me.
To Grandma and Bob-Bob—I hope wherever you are,
this makes you proud.

Contents

Acknowledgments

We are grateful to all of you who helped guide us through this long and complicated history of Boston's organized crime dating back to the 1960s through the present. Thank you for taking the time to provide us with exclusive behind-the-scenes interviews for this book. A special shout-out to the U.S. Marshals who ran everything so smoothly at the John Joseph Moakley Federal Courthouse. You always greeted us with smiles, and brightened even the darkest days of the trial.

Thank you to Tom Doherty and Bob and Susan Gleason for believing in this book and our partnership. We also appreciate your friendship and guidance. Thanks to Kelly Quinn for putting up with all of the e-mails and calls to make sure things were just right. We applaud all the hard work and camaraderie from everyone at Tor/Forge.

Margaret: Thank you to my parents, Robert and Carol McLean, for your support, and to my children, Sarah, Dave, and Kate Barcomb, for your patience all summer as I attended the trial. I'd like to extend a special thank-you to Patricia Donahue for welcoming me into your family with open arms. I appreciate all the new friendships that have blossomed from covering this trial: It brought good people together, ranging from victims' families to law enforcement. Thank you to all my friends. A special thanks to everyone at NECN and WGBH for bringing me on board to provide trial analysis every morning.

A big thank-you to my coauthor, Jon, for all his hard work, for making me laugh, and for being so encouraging and upbeat when the deadlines loomed.

* * *

Jon: Thank you to all of my family, friends, and colleagues for all of the encouragement. It has meant the world to me during this daunting undertaking. I love you all. And I'm sorry to those of you I neglected during this laborious process. I hope this work makes you proud.

Thanks to my coauthor, Margaret, for weaving this amazing tale.

Whitey on Trial

All causes shall give way: I am in blood
Stept in so far that, should I wade no more,
Returning were as tedious as go o'er.
       —William Shakespeare, *Macbeth,* Act III, Scene IV

chapter

1

CONFLICTS

At the center of all this murder and mayhem is one man, the defendant in this case, James Bulger.
  —*Assistant U.S. Attorney Brian Kelly, opening statement*

IT WAS A NOTE FROM A KILLER. A HANDWRITTEN LETTER, NESTLED BEtween bills in the mailbox, and postmarked ten days after a jury rendered a verdict at his trial. From: *Whitey Bulger.* The man accused of murdering nineteen people had written to us, wanting to tell his side of the story.

We couldn't open it.

We, Margaret McLean and Jon Leiberman, had joined forces to cover the sensational trial and write about it. Margaret is a former Boston-area prosecutor, legal analyst, and law professor at Boston College. Jon reported for *America's Most Wanted* and traveled around the world with the FBI task force searching for Whitey while he was a fugitive from justice.

Why couldn't we open that letter? We had formed intimate bonds with victims' relatives and members of law enforcement who had pursued Whitey for decades. They had helped us for months with this complicated case, given us their time.

Including a letter from Whitey in our coverage of the story felt like a betrayal. We fought about it. Was it the right thing to do? Our friends

James "Whitey" Bulger shown here as a young man. The defense submitted this photograph toward the end of the trial.

had experienced the murder of loved ones. Other friends had been tortured and beaten by Whitey. Those memories were painful for them, but they had learned to trust us and had shared private moments and feelings. Allowing Whitey to have his say felt wrong.

The trial itself had been overwhelming. Another friend and key prosecution witness had been murdered mid-trial. *Silenced*. He never had the chance to testify.

We became aware of the conflicts raging beneath the surface before the trial even started. Victims' relatives came to us for advice, torn over which side to root for at trial. We wondered how could that be? Don't victims always want the prosecution to win? Neither of us had

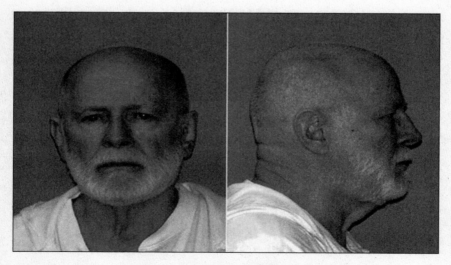

James "Whitey" Bulger following his arrest in Santa Monica, California, after spending sixteen years on the lam.

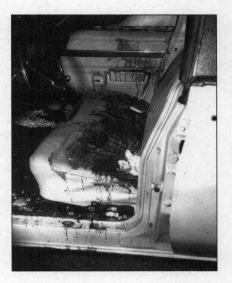

Photograph of the bloody interior of an automobile that Al Plummer, Hugh "Sonny" Shields, and Frank Capizzi rode in on March 19, 1973, in the North End. It was the target of a gangland hit. Plummer was killed.

seen that. We knew the trial would reveal decades of terror, extortion, and bodies buried in unmarked graves. Machine guns. A beautiful girl, strangled and buried in the basement. A brown-stained, grinning skull . . . *and she was known for her smile.*

The evidence of violence was overwhelming, so why weren't the victims rooting 100 percent for the prosecution? The government typically upholds the principles of truth and justice, right?

We learned that Whitey's trial was far from black-and-white. It contained murky layers involving government leaks of top secret information that had caused innocent people to be killed. The massive-scale cover up and corruption went all the way up from Boston to the Department of Justice in Washington, D.C. Top echelon FBI informants were murdered while the government looked the other way.

We opened that letter, and we are sorry for the pain it will inflict on some of our friends. We did it to expose the truth, and sometimes we need to hear it from all angles. A copy of Whitey's letter has been included toward the end of the book.

What follows is an eyewitness account of the Whitey Bulger trial and countless interviews with people intimately connected to the case.

chapter

[**2**]

ALL RISE

I don't think you know how big this case is really going to be until
you step in that courtroom. It's been thirty-one years since my husband was murdered. I'm in a catch-22 situation. We want Whitey to
lose but we don't want the government to win either.[1]
—*Patricia Donahue, on the eve of the trial*

A MOTORCADE OF FOUR VEHICLES WITH SIRENS BLARING BARRELED
single file along Boston's Seaport Boulevard. Two federal squad cars
flanked identical SUVs in the center. They looked the same, but we
knew only one was armored. That armored car contained the prisoner,
James "Whitey" Bulger, arriving for the first day of trial on that humid
Wednesday morning, June 12, 2013. The motorcade sped past television satellite trucks and down a side alley next to the John Joseph
Moakley United States Courthouse. Helicopters hovered overhead.

Even the setting for Whitey's trial presented a conflict between the
beautiful and the ugly. The Moakley courthouse is arguably one of the
most opulent government buildings in the country. It's located on Fan
Pier overlooking the historic harbor, the site of the Boston Tea Party. The
harbor teemed with sailboats, fishing vessels, and yachts that morning.
The eighty-eight-foot-tall courthouse, with its curved glass facade, jutted
into the harbor on a peninsula. Visitors from all over the world could
see it glistening in the sun as they flew into Logan airport. The Moakley

courthouse was designed by renowned architect Henry Cobb at a cost of $170 million. The building is surrounded by two acres of manicured shrubs, pristine flowers, and ornate wooden park benches.

The Moakley courthouse is a spectacular stage, yet during its largest, most featured production, the government was about to unveil a grotesque portrait of itself.

It was the summer of Whitey.

"It's time." The deputy United States marshal unlocked the spotless glass doors of the courthouse.

We watched a crowd burst through the lobby at 7:30 A.M., past several agents from the Department of Homeland Security with their bomb-sniffing black Labs.

No one dreamed this day would come, especially after Whitey spent sixteen years on the lam. Many thought he'd never be caught. Whitey had become a legend, a ghost of the past.

BEHIND THE SCENES

"We believe he has stashed millions of dollars in safe deposit boxes all over the world," FBI case agent Richard Teahan told us while searching for Whitey with *America's Most Wanted* in 2008. "He set himself up for a lifetime on the run."[2]

We walked through the courthouse doors on that first day of the trial and entered straight into a commotion befitting three decades of waiting. The lines to get through security snaked throughout the lobby. People yearned for a glimpse of Whitey finally taking a seat in that empty spot at the defendant's table.

"Check phones in over here." The marshal pointed to the guard desk behind him, where two more lines had formed.

We flashed our media identification cards, which would allow us to bring electronics into the courtroom.

"Media to the right." The marshal pointed toward the far security beltway and metal detector.

A man pushed in front of us. "I'm here for the Whitey Bulger trial. Can I get into the courtroom?"

"First ten people on the list," the marshal said.

"Where's the list?" the man asked.

"Fifth floor. Courtroom 11. And it's first come, first served. We had people lined up since early this morning."

The man cut into a security line.

"Wait a minute, sir! You still have to check your phone." The marshal cupped his hands like a megaphone. "All electronics have to be checked."

After making it through security, we had to wait again with the crowds for an elevator up to the fifth floor. After missing at least six packed cars, we finally made it, our backs pressed against the far wall.

Patricia "Pat" Donahue squeezed into the same elevator, along with her three grown sons, Michael, Shawn, and Tommy. While many Boston-area families would spend the months ahead on Cape Cod, the Donahue family would not. They would spend their summer en route to and from the courthouse. This elevator would become their conduit between the pain of the past and hope for the future.

Pat waved at us and waited for the elevator doors to close. She had been waiting over three decades, ever since her husband Michael was murdered in 1982. She wore her blond hair short and stylish. She always appeared put-together in a conservative summer skirt, matching top, and colorful scarf or vintage necklace. Pat often welcomed others with a full bear hug and a kiss on the cheek. She was exuberant and full of life. When Pat walked into a room, heads turned. She had never remarried and we often wondered why.

Two marshals managed the crowds outside Whitey's courtroom on the fifth floor. We knew they'd maintain order in the actual halls of justice, but would the government control this case on the inside, where it really mattered?

"Sorry, public seats filled." The first marshal showed a handwritten list of ten names to the pushy man who we'd seen downstairs. "You'll have to watch the trial in one of the overflow rooms down the hall. They've got big-screen TVs all set up." He turned toward an attractive woman who had squeezed past and raised a finger. "Hold on."

"CNN," she said.

"Did they put your name on the list?"

"Right here."

"Okay." The marshal placed a check mark next to her name. "Head on in. The benches on your left are labeled for media. The first row's reserved for the sketch artist."

"Oh, good morning, Pat." The marshal stepped aside and held the door open for the Donahue family.

The Donahues squeezed into the second row of benches, labeled RESERVED.

Steve Davis turned around in his front-row seat and nodded at them. We knew his sister Debra had been strangled years ago. Whitey stood trial for that, too. The Davis family wanted answers. Debra was a beautiful twenty-six-year-old blond, full of life. Why were all her teeth pulled? Why was she buried in the basement? Why had three decades gone by without any justice for Debra?

Carmen Ortiz, the United States Attorney for the District of Massachusetts, sat in the front row with her legs crossed and chin slightly raised. She wore her shoulder-length dark hair in a simple, no-nonsense style. Her pressed and starched suit made her look like an influential business woman. The national spotlight shone down on her office that day. Ortiz had assigned three of her top lawyers to prosecute Whitey. We knew the government had nine hundred exhibits at the ready. Carts loaded with fat three-ring binders lined the railing behind the government's trial table. We watched Ortiz glance toward Richard DesLauriers, the top gun of the Boston FBI, who sat on the bench designated for law enforcement. The defense team would attack Ortiz's office and the FBI for years of government corruption and leaks of top secret information to Whitey and his men. Leaks that killed informants along with innocent people. The dark days had occurred before Ortiz's time in office, yet questions still lingered. Top secret documents dating back to the 1970s remained hidden under lock and key. Would they finally be unsealed during Whitey's trial? How high up did the corruption go? Would anyone else take the fall?

The lead investigators took their seats: DEA agent Dan Doherty, State Police Lieutenant Steve Johnson, and Department of Justice lawyer James Marra. They'd been consumed with the Whitey Bulger case long before he was caught.

One man sat at the end of the bench in the front row reserved for the defendant's family: Whitey's brother John. It was a tough day for the Bulger family. We knew family members felt conflicted. Most chose not to attend.

A side door opened and a hush descended upon the packed gallery. "There he is!" A man in the public section rose halfway and pointed. Whitey Bulger entered the room. *The Whitey Bulger.*

People craned their necks to catch a glimpse. Several stood. Many likely remembered the snapshot of Whitey in dark sunglasses wearing a Red Sox cap as he had appeared years before, a free man, walking along the pedestrian paths at Castle Island in South Boston. This man was no longer on the run, no longer shielded by sunglasses or disguises.

BEHIND THE SCENES

Howie Winter, former head of the Winter Hill Gang and Whitey's partner in crime, told us, "He's always four or five steps ahead of everyone. I don't think they'll ever catch him. I'd say no to be honest with you. . . . He's very clever and a master of disguises. He always had wigs and makeup."[3]

Marshals escorted the pale white-haired eighty-three-year-old to his seat behind the defendant's table. He looked like an ordinary man: no handcuffs, no prison jumpsuit. For the big day, he had chosen a kelly green long-sleeved Henley shirt tucked into Levi's jeans with bright white sneakers. Nothing formal. A suit and tie would've been out of character for Whitey. He glanced into the gallery, making eye contact with his brother.

Spectators murmured.

"Quiet in the courtroom!" a marshal yelled.

We watched the lawyers taking last-minute notes. This would be a tricky trial for both the prosecution and the defense.

$$3$$

THE BELL TOLLS
NINETEEN TIMES

He did the dirty work himself, because he was a hands-on killer.
—Assistant U.S. Attorney Brian Kelly,
opening statement

ASSISTANT UNITED STATES ATTORNEY BRIAN KELLY PURSED HIS LIPS and chewed the tip of his pen. He sat behind the government's table with his two colleagues, waiting for the judge and then the jury to enter. We knew Kelly would deliver the opening statement for the government in a matter of minutes. The government always goes first, as the party with the burden of proof. He had chosen a dark suit with a bright red tie. His sandy brown hair appeared freshly trimmed. Kelly had a receding hairline, yet looked young and cherubic for a man in his early fifties. Kelly's family sat in the gallery, appearing fidgety and anxious for him.

Kelly and lead prosecutor Fred Wyshak were seasoned veterans of Boston's war on organized crime. Wyshak, age sixty, looked stockier than Kelly, with cropped gray hair and a large, creased brow. They fought together for over two decades tearing down Whitey's empire. They had recently added Zachary Hafer to the team. He was a handsome lawyer in his midthirties with a full head of dark hair.

Kelly turned and whispered to an assistant seated at the table behind him. She nodded and checked something on a courtroom computer.

Kelly's eyes appeared puffy. Had he slept the week before? He had to be conflicted about his case. We knew he was a good man, a man of high integrity and moral character. How would he deal with the underlying current of government corruption? What was the government setting out to accomplish? A win across the board with guilty findings on every count in the criminal indictment, or the truth?

The clerk rose from her seat just below the judge's bench. "All rise!" she said.

United States District Court Judge Denise Casper whisked into the courtroom from a door located behind the bench.

"Court is in session. Please be seated." The clerk remained standing. "Criminal Action 99-10371, United States versus James Bulger."

"Good morning." Judge Casper scanned both counsel tables, which were positioned side by side in the center of the lawyers' section, called the bar.

"Good morning," the lawyers said.

Casper regarded Whitey for a moment. "Good morning, Mr. Bulger."

Whitey nodded and returned the judge's greeting.

Judge Casper commanded attention. This was her courtroom and the biggest trial so far of her career. Critics snickered, telling us she was far too inexperienced to handle a trial this big. Others praised Casper as intelligent, no-nonsense, and a good listener.

"We'll be here until Christmas," a reporter whispered when the final pretrial conference carried on until 6:00 P.M.

"She's slow. Very slow," said a lawyer who had appeared before her on another case. Most lawyers hadn't practiced before Casper. She was an unknown commodity.

While Casper's personality was a wild card, her pedigree stood out: Wesleyan University, Harvard Law School. President Obama appointed her to the bench in 2010 as the first African-American woman to serve on the First Circuit. Casper had practiced civil litigation for a prominent Boston law firm and worked as a federal and state prosecutor.

The slender forty-six-year-old woman in the black robe and shoulder-length hair adjusted her glasses and shuffled papers. How would she handle five experienced male attorneys . . . and Whitey? Six against one? Will she command respect? Will she favor one side over the other? How will she control her courtroom with the anticipated high drama of convicted killers coming face-to-face with Whitey for the first time in decades?

"All rise for the jury."

Whitey rose, along with his lawyers and the rest of the gallery. His gaze shifted toward the door to the left of the judge's bench as the jurors entered. Twelve would decide his fate. Did they have any idea of the enormity of the case at hand?

The court had called 858 people for jury selection, which is also called *voir dire*. It took six days of questioning and criminal background checks to reach twelve, the magic number. Lawyers had bickered, yet finally agreed upon a fair and impartial jury of ten whites, one Asian, and one African-American. Altogether, eight men and four women. Six alternates had been chosen to sit through the trial, and all would be paid fifty dollars a day for their service. They would not be sequestered.

"You may be seated," the clerk said to the spectators' gallery. The jurors took the seats they would inhabit for the next several months.

As Judge Casper explained trial procedure, most jurors appeared uncomfortable as they absorbed their surroundings and peered at the crowd. They had watched a video in the jury assembly room on the second floor about the importance of jury duty in a democratic society. Did they know they held the national spotlight? They couldn't miss the throngs of media outside the courthouse and the long row of microphones they had to slip past every morning. Whitey's fate rested with them.

Judge Casper scrutinized the government's table. "Mr. Kelly?"

"Yes, thank you, Your Honor." Kelly rose and casually walked toward a podium in front of the jury box. This was it. All eyes focused on Kelly in courtroom 11, along with scores of people in the overflow rooms watching on television monitors.

"Good morning." Kelly took a moment to adjust the microphone and make eye contact with each juror. He had to connect with them in his opening statement. The government's legal strategy: hook them right away. Expose the violence, shock the conscience.

"This is my chance to give you an overview of the case." Kelly paused. There was so much to tell. Could he simplify the massive history of Whitey Bulger and his complex criminal network for the jury? That was the challenge—they were starting from scratch.

"It's a case about organized crime, public corruption, and all sorts of illegal activities ranging from extortion to drug dealing to money laundering to possession of machine guns to murder, nineteen murders." Kelly lingered on the word "murders," and puckered his lips. "It's about a criminal enterprise, which is a group of criminals, who ran amok in the city of Boston for almost thirty years." Kelly didn't look at his notes. His voice sounded sincere, not blustery, more like a conversation than a lecture. It was all about the jury now.

"And at the center of all this murder and mayhem is one man, the defendant in this case, James Bulger." Several jurors studied Whitey, who sat at his table scribbling notes on a legal pad. The Whitey they saw didn't appear dangerous at all. He was a pale old man wearing glasses, like a benign, perhaps beloved grandfather.

Kelly had to erase that image. We knew he wanted jurors to go home at night with a visual of Whitey as a cold-blooded murderer.

Kelly carefully chose one murder to paint a new portrait of the defendant. And it was a good one. He featured the murder of Arthur "Bucky" Barrett, a father and husband who Whitey chained to a chair and psychologically tormented for hours. "As Barrett walked down the stairs, this man over here—" He pointed at Whitey. "—James Bulger, shot him in the back of the head, killing him. Bulger didn't get involved in the burial process, he let his other gang members do that. He stayed upstairs and rested on the couch.

"He did the dirty work himself, because he was a hands-on killer," Kelly said, before he touched upon other murders, adding color here and there, foreshadowing a tale of savagery.

Kelly drew the curtain back on Whitey's fearsome criminal empire: "It's crimes like these, vicious crimes, that made Bulger and his gang widely feared. And that's how they made a lot of money. . . ." Kelly promised jurors they would hear from a slew of witnesses. Whitey and his gang "made millions" extorting countless drug dealers and bookmakers operating across New England, along with legitimate businessmen.

How did Whitey stay in business for so long without getting caught? According to Kelly, "Bulger and his friends made a point of paying off members of law enforcement. They did that so they could get tipped off to investigations and stay one step ahead of the honest cops who were actually trying to make a case against them. So it was part of a strategy they had, and it worked."

Kelly hit a home run when he announced all nineteen murder victims' names and flashed their pictures on the video screens: "Michael Milano, Al Plummer, William O'Brien, James O'Toole, Al Notorangeli, James Sousa, Paul McGonagle, Edward Connors, Thomas King, Francis 'Buddy' Leonard, Richard Castucci, Roger Wheeler, Debra Davis, Brian Halloran, Michael Donahue, John Callahan, Arthur 'Bucky' Barrett, John McIntyre, and Deborah Hussey."

A somber mood veiled courtroom 11. It felt like the 9/11 memorial services. Jurors must have imagined a bell tolling after each name. How could they not convict? What could the defense possibly say next?

chapter

4

THE PROSECUTOR'S KITCHEN

This process may be a pretty good recipe to get testimony, but it's an unreliable recipe to get the truth.
—Defense attorney J. W. Carney Jr., opening statement

"MR. CARNEY." JUDGE CASPER GAZED AT DEFENSE ATTORNEY J. W. Carney Jr. as he pushed his chair out and slowly rose from the defense table.

"Thank you, Your Honor," he said in a quiet, slightly hoarse voice. Carney walked toward the jury box. He was slender, bald headed, and sported a trimmed white beard with a thin mustache. He wore oval glasses and looked more like a professor than a lawyer. Could he break through the storm cloud that had cast an ominous shadow over the courtroom? we wondered. Was he conflicted about representing this client? Deep down in his gut did he believe Whitey was guilty of the crimes, the nineteen murders? How could he defend someone who was just described as a "hands-on killer"?

Legal experts will say that cases are often won during opening statements, and the government had scored. Kelly was a tough act to follow, but Carney came seasoned. He graduated from Boston College Law School and began his career as a public defender and an assistant district attorney. Carney is a named partner at the prestigious criminal defense firm of Carney & Bassil, and has handled cases for many high-profile defendants. Carney has earned a reputation for being a legal mastermind, known for his poised, quiet demeanor, and passion for the law.

"My name is Jay Carney, and with my cocounsel, Hank Brennan, we'll be representing the defendant, James Bulger." Carney gestured toward Brennan, a nice-looking, dark-haired man in his early forties with an endearing, easygoing personality. Brennan was a skilled prosecutor in a high crime area and has quickly become one of Boston's rising stars. He is persuasive and passionate, quick to rattle off case law, and more theatrical than Carney. He is famous for his rapid fire cross-examinations complete with animated facial expressions.

"When we were appointed by a judge in this court to represent him, we knew we had a challenging task." Carney paused, making eye contact with each juror. Right away, he had informed them that Whitey hadn't hired some high-powered, expensive legal team. Jurors wouldn't know that Carney's firm handled court-appointed cases along with clients who could afford the full boat. The Whitey Bulger case would bring in business for years to come. Carney was smart to point out that defending their client would be an uphill battle; they were the underdog.

BEHIND THE SCENES

Defending Whitey was a thankless job. He had been vilified in the media for decades. The popular television show *America's Most Wanted* profiled Whitey eighteen times, more than any other fugitive. According to host John Walsh: "Whitey is probably the most narcissistic, sociopathic, cold-blooded, and smartest fugitive I have ever profiled."[1]

Carney thanked jurors on behalf of his client, "Jim," for their service and the "extraordinary sacrifice" they were making. We had noticed earlier that Whitey poured his lawyers glasses of water. This was likely orchestrated as a small gesture meant to show that the gangster on trial was courteous. Lawyers know that every word, gesture, and facial expression is fair game for judgment. The courtroom is both a battleground and a stage when the jury is present. Jurors notice details.

Carney cocked his head as if a thought had just occurred to him: "Listening to Mr. Kelly's opening statement kind of reminded me of a restaurant and how when you go to a restaurant, you're served a meal, and the food has been prepared in the kitchen. By the time it gets to your table, there's a beautiful presentation." He spread his arms. "A lot of time has been spent on it to make it look as appealing as possible."

Several jurors nodded, perhaps visualizing their favorite restaurant and the various garnishes used to decorate the dish du jour. But where was Carney going with this? How did it relate to a case with nineteen murders?

"And that's sort of like what it is when the government presents a witness in the courtroom," Carney said. "They've spent a lot of time with the witness, they've done a lot of negotiating with the witness, things have evolved with the witness, and then it leads to the point where the witness is ready to come to the courtroom and testify, just like food when it's brought to your table."

Did jurors picture the prosecutors dressed as waiters balancing large black trays on their shoulders? We glanced at the prosecutors. Those waiters wouldn't make a mistake after years of practice. The plated dinners would be placed on crisp white linen with sophisticated table settings, the kind with multiple forks and spoons. Those types of settings intimidate ordinary people who aren't sure which fork to use first.

"What Hank and I are going to do is try to show you what happens in the prosecutor's kitchen before this witness gets out here and tells you things that went on that Mr. Kelly didn't tell you . . . the factors that shaped not just the witnesses, but more importantly, what the witness is going to be saying to you." He spoke slowly, like a good storyteller, connecting with the jury.

Before opening the swinging doors to the government's kitchen, Carney provided jurors with a history lesson about federal law enforcement in Boston—explaining how the table was set, and the precise placement of the silverware. Starting with the J. Edgar Hoover days, the federal mandate was to "smash the Mafia" in the North End and

Providence. The FBI developed a "Top Echelon Informant Program" to take down the Italian Mafia leadership. Carney insisted that his client was never an informant for the government. It was the other way around. Whitey paid law enforcement agents "tens of thousands of dollars" for information to keep his criminal enterprise running, and corrupt FBI agents accepted those bribes because they wanted to make names for themselves and "live the lavish lifestyle."

Carney explained why his client was never an informant: "James Bulger is of Irish descent, and the worst thing that an Irish person could consider doing was becoming an informant, because of the history of the 'Troubles' in Ireland." In addition, "James Bulger was not deeply tied to the Italian Mafia. You'll hear that La Cosa Nostra centered on people of Italian, in particular Sicilian, descent. They wouldn't let someone who wasn't of that background be knowledge-able about what was going on in their activities. . . . Bulger would never be provided with information that he could give, even if he wanted to."

Whitey apparently wanted the world to know that he never provided information to law enforcement, he merely received it. He operated on a one-way street. Did he care more about clearing his image as a rat than as a murderer? We watched as he wiped his glasses clean and scribbled more notes on his legal pad. Was he considering his legacy at the ripe age of eighty-three?

Carney's legal strategy throughout the opening statement was to flip the case on its head and place the government on trial. The depth of corruption within the FBI ran deep, and he would use that to his client's advantage. He pointed out that during Whitey's years of operation, from the early 1970s to the mid-1990s, law enforcement looked the other way, giving him free reign to commit crimes. Whitey was never arrested or prosecuted during that time. This was a risky defense strategy for Carney admitted that Whitey was "able to do illegal gambling, make illegal loans, be involved in drug trafficking and extortion of people, and never, ever be charged, and on top of that, make millions upon millions of dollars doing so."

Wasn't that a major concession? Jurors could find Whitey guilty on just two extortion acts and that would be enough to convict him for racketeering and send him away for life. It didn't make sense. Was

Carney going for jury nullification? Would he come up with enough evidence of FBI corruption to cause jurors to acquit Whitey on principle, to punish the government?

Carney switched gears, taking us back to that fancy restaurant. This time he opened the swinging doors to the kitchen and beckoned us to enter. Carney would show us secret government recipes along with the garnishes used for presentation at the table.

The three biggest stars in that kitchen were killers: John Martorano, Stephen "the Rifleman" Flemmi, and Kevin Weeks. Would their testimony be truthful or were they merely parrots repeating exactly what the prosecutors wanted them to say?

"He is the scariest criminal, most violent psychopath in Boston history," Carney said, referring to government witness Martorano. "He would kill people almost randomly, just as the mood befit him. He would kill people because they crossed him. He would kill people because he wanted their money. He would kill people because he didn't want to pay a gambling debt. He would kill people as easily as we would order a cup of coffee in a store."

Did Martorano have a conscience? What would he look like on the witness stand? How would the government dress him up to be served at the table? What did it take for prosecutors to convince a cold-blooded murderer like Martorano to flip against Whitey and be labeled a rat?

Carney informed jurors of the sweetheart deal the government cut with the devil: for twenty murders, Martorano would get twelve years, no death penalty. On top of that, they paid him thousands of dollars. Martorano had served his time and now strolled the streets of Boston. He'd been spotted dining out in the Back Bay.

Kevin Weeks was the second witness prepared in the prosecutor's kitchen. Carney pointed toward the courtroom doors and emphasized that he was also roaming around the community "free from all restraints." Weeks pled guilty for his involvement in five murders in exchange for five years in prison and the ability to keep movie rights and book deals. "I submit that Kevin Weeks can't tell the truth, even when there is nothing at stake for him," Carney said.

Stephen Flemmi was "next into the Department of Justice kitchen," where prosecutors would prepare for years to serve him up on a fancy platter for the big feast. Flemmi bargained for his life. Prosecutors in

Massachusetts worked deals with Oklahoma and Florida to spare Flemmi from the death penalty in exchange for implicating Whitey. For that deal, he started blaming Whitey for crimes that "Stevie Flemmi himself had carried out." Carney promised jurors the evidence would show that Flemmi, not Whitey, strangled his girlfriend, Debra Davis, and his stepdaughter, Deborah Hussey.

"When you add to the recipe the unbelievable incentives the prosecution has given these three men so they will testify in the manner that the government wants . . . do you believe them beyond a reasonable doubt?" Carney asked. The mention of a recipe conjured images of Wyshak and Kelly in the kitchen with tall white chef hats, furiously cutting deals on the prosecutor's worn wooden chopping block.

Carney walked out of the prosecutor's kitchen and left jurors with a parting thought: "This process may be a pretty good recipe to get testimony, but it's an unreliable recipe to get the truth."

Jurors appeared pensive as Carney took his seat, and that's likely what he wanted—to make them think. The government would soon launch its case against Whitey with hard evidence such as machine guns and emotional testimony from victims' relatives. Carney had to get through to them by raising questions about the foundation of the government's case and the credibility of their key witnesses. He had to persuade jurors to question the system.

chapter

5

THE VOLCANO

In the morning, the garage "operated like a local car repair service whose atmosphere changed around noontime" into "a cauldron of who's who in organized crime."

—*Massachusetts State Police Lieutenant Robert Long,*
trial testimony

"MR. HAFER?" JUDGE CASPER GAZED AT THE YOUNGEST PROSECUTOR.

"Yes, Your Honor. The government calls Robert Long." Assistant U.S. Attorney Zachary Hafer positioned himself behind the podium. All heads in the packed gallery turned toward the closed double doors. It was the perfect moment for a drum roll. Who was the very first witness of the biggest case of the year? We knew prosecutors spent months determining the order of their witnesses. They had to start off on the right foot.

Retired State Police Lieutenant Robert Long, a robust-looking man with a full head of brown curly hair, entered the courtroom. He exuded confidence in his dark suit and red "power tie."

BEHIND THE SCENES

Before the trial, Bob fell from a ladder and sustained a severe compound fracture in his leg. He was confined to a wheelchair and later spent months in rehab and on crutches. He knew he

was scheduled to be the first witness, and he'd been waiting
for this moment for thirty-three years, ever since those long,
sweltering evenings spying on Whitey from the flophouse. "I
wasn't using crutches, but my leg was still healing. I didn't
want to trip and embarrass myself. I didn't want to show any
signs of weakness in front of Whitey."[1]

Long ignored the pain in his recently broken leg, and marched
down the aisle, past Whitey. He looked serious and ready to get down
to business.

"Sir, please raise your right hand to be sworn," the clerk said.

"Do you swear to tell the truth, the whole truth, and nothing but
the truth, so help you God?"

Long raised his hand. "I do," he said, in a deep, confident voice.

"Thank you. Please be seated."

Long sat in the witness box to the right of the judge's bench and
exchanged greetings with Judge Casper and the lawyers. He was the
perfect witness to kick off the government's case due to his years of
experience and ability to set the stage. Long could provide jurors with
vivid descriptions of Whitey's underworld through surveillance photographs and video.

Hafer began his direct examination by questioning him about
his investigations and distinguished career. Long had testified many
times in the past, and came across as personable and trustworthy.
Long was a highly decorated twenty-two-year veteran of the Massachusetts State Police, and retired with the rank of detective lieutenant
inspector. He received awards for his undercover work involving the
Hell's Angels motorcycle gang and for "Operation Lobster," a massive state and federal investigation of organized crime involving
truck hijacking in the late 1970s, in which "Massachusetts led the
nation."

"What was your understanding about who the major organized
crime groups in Boston in or about 1979 and 1980 were?" Hafer asked.

Long addressed the jury. "There were two. First was the Italian
Mafia run by the Angiulo family. And then there was the Winter Hill

Gang. The Italian Mafia had most of the rackets in downtown Boston and points going up to the North Shore. The Winter Hill Gang had most of the rackets in South Boston, Dorchester, and other metropolitan cities and towns going north to Lowell and into the South Shore down to Quincy."

Winter Hill is a neighborhood in Somerville, Massachusetts, which is named for its 120-foot hill. Winter Hill dates back to the 18th century where it can be viewed on old Revolutionary War–era maps. Winter Hill is where the Winter Hill Gang had its headquarters for many years. The Winter Hill Gang is not named after Howie Winter, its longtime leader.

Hafer displayed an organizational chart of the Winter Hill Gang, circa 1975, with photos of Whitey and his five partners along the top row. Whitey's lawyer, Hank Brennan, objected and requested a sidebar conference, which was granted. We watched the lawyers whispering to the right of the judge's bench.

Brennan argued that the chart showed Whitey at the top, thus, "It gives an opinion that there's a RICO conspiracy, that the person on top is responsible for all of the acts of the people below them." Judge Casper ruled against him and the chart was allowed into evidence.

The Winter Hill Organizational Chart (Whitey Bulger depicted in the top row, far left next to Stephen Flemmi).

BEHIND THE SCENES

According to juror Gusina Tremblay, the organizational chart would become a sticking point in the deliberation room. The date of 1975 from the chart served as a cutoff point: "It ultimately screwed us up with the earlier murders."[2]

When we later informed the prosecution team, they were astounded. "The chart hurt us? I can't believe it. I loved that chart!" Fred Wyshak said.[3]

"Lieutenant Long, do you recognize the individual there in the tight white shirt?" Hafer asked, not long after the sidebar conference. It's essential for the witness to identify the defendant.

Long stared at Whitey, who kept his head down, scribbling notes. "Yes, James Bulger." Long enunciated Whitey's name, venom seeping from his voice.

BEHIND THE SCENES

We asked Bob Long what he thought about as he testified against Whitey. He recalled: "It repulsed me how Whitey just sat there drumming his fingers—I kept thinking about all those people whose lives he ruined. One time when all the lawyers were at sidebar with the judge, he sat there alone, so I stared at him. He must've sensed me looking because he stopped drumming his fingers and we locked eyes. I wouldn't look away. He was the one who looked away first."[4]

Long testified about the undercover surveillance of Whitey that he and two others had conducted in the spring of 1980 at the Lancaster Foreign Car Service Garage on Lancaster Street near Boston's North End, where the Italian Mafia had its headquarters. They had rented a third-floor room in a flophouse across the street.

TOP: Whitey Bulger (on left) with George Kaufman at the Lancaster Street garage.

BOTTOM: Bulger (middle) caught on surveillance in 1980 meeting with Ted Berenson (left) and Phil Wagenheim (right).

BEHIND THE SCENES

Bob Long, Rick Fraelick, and Jack O'Malley spent three months, day and night, in a sweltering, cockroach-infested flophouse with thin paneling serving as walls between rooms. "There were derelicts, all sorts of crazy people in there. You could hear everything," Long recalled. "One night during a full moon, around 1 A.M., we heard howling. We looked out the window and saw a man on the roof across the street screaming while exposing himself . . . for the whole world to see him."[5]

Whitey Bulger (middle) talks with Stephen Flemmi and George Kaufman in a surveillance photo taken at the Lancaster Street garage in 1980.

Jurors appeared captivated by the multiple black-and-white photographs and short video clips from Long's surveillance that were introduced and displayed on the giant monitors in the courtroom. Long pointed out key individuals like "James Bulger, Stephen Flemmi, George Kaufman, and other members of the Italian Mafia" who operated in Boston's underworld. George Kaufman was the manager of the garage and a key player in Whitey's enterprise. He could be seen exchanging envelopes and paper bags of cash with Whitey and Flemmi. Other Mafia figures included Donato "Danny" Angiulo, a Capo and brother of Gennaro Angiulo, underboss of the Patriarca crime family, which ran New England. Also featured with Whitey: Larry Zannino, a Mafia consigliore; Phil Wagenheim, a Mafia hit man; and Frank Salemme Jr., whose father would later become the LCN (Mafia) underboss in Boston. LCN stands for La Cosa Nostra, which means "this thing of ours" in Italian.

BEHIND THE SCENES

Long told us: "The first time we went into the garage, we looked everywhere for a key in order to get back in. Dust and debris kept falling down from the ceilings, so one of the guys had to follow us around like a maid with a vacuum. We never found the key." The bug placed in a chair got crushed when a fat Mafia guy sat on it. Others didn't work well due to interference from one of the nearby hospitals. They eventually planted working bugs.[6]

The old photos represented a window into the past, reminding us of clips from the Godfather movies, with gangsters wearing jeans, tight shirts, and dark oversized 1980s-style shades, standing next to boxy sedans from the late '70s, counting currency. At night, their white shirts glowed in the dark like ghosts from the past coming back to haunt Whitey. One photo advertised donuts for eighty-six cents a dozen, and another showed Whitey standing next to a long bank of pay phones. Back in the day, Long explained, pay phones were "used to avoid electronic surveillance."

What was Whitey thinking as he examined the old pictures of himself from thirty-three years ago? He appeared fit and in control back then. Gangsters came to him. One video showed him swinging his fists and laughing as if explaining how a fight went down. It was like watching an old silent family movie.

Long testified that "Bulger and Flemmi were almost inseparable." Several jurors smiled at the photograph of the pair walking together and eating bananas. The government was doing its best to tie the two mobsters together as partners in a vast criminal enterprise.

After months of surveillance, Long applied for a warrant and received permission to plant listening devices inside the garage.

BEHIND THE SCENES

Long explained the challenges of planting bugs back then: "We had to use an electrical power source, plug them in. Batteries only lasted twenty-four hours and we couldn't just break in every day to change the battery." When asked how they got into the garage to plant the bug, Bob replied, "We had a woman drive down Lancaster Street in a van filled with furniture, which broke down in front of the garage. She asked the mechanic if she could leave the van inside the garage overnight because she worried about the furniture getting stolen. The mechanic agreed. Little did he know Trooper Jack O'Malley was lying flat, cramped up in a secret coffinlike compartment with furniture piled on top of him, from 4:00 P.M. until after midnight."[7]

The government's legal strategy was to establish Whitey as a connected leader in Boston's criminal underworld, and what better way to do it than with visuals: photos and video clips. The images also contradicted what Carney had said in his opening statement, that Whitey could not have been an informant against the Italian Mafia because he was of Irish descent and would not have the knowledge. The photos painted a far different story.

Jay Carney got up for the first cross-examination of the trial. Lawyers had to ask all questions from behind the same podium; dancing around the room was not allowed. We wondered what he would do with this experienced witness? Cross-examination boiled down to scoring points. Carney knew better than to challenge Long in his area of expertise.

BEHIND THE SCENES

"I prepared for that cross for months," Long said. "Went over old reports and documents. I didn't know what Jay was going to throw at me." He'd known Carney from the time he was a young prosecutor in Middlesex County. He was well aware of Carney's skill.[8]

"Your intention was to get a wiretap to put a listening device into a certain location to transmit to another location?" Carney asked.

"Yes," Long said.

"Did you approach Jeremiah O'Sullivan for assistance?"

"Yes."

"Was the listening device compromised at Lancaster Street garage?" Carney rubbed his beard.

"Yes."

"And explain, please, to the members of the jury, what the word 'compromised' means?"

"Compromised." Long gazed at the ceiling for a moment. "An individual who you're targeting has become aware of it."

"How quickly after the bug was put into the Lancaster Street garage was it compromised?"

"Within days."

BEHIND THE SCENES

The compromised Lancaster Street garage investigation started the ball rolling. According to Long, "It was the beginning of everything. Out of failure came a demand for answers, finger-pointing. We accused the Boston FBI of leaks . . . all hell broke loose . . . it caused the volcano to explode."[9]

Carney informed the judge he had no further questions. The secret to effective cross-examination is to score points and sit down. Carney's cross was short, yet effective. He scored by planting the seed of government corruption by mentioning Jeremiah O'Sullivan, the former federal prosecutor and head of the Justice Department's New England Organized Crime Strike Force. Whitey claims O'Sullivan gave him immunity to commit crimes during the 1970s and 1980s. O'Sullivan died in 2009. Carney wanted jurors to connect O'Sullivan with a possible leak of information pertaining to the Lancaster Street garage surveillance. His legal strategy was to plant the seed that Whitey was being protected by the federal government.

chapter

6

BIG GUNS

We started at the bookmaker level with low-level informants, and
worked for years going up the chain. . . . If you want to do the foot-
work and work at it, it can be done. It's very demanding, but that's
your job.

—*Retired Massachusetts State Police Colonel*
Thomas Foley, interview

"COULD YOU PLEASE STATE YOUR FULL NAME AND SPELL YOUR LAST
name?" Wyshak asked, as he arranged his notes on the lawyers' podium for direct examination of the second witness late Thursday
morning on June 13th, the second day of the trial.

"Thomas J. Foley, F-o-l-e-y."

Retired Massachusetts State Police Colonel Thomas Foley appeared handsome and distinguished-looking with a full head of
white hair. Over the years, Foley earned the reputation of being
a classy, honest state trooper. He would never give someone the
brush-off, he wouldn't look over a person's shoulder to see if someone more important had entered the room. He looked people square
in the eyes and listened to every word they said. He sized up Whitey
from the witness stand. This was a big moment for Foley. What was
he thinking?

We asked Colonel Foley what his thoughts were as he gazed down at Whitey from the vantage point of the witness stand. He said, "I was dying for so many years to get to that point. . . . When you are taking the stand my concern is you want to make sure you testify appropriately and you are prepared. I didn't feel like it was about me and Bulger. I felt more like I wanted to do my job up there. I looked at him several times to get his attention, but he never looked at me eye to eye. I wish he had but he never did. . . . I am surprised. I know he knows that my crew was dogging him all those years, and we caused a lot of his heartache. I would expect he would have had a lot more consternation with me than he had."[1]

Foley had pursued Whitey for decades, following every small lead, and often coming up empty-handed. We knew he had fierce run-ins with the FBI. The feds and the state police had waged a war over Whitey. Mistrust and bitter feelings still lingered. Both sides had been embarrassed by bad cops within the ranks.

The government needed Foley to lay the foundation and explain to the jury just how vast and powerful Whitey's criminal empire had become throughout the 1980s. Foley picked up where Bob Long left off earlier that morning, educating the jury about the structure and business model for organized crime.

Foley testified about working in the organized crime section in the mid-1980s, along with the FBI's organized crime unit, called C-3. Foley explained his duties: "We went out and gathered information on a particular target . . . we'd monitor wiretaps, interview individuals, gather information." Wyshak established Foley as an expert in the field of organized crime investigations. He was a credible witness, similar to Bob Long: trustworthy and likable.

Wyshak led Foley through accounts of multiple investigations against the Italian Mafia in Boston, including the attempted assassination of "Cadillac Frank" Salemme at an IHOP in Saugus in 1989.

BEHIND THE SCENES

A source in the Italian Mafia explained the significance behind the attempted hit on Salemme: "Frank Salemme was capo regime, along with Vinnie Ferrara, in 1989. That means all the made guys (soldiers) reported directly to either one of them. Capos work under capo regimes or lieutenants. The attempted hit on Salemme and murder of his underboss, Billy Grasso, marked the beginning stages of a mob war over leadership which lasted until 1997. Over two dozen men were killed." We asked why the mob war came up at Whitey's trial? "The bottom line is that Whitey and Stevie played both sides of the Mafia and the feds."

—Anonymous source, Mafia soldier

Foley investigated the Winter Hill Gang and the Mafia, and ultimately became commander of special services.

"And can you explain to the jury how, in general, these organizations made money?" Wyshak asked.

"Any way they possibly could, mainly, but the primary areas where they tried to make money was bookmaking, loan sharking, drug distribution, extortion, and, at times, murder."

"And those activities, loan sharking, gambling, extortion, were those known as the 'rackets'?"

"Yes."

Foley educated jurors about the structure of the Winter Hill Gang using Wyshak's favorite organizational chart, circa 1975. The key players were Bulger, Flemmi, John Martorano, Howard Winter, Joe McDonald, and Jimmy Sims. He testified that informants had been "giving extensive information on the activities of James Bulger." Foley's plan for taking down the Winter Hill Gang was to "attack the organization through the bookies" because gambling proceeds were a "huge source of revenue." Foley explained that "a bookmaker takes bets" on any kind of sports, and back then, there was "heavy betting on games." They also made money through loan sharks "by lending out money at usurious rates or at a high percentage rate." The Winter Hill Gang and the Mafia would make boatloads of money by collecting tribute, or rent, which is "a fee that a bookmaker or drug dealer would have to pay organized crime leaders . . . to operate in an area."

"And what were the consequences of nonpayment?" Wyshak asked.

"Well, it could range from being put out of business, to taking a beating, or actually, at times, some people were killed." Foley paused and made eye contact with the jury. He had to connect with them regarding the gravity of the situation on the streets when Whitey ran the show.

"Based upon your experience in this area and conducting the investigations of organized crime over the years, did you learn that this organization had a reputation for violence?"

"Yes, I did."

"And did that assist them in being successful in extorting individuals?"

"Yes."

Ultimately, Foley's aggressive investigation and pressure on bookmakers led to information regarding the whereabouts of notorious hit man John Martorano. He had been living as a fugitive in Palm Beach County, Florida, ever since he fled a federal indictment for fixing horse races. Foley's team, which included Steve Johnson, a hard-digging state police investigator, discovered that Martorano had been living under the alias Vincent Rancourt. They arrested him on a charge of racketeering in January of 1998, and brought him back to Massachusetts.

Jurors perked up as they listened to testimony about the Martorano arrest. Carney had referred to him in his opening statement as "a violent psychopath" who would kill people as easily as "we would order a cup of coffee." He had accused the government of working a deal with the devil: twelve years for twenty murders. Jurors regarded Foley with keen interest. The man testifying before them had been responsible for arresting and debriefing the devil. Foley had worked that deal. How and why did he do it?

BEHIND THE SCENES

We asked Colonel Foley how he and his team received the pertinent information to locate and arrest Martorano. He told

us: "We started at the bookmaker level with low-level informants, and worked for years going up the chain. We started
with a series of wiretaps, and each time we went up a level.
We would use the previous wires as probable cause to go up
the ladder. We weren't giving serious criminals a pass to go
out and commit serious crimes. We might give some bookmakers a pass along the way, but if you want to do the foot-
work and work at it, it can be done. It's very demanding, but
that's your job."[2]

It took over a year for Foley and his team to reach a deal with Martorano. They didn't have solid evidence against him to prove he had
committed murder.

"And in 1998, when Mr. Martorano first cooperated with you, had
he been charged with any murders?" Wyshak asked.

"No."

"Do you recall what he was charged with at the time?"

"I believe it was a racketeering count at the time," Foley said.

"When he agreed to cooperate, did you take a proffer from him?"

"Yes."

"And what is a proffer?"

Foley addressed the jury. "A proffer is used to gather information
from the individual so we could evaluate that information to decide if
we were going to go into an agreement with that individual or not." He
knew he had to explain the common legal term to jurors, for they would
be hearing it throughout the trial. A number of witnesses had provided
the government with details about their crimes in a proffer as part
of their cooperation agreement. The proffer could not be used against
them later on. Many had been granted immunity from prosecution as
long as they testified truthfully.

"And during the course of this proffer, did he admit to his participation in any murders?" Wyshak was referring to Martorano.

"Yes, he did."

"How many?"

"Twenty," Foley said, with authority.

"And after you took the proffer from him, was that the first time you had enough evidence to charge other individuals with their participation in those murders?"

"Yes."

Wyshak flipped a page from his notes. "And just generally, can you tell us when those murders that Mr. Martorano told you about had been committed?"

"A lot of them in the 1960s, '70s, and the beginning of the 1980s."

"So what do they call a case that's twenty or thirty years old that's never been solved?"

"Cold case."

"And generally, those cases are never solved, are they?"

"A lot of them aren't," Foley said.

BEHIND THE SCENES

The big question for many watching the trial was why did Martorano receive such a sweetheart deal? We asked Colonel Foley, and he explained: "We were sick over making the deal with Martorano. But, as the case started languishing, Bulger was a fugitive and we were at a crossroads. We had an opportunity—if a guy like Martorano came in first, other people would follow. We knew he would be able to give us a lot of murders going back to the 1960s that were never going to be solved. There was no activity on those at all. If we let him walk—the public corruption part of this would not have been resolved. There would have been zero closure. We solved fifty murders because of information Martorano brought in. Guys like Weeks came in, and said, 'If Martorano can do it, I can do it too.'"[3]

Martorano's cooperation was like an earthquake that caused the stone walls of Whitey's empire to crack and tumble. Foley and his team worked with prosecutors in several states and with Massachusetts U.S. Attorney Donald Stern. As a result, prosecutors brought murder charges against Flemmi, Bulger, and former FBI agents H. Paul Rico and John Connolly. Rico died in 2004.

Donald K. Stern, former United States Attorney for the District of Massachusetts, approved the controversial Martorano plea bargain and explained his reasons to us: "Martorano was not making a deal. The only charge we had him on was extortion, and he was facing six years. He hadn't been charged with any of the murders—we didn't have enough evidence. Bulger and Flemmi had not been charged, the bodies had not been found. You see, back then guys just disappeared. It took a long time, a lot of negotiating, to work out the details of his proffer. Martorano did a lot of dancing around. It took a year until the dancing finally stopped. He learned that Bulger had been an informant all those years (a rat). The corruption involving FBI agents Connolly and Morris was just coming out. Kevin Weeks was still out there, and he didn't know if Weeks would start cooperating. He wanted to get in first because he worried over who else might roll. If it wasn't for Martorano's deal we may not have built a solid case against Bulger. Martorano got the ball rolling. Weeks and Flemmi started talking after that. I do believe it would have been worse not to make the deal with Martorano."[4]

Following Martorano's cooperation, Kevin Weeks quickly caved and showed them a "hide" located in a secret wall in a screen house in South Boston.

Jurors perked up at the word "hide." It sounded like something out of an old mob movie.

"What did you find?" Wyshak asked.

"We found gun racks inside there. We found an extensive amount of ammunition, and we also found one handgun," Foley said.

Jurors and spectators leaned forward and focused on the courtroom monitors. Sure enough, photos of the "hide" revealed a secret room behind a fake wall with empty gun racks and a big Tupperware box filled with ammunition, silencers, clips for automatic weapons, brass knuckles, handcuffs, and a handgun. More bullets and silencers had been stored in a U.S. Navy bag. We wondered where they got that. Foley was about to talk about finding more guns when Judge Casper decided it was best to take the morning break. Foley looked disappointed, and so were we.

We pulled tables together in the cafeteria, and talked about Colonel Foley and his dedication to the job.

"I still don't think Martorano should be out walking the streets," Pat Donahue said, as she made room for her lunch tray. "Twenty murders." She shook her head. "You know what I mean?"

"You think he's out there committing crimes?" a female reporter asked.

"If he is, I'm sure the government's protecting him—that's what they do." Tommy Donahue bit into his pizza.

"Flemmi's in jail for life and he's testifying, so why not Martorano?" Pat took a bite of her fish with rice pilaf. "He got off easy."

We argued back and forth about whether the hit man had officially retired. He had grandchildren now, but we had also heard through organized crime sources that he was a compulsive gambler.

After the morning break, Foley dove right into the meat of his testimony. The idea that he was going to talk about "finding some weapons" was an understatement. Foley explained how they recovered additional weapons in a Somerville, Massachusetts, home, and in a safe house in Florida. By the time he finished there were more guns piled on the clerk's table than the courtroom had likely ever held. And that wasn't all of them.

The huge cache of weapons included pump-action and sawed-off shotguns; rifles; Derringer pistols; Smith & Wessons of various models; .38, .44, and .357 caliber revolvers; semiautomatic pistols. The military-style machine guns included heavy M1 carbines, M-16s, and an Uzi. They came in so many shapes and sizes. They also found illegal knives, daggers, a Boston Police Department badge, and eerie rubber Halloween masks, which Foley testified, "are commonly used in the commission of a crime to hide your identity." There were so many lethal weapons that it took Foley over half an hour to go through them all. We chuckled when he held up a random stapler, regular size, that you'd find in an office. It seemed out of place. Foley never offered an explanation as to why is was there—perhaps it was tossed in with the guns by accident.

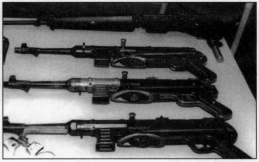

LEFT: Guns, knives, and a Boston Police badge recovered from the Weeks home at Pilsudski Way in South Boston.

RIGHT: Military-style machine guns recovered from a "hide" in South Boston.

Foley identified six powerful machine guns on the stand. He showed the jury how they worked (without firing them). Whitey couldn't resist checking out the guns. He must have been impressed with his own collection, yet disappointed that they would all be destroyed. How many of those weapons had he intimidated people with? How many had he fired? How many others had he disposed of? How many had been wiped clean of blood spatter?

Strategically, it was a good move for the government to call Foley second. All those guns became tangible evidence that Whitey operated a vast criminal enterprise. These were the tools of the trade—*for gangsters.*

"Nothing further," Wyshak said. We didn't catch his last question—we were still staring at the arsenal.

chapter

7

LAST MAN STANDING

They [the FBI] put a higher priority on protecting their informants than public safety.
—Retired Massachusetts State Police Colonel Thomas Foley,
trial testimony

HANK BRENNAN POPPED UP FROM HIS SEAT LIKE A PIECE OF TOAST, took over the podium, and began cross-examining Foley with his book, *Most Wanted: Pursuing Whitey Bulger, the Murderous Mob Chief the FBI Secretly Protected*. Brennan specified that when the book came out, Foley presented it to the public as "the truth."

Foley agreed, yet blamed his coauthor for any inaccuracies: "Some of the information he came out with, I questioned as to where he got it." Someone must have advised him to say that.

"And you wanted this book to help the public know about the truth of what you went through?" Brennan raised his eyebrows and stressed the word "truth."

"Yes," Foley said.

Brennan read the following passage from the book: "The feds stymied our investigation of Whitey, got us investigated on bogus claims, tried to push me off the case, got me banished to a distant barracks, phonied up charges against other members of the State Police, lied to reporters, misled Congress, drew in the President of the United States to save themselves, nearly got me and my investigators killed." He regarded Foley for a moment. "That was the truth, wasn't it?"

"Yes, it was."

The specter of government corruption materialized across the courtroom with Brennan's rapid-fire questions.

"In fact, sir, the agencies sometimes gave you more difficulty in pursuing the crime than the people you thought were the criminals? Isn't that true?"

"At times."

"At many times the FBI, according to you, undermined your investigations?"

"Yes."

"At many times the Department of Justice themselves, members of the DOJ, were undermining your investigations?"

"Yes."

"In fact, sir, it led you to the despondent conclusion that the mobsters, and the FBI, and the United States Attorney's Office, didn't traffic in the truth, it wasn't their language, they said everything but, it was all lies and half-truths and deceptions?" Brennan asked.

"At times, yes." Foley sighed.

"And you were referring to mobsters?"

"Yes."

"FBI?"

"Yes."

"The United States Attorney's Office?"

"Yes."

"Throughout the history of your investigations in trying to find the truth, were you surprised that law enforcement was undercutting you and fighting with you?" Brennan placed a hand on his hip.

"Yes."

"Were you surprised that lawyers in the Department of Justice were doing the same?"

"Yes."

Mobsters, cops, and lawyers lied? Did anyone tell Foley the truth? Brennan pressed Foley, getting him to admit that the Department of Justice attorneys prevented him from taking out indictments against organized crime figures who were being protected by the government. In fact, the lawyers actually "tanked" indictments.

Brennan questioned Foley about specific examples where his investigations had been blown wide open in order to protect organized crime figures. "You were tapping Frank Salemme's phone, weren't you?"

"Yes."

"And you believe that the federal agents corrupted that wire, didn't you?"

"I believe it was compromised." Foley nodded. "Yes."

"When you say 'compromised,' you believe it was compromised by the FBI?"

"Yes."

When Foley placed a bug in the napkin holder at the Busy Bee Diner, the mobsters suddenly stopped talking. As soon as he bugged a hair salon where the mobsters hung out, it closed. Foley believed those investigations were leaked by the FBI as well. It's surprising he kept at it. Most would've given up with all that resistance.

Brennan pointed out that a stenographer who had worked for the FBI's organized crime section had leaked information to the Mafia, and Foley complained that they handled it internally and allowed her to retire with a full pension.

"Did they prosecute her?" Brennan asked.

"No, they didn't." The muscles along Foley's jawline tightened. "No."

Brennan appeared to be sympathizing with Foley as he brought up many other instances where the Department of Justice undercut, fought, and "circumvented" Foley and his team. Foley had numerous fights with the DOJ over those leaks, and, back then, he always seemed to come out on the losing end.

It was hard not to feel sorry for Foley. He came across as a solid, conscientious cop. How did he ever get anything accomplished with all those government agencies working against him behind the scenes? We pictured a red-faced Foley banging his head against the wall.

Brennan switched gears and zeroed in on the government's sweetheart deal with Martorano.

"And in considering what the deal would be, some things you had to consider is what John Martorano wanted as well, didn't you?" he asked.

"We would listen to what he wanted, sure."

"And it was important to John Martorano that he not be labeled as a rat, right?"

"Objection!" Wyshak rose halfway up.

"Overruled."

"That was important to him, yes," Foley said.

"John Martorano made it clear to you that if he was going to cooperate, there were some people he was not going to offer evidence against."

"There were people that he preferred not to," Foley admitted.

"One of those persons was his brother, Jimmy Martorano?"

"Yes."

"And another person was Pat Nee?" Brennan stared right into Foley's eyes. Nee had been a criminal associate of Whitey's for years.

Foley shifted in his seat. "He denied—I had no specific conversation with him about Pat Nee."

Brennan pinched his lower lip, and regarded Foley with a long look of incredulity. "Another is Howie Winter?"

"Again, he would prefer not to."

"And as a state police officer, you have a duty and also you have a right to pursue charges against people who are alleged to have committed murder in the state of Massachusetts, right?"

"Yes."

"And you had information from John Martorano that Patrick Nee had committed murder, *was a murderer,* didn't you?" Brennan raised his voice every time he said the word "murder."

"The information that we had at the time was about people that were—that we were actually able to indict, and we indicted them," Foley said. "Information was passed to the state authorities prior to our agreement with John Martorano regarding what John Martorano had told us."

Brennan whipped out a transcript from the John Connolly trial where Foley had specifically said that Martorano was not going to testify against his brother, Nee, or Winter. That was part of the deal.

"You've encouraged prosecutors to hold people accountable for the murders they've committed in the past, haven't you?" Brennan asked.

"Yes, I have."

"Mr. Foley, did you make any efforts to take the information Mr. Martorano gave you to try to develop a case against Mr. Winter and Mr. Nee?"

"We were working on this case, which was taxing us for years, Mr. Brennan." Foley sounded exasperated. "If I sent my people off in every direction that we had a lead on, this case would never have been completed. And the reality of it is, this was the more serious crime that I felt we could investigate at the time."

"You don't think that the murders of Pat Nee were important to the murder *victims* of Pat Nee?" Brennan gave the jury a long, horrified look, and then glanced back into the spectators' gallery where the victims' relatives sat.

"Objection," Wyshak sprang from his seat and opened his mouth wide. "This is argumentative."

"Overruled." Judge Casper regarded Brennan. "I'll let you have the question, counsel."

Foley answered: "I didn't have information that Pat Nee killed nineteen people or Stephen Flemmi killed people." He spoke rapidly, sounding defensive. He must have meant to say Howie Winter instead of Flemmi. He added, "I had information that Stephen Flemmi and James Bulger killed many people, and that's where I was focusing on, because that's where I had to put our resources. I would have loved to have taken out Pat Nee and anyone else he named in that. But realistically, Mr. Brennan, it was not going to happen."

"You took what you could get from John Martorano," Brennan said. He had to regain control of the witness.

Foley nodded. "I took what I could get to get to the bottom of what was going on here for a long time."

BEHIND THE SCENES

We reminded Colonel Foley of the inferences Brennan made during cross-examination, in particular, about how Martorano didn't have to testify against Nee or Winter. Foley defended the deal: " In the case of Bulger and Flemmi, they were operating as FBI informants for twenty years, and being allowed to go out and commit these crimes under FBI knowledge and approval. It's different with Martorano. We did not authorize him to commit the crimes he committed. We used him as a *witness,* not an informant. We weren't operating with him, and saying, 'It's okay to kill those people. It's okay to have drugs come into South Boston. It's okay to do what you want. We will take care of you, and tip you off to law enforcement,' and so forth. If we're going to take down Bulger and Connolly and Flemmi, and bring home the bodies to the families, this was the only option.

"To start veering off on Nee and Winter when their crimes were so far back, and for us to make a RICO case . . . it had to be within the five years. Nee was in jail most of the time, as was Winter. You can go with a shotgun and spray into a thousand different directions, or you can use a laser like we did with Bulger and Flemmi."[1]

Brennan also pointed out that none of the masks, guns, ammunition, or weapons were found in Whitey's home in South Boston. There was no forensic evidence like DNA or fingerprints linked to Whitey.

Wyshak attempted to rehabilitate Foley during redirect examination: "Can you tell us what the—in your view—the cause of the heartache you had regarding the FBI was? What's the basis for that?"

"Well, the basis was that I think they put a higher priority on protecting their informants than they did actually looking at public safety," Foley said. "It was—there were investigations that we were trying to accomplish and take care of that were being compromised as a result of their relationship with informants."

"Colonel Foley, do you know if the defendant in this case was an FBI informant?" Wyshak asked, pointing at Whitey. He knew that Whitey didn't like being labeled an informant. That word alone made him squirm.

"He is," Foley said with conviction. He gazed at Whitey, who did not look up.

"How do you know?" Wyshak asked.

"Because the FBI identified him as one."

Foley also testified that he reviewed both Whitey's and Stevie's voluminous FBI informant files.

Wyshak informed jurors that Whitey's handler, former FBI agent John Connolly, was convicted of second-degree murder and was doing time in Florida. Most jurors jotted that down in their notebooks.

Mafia underboss Gennaro "Jerry" Angiulo (left) with Whitey Bulger (right) from state police surveillance from Lancaster Street garage.

"To say the least, the informant program was poorly run at the time," Foley said.

On recross, Brennan jumped all over the informant issue. If Foley didn't trust the FBI, if they had been lying to him and leaking his investigations, why would he believe anything he saw in Whitey's informant file? "You'd be relying on a document written by somebody else . . . if they wrote a lie, you'd be relying on a lie, right?" Brennan stretched his arms wide.

"Yes." Foley nodded once.

Brennan hammered on the reality that the government picks and chooses who gets prosecuted and who gets a sweetheart deal. Sometimes the government simply looks the other way . . . and sometimes they just make things up.

It was raining when we left court that day. Most of us had forgotten our umbrellas, including Foley. He had to stand in the rain while enduring the questions from the swarm of media in front of the courthouse. He could have walked away, but instead he gave people his time. The reporters were obsessed with the guns.

"The weapons themselves are pretty impressive," Foley commented when asked for the tenth time about the massive artillery of machine guns piled high on the clerk's table. "You don't find those weapons around anywhere, actually. They're all military-style weapons, they're very heavy, heavy-caliber machine guns, and just even from a law-enforcement perspective, to see those types of weapons and to think about the type of hands they were in for so many years is pretty chilling."

Whitey's guns were the lead story on the evening news. Even the national media outlets displayed photographs of the impressive stockpile in Boston. However, the bigger picture—bigger than the big guns— was the concept of government corruption and how deep it ran for years. We also wondered why Pat Nee and Howie Winter were never prosecuted for some of the murders. It didn't seem right. Foley's explanation didn't quite satisfy us. How much more would we learn as the trial progressed?

chapter

$$\boxed{8}$$

THE RACKETS

Well . . . they had somewhat of a gang war in South Boston and people were shot, and Mr. Bulger ended up on top, so you can draw your own conclusions.
—Richard O'Brien, trial testimony

FRIDAY WAS BOOKIE DAY. WE HAD HEARD FROM LAW ENFORCEMENT about how Whitey extorted the bookmakers, and now it was time to hear it directly from them. How much money did they make? How did the pyramid work? How difficult was it to get them to flip? What deals would Foley and prosecutors cut to convince them to cooperate? Were they telling the truth about Whitey?

James Katz took the oath and sat in the witness chair at 9:00 A.M. sharp. The seventy-two-year-old had groomed white hair and glasses, and wore an orange plaid button-down shirt. He kept twisting his fingers and sniffling into the microphone. He averted his gaze from the defense table. Did Whitey still invoke fear in the old-timers? We later learned that Katz's nickname on the streets was "Jimmy the Sniff." No wonder.

Katz made a career out of bookmaking from the early 1970s into the 1990s. He educated jurors about the math behind the business. The "vig," or vigorish, was 10 percent on the bets he took in. At one point, Whitey and Stevie changed the vig to 20 percent, which made it hard on customers . . . and everybody else in the business.

"What happened if you didn't comply with the directive?" Wyshak asked.

Katz snickered. "If they caught you, you could wind up in the hospital."

That was an understatement. With all the guns we'd seen the day before, it could be a lot worse than the hospital. Whitey must have been suppressing a smile. Wyshak reviewed his notes; he was likely thinking along the same lines.

Wyshak asked Katz to identify the defendant, and he quickly pointed at Whitey. Whitey gave him a cold, hard stare. Katz flinched—it was slight, but we caught it. Deep down, Whitey must have felt some satisfaction that he still had an effect on people after so many years.

Wyshak moved on: "What if customers win and beat the bookmaker?"

Katz explained that was called a "makeup." The bookie would get nothing and owe a bigger bookmaker for covering the loss. "You'd be placed on makeup the following week and owe it."

Wyshak nodded. "What's a layoff?"

"When a bookmaker wants to even off his book, even off his odds, bet on both sides," Katz said. That would happen when too many gamblers bet on the same team to win a game. If too many people win, the bookie loses.

At one point, Katz explained, Whitey and his gang decided to shake down the bookmakers and collect rent. It was easier. The bookies would have to pay George Kaufman, Whitey's rent collector, on a monthly basis for the privilege of doing business. They were charged a thousand dollars during football season and five hundred per month the rest of the year. Some bookies paid rent to the Bulger group while others paid the Mafia. Some had to pay rent to both groups. Katz explained, "You can't change your affiliations; once you're with somebody that's who you're with."

Katz had customers all over, including some out of state. They wrote checks for bets made out to Babe Ruth and John Hancock instead of sending cash through the mail. Katz would sign those fake names and cash the checks for a one percent fee. The checks were drawn on U.S. banks, which left a money trail, leading investigators right to Katz. He was caught red-handed and indicted.

The government pounced, pressuring Katz. Foley and prosecutors had something to work with. We pictured them sitting in a circle, grinning and rubbing their hands together. At first, no deal. *No way.* Katz testified that he would rather go to prison than be a rat, so he ended up with four years for money laundering. But, the government still had something to work with. It's all about bargaining power. Katz had a wife, three daughters, and property. Could he do hard time? Most people cannot. The government knew it and subpoenaed Katz to testify before the grand jury in 1994. He explained why he lied: "If I were to testify—my safety would've been compromised. . . . The people, they could reach me in jail . . . the Bulger group, Stevie and Whitey."

Prosecutors held Katz in contempt and told him his prison sentence wouldn't start until he cooperated. He had to sit in jail and wait. That's called "dead time." It sounded like indefinite detention to us. We wondered if he did any time down at Gitmo.

The government also threatened to take his home and toss his wife out on the streets. In exchange for his "truthful" testimony, Katz would be released from prison, keep his property, and be placed in witness protection. They'd throw some cash into the equation as well by covering living expenses and health insurance for his wife. Katz finally caved: "The government was going to take my house—my wife would've been out of the house . . . they reduced my sentence to five years' probation and vacated the forfeiture judgment. The government gave me a new name when I entered the witness protection program."

When Wyshak finished his direct examination of Katz, it was clear that his legal strategy was to educate the jury about how millions of dollars came in through the vast network of illegal gambling. It was like a structured pyramid with money flowing up to Bulger and Flemmi at the top. He also accomplished the legal goal of exposing that element of fear associated with Whitey. Katz had to be placed in the witness protection program and given a new identity. That lingering fear of Whitey came through in his body language.

Jay Carney's legal tactic during cross-examination was to make a big deal out of Katz's favorable treatment by the government in return for his cooperation.

"In prison, you're surrounded by criminals, right?" Carney asked.

Katz smiled. "We're all criminals in prison."

"What was the worst thing about prison?"

"Being away from my family," Katz said. We could hear the conviction in his voice.

"You made an agreement to come before the grand jury and testify again. . . . Your house was going to be forfeited to the government, the house your wife was living in . . . ?"

"Yes."

"You could be released that same day?" Carney implied that if Katz had testified in accordance with the government's wishes, he'd get to go home to his family.

"Yes."

Carney also emphasized that Katz only met Whitey once; most of his dealings were with Flemmi, and Katz was terrified of Flemmi.

"You knew Stevie Flemmi had a reputation—that he had killed several people?"

"I would never want to run into him," Katz said. Again, we heard the conviction in his voice.

Carney scored with that answer. It played into the defense strategy of vilifying and placing the blame on Flemmi, a key government witness.

When finished with Katz, the prosecution team pushed an eighty-four-year-old man down the aisle in a wheelchair. He looked like a Southern gentleman on his way to church, or perhaps the Kentucky Derby. The former bookie was dressed in a spiffy navy suit with brass buttons and a red tie. He had a full head of white hair. We wondered if the jury had heard enough about the gambling business. Was it overkill?

"Good afternoon, sir," Judge Casper said.

"Good afternoon." The witness looked up toward the ceiling. He appeared perplexed. "Who's speaking to me?"

It was the almighty voice from above.

Judge Casper smiled and waved. "It's me. It's over here."

"Ahhh." He smiled and acknowledged the judge.

We soon learned that Richard "Dickie" O'Brien was no ordinary bookmaker, as Zach Hafer began his examination. He ran a vast, and at times, very lucrative gambling network throughout several states.

"What do you mean by a bookmaker?" Hafer asked.

"Well, an individual that takes bets on horse races, numbers, sports," O'Brien said.

Bookmaker Richard "Dickie" O'Brien (right) with Stephen Flemmi (left) in a June 1980 surveillance photo from Lancaster Street garage.

"And what do you mean when you say 'numbers'? What are numbers?"

"Well, numbers are a number that was put out at the time, printed in the newspaper every day, and bookmakers would take bets on the numbers . . . they paid six hundred dollars for one dollar," O'Brien explained. This was before the state lottery came in.

"Is bookmaking in Massachusetts legal or illegal?"

O'Brien's eyes widened. "It's illegal." He raised his voice at the absurdity of Hafer's question and the gallery burst out in laughter.

O'Brien learned the bookmaking business from his father, and often took bets over the telephone from his South End betting "office" in Boston. Agents (smaller bookmakers) worked for him. He often had over thirty agents reporting to him from several states. If they had a winning week, the agent would keep 50 percent and the other 50 percent would go to O'Brien's office. He explained what happened if the agents lost: "Now, the office obligation was to pay whatever that agent lost. So, say that he lost five thousand dollars for the week. Well, the office paid that five thousand. That five thousand dollars would be set aside, called makeup. Until he won that five thousand back and got the office even, he wouldn't receive a commission. So, it was an unwritten law you stayed with an office."

O'Brien was associated with the Italian Mafia, but became independent in the early 1970s until he "was told that he had to meet with Whitey Bulger." O'Brien glanced at Whitey sitting at the defense table and smiled at his old acquaintance. At the meeting, Whitey told him: "You're by yourself now, I think you should be with us . . . forget the North End." O'Brien had no choice in the matter: "It was put down as law." Whitey and his gang had a reputation.

"And what was that reputation?" Hafer asked.

"That they were very capable." *Simply put.* Again, we thought back to the arsenal of machine guns.

"And by 'capable,' what do you mean?" Hafer glanced toward the jury.

"Well, that they had somewhat of a gang war in South Boston and people were shot, and Mr. Bulger ended up on top, so you can draw your own conclusions." O'Brien smiled. He should have given Hafer a wink.

In the bookmaking business, there were benefits to being aligned with Whitey's organization. Whitey threatened an agent who owed O'Brien money: "You were treated right by Dick," Whitey told the agent. "You owe him a big amount of makeup . . . we have a business besides bookmaking—that's killing assholes like you." Whitey tossed his head back and laughed when he heard the testimony. He must have remembered the conversation. O'Brien was an entertaining witness.

Eventually, O'Brien had to pay rent to Whitey's organization. "I paid rent because I valued my own life as well as those with me," he testified. O'Brien paid rent as high as two thousand dollars per month for fourteen years. In addition, Whitey "charged" him extra if law enforcement got a wiretap installed against one of his agents. O'Brien testified that he "paid cash to Stevie . . . Bulger never took the cash." He also noted that "Flemmi wasn't always a happy person."

In the early 1990s, O'Brien moved to Florida and his college-educated daughter, Tara, took over the family bookmaking business. John Martorano informed O'Brien that law enforcement had people "who were going to roll over on Whitey and Stevie." There were rumors about a young lady and her father who were cooperating, so Flemmi flew down and arranged an abrupt meeting with O'Brien. He was uncertain whether he'd come back alive, knowing Flemmi's reputation for violence. O'Brien instructed his daughter to go to the FBI in Miami if he didn't make it back. At the meeting, Flemmi told O'Brien about Chico Krantz, another bookie, who had "turned over." Flemmi kept repeating that he "should've taken care of him" when he had the chance. O'Brien assured Flemmi, "I'm the last person in the world that would turn over on you."

O'Brien miraculously survived.

Not long after, O'Brien received a grand jury subpoena. He said: "I didn't tell the truth, knowing what I thought I knew. I wouldn't testify against those people because of the repercussions I could have." O'Brien went to jail for contempt and Flemmi got to him in jail, instructing him "not to involve any one of them. Put the blame on someone else."

The government's main legal strategy in calling O'Brien was to emphasize how massive the bookmaking business was at the time. When O'Brien turned independent, he had no choice but to go with Whitey's organization and pay high rent and surcharges. Clearly, Whitey's enterprise established a monopoly over the lucrative illegal gambling business.

During cross-examination, Carney pointed out the benefits of being associated with groups like Winter Hill and the Mafia. These bigger organizations could provide protection, solve problems, and loan book-makers money. Carney's questions brought out the positive aspects of being protected by Whitey: "It benefited you in your business . . . it wasn't meant to be a secret by you . . . it was common knowledge by everyone on the street. And it was to your benefit!" O'Brien agreed.

Carney tried to paint Flemmi as the enforcer, the guy who instilled fear in others—the real monster of the organization. He noted that both O'Brien and his daughter were terrified of Flemmi, and sug-gested that Flemmi had killed his girlfriend, Debra Davis.

"I did not trust Stephen Flemmi," O'Brien admitted.

Carney suggested that Flemmi caused his daughter Tara to have a nervous breakdown, and she ended up in a hospital due to Flemmi's Florida visit. "Did you feel in any way responsible that your daughter had this breakdown?" Carney asked.

O'Brien sparred with Carney, but finally admitted, "It really upset her."

Carney finished his cross by emphasizing the unbelievable deal that the government gave O'Brien in exchange for his testimony. His daughter was also going to be charged with illegal gambling and money laundering, so he worked a "package deal" for her as well: "I would do about anything to get her out," O'Brien said.

Combined, the bookies provided an inside glimpse into how much power and reach the Winter Hill organization had throughout the un-derworld. We could picture O'Brien's "office" littered with newspapers, telephones constantly ringing, guys placing bets, envelopes stuffed with cash, and the occasional beating if somebody didn't pay up.

Whitey and Stevie Flemmi ran the show.

MURDER BY THE NUMBERS

> I shot three times and killed three people. My ride didn't pick me
> up so I had to walk and wash up in the snow.
> —*John Martorano, trial testimony*

THE KILLER RAISED HIS RIGHT HAND FOR THE OATH. THE AIR INSIDE
the courtroom suddenly felt like winter. John Martorano was the
real thing—a scary-looking mass murderer. What would Whitey do?
It had been thirty-one years since they'd been face-to-face. Would
they go at each other? We could sense the tension, the hatred between
the two. The marshals stood guard, ready to draw their weapons.
Anything could happen. The jurors sat forward in their seats, appearing anxious. They could sense danger.

Martorano was stocky, thick-looking . . . menacing. He breathed
heavily into the microphone, which amplified the sound across the
courtroom. He sounded like Darth Vader on the stand. He had dark
brown, graying hair with a round, saggy face and creased brow. His
lips formed a downward scowl and his nearly black eyes surveyed the
people in the gallery. He wore an expensive Italian dark blue suit and tie.
The large oval-shaped glasses failed to disguise the dark purple bags
beneath his eyes. He was a divorced father of five and a grandfather.

In the courtroom, he was out of his criminal element. On the streets,
this guy would walk up to his victims and shoot them point-blank in

the back of the head, the temple, or between the eyes. Most victims wouldn't see it coming. Martorano just got the job done, and with precision.

Wyshak started his direct examination with Martorano's plea deal. He had no choice but to expose the bad stuff up front to lessen the blow of cross-examination. This deal was a whopper—an unheard-of bargain with the devil. Martorano was sentenced to fourteen years for twenty murders and multiple racketeering counts. He agreed to cooperate and testify to avoid the death penalty in Florida and Oklahoma. He served just twelve years in a much nicer federal witness security facility where the government kept his commissary account filled so he could buy things, costing taxpayers approximately six thousand dollars. They also gave him twenty thousand for "start-up" money when he got out. Why did this killer get such a bargain? Couldn't they just take the death penalty off the table and give him life?

To rub more salt in the wound, the government allowed Martorano to profit from a two hundred and fifty thousand dollar movie option. If they make a movie, he'll get another quarter of a million.

Martorano was now a free man—a mass murderer walking the streets of Boston. Was he really retired from "the life"? Would he kill again?

BEHIND THE SCENES

"Don't be fooled. Johnny still knows how to shoot a gun," according to an anonymous source from the Italian Mafia. On the eve of the trial Whitey's defense team claimed that Martorano was still involved in criminal activity. The defense believed that the government shielded and protected their star witness. They fought for privileged state police reports, but were denied.

"What did your relationship with James Bulger and Stephen Flemmi entail?" Wyshak asked.

"They were my partners in crime, best friends, and my children's godfathers." We knew that Martorano had named his youngest son after his two "best friends."

"What motivated you to testify against them?" Wyshak asked.

Martorano scowled and looked right at Whitey. "After I heard they were informants, it broke my heart, broke all trust, all loyalties." In the criminal world it was understood that you can't rat on a rat.

Wyshak laid the foundation of Martorano's career as a hit man in organized crime, going back to the gang wars of the 1960s between the McLaughlins in Charlestown and the Winter Hill Gang, led by James "Buddy" McLean in Somerville. Martorano had his hands in everything from bookmaking and loan sharking to fencing stolen goods, and, of course, murder. Martorano's career as a killer started back in his early twenties. He described hit after hit in a flat monotone, without emotion, very matter-of-fact. Sometimes he'd kill in retaliation for a beating his brother Jimmy received or if somebody failed to pay a debt. His violent reputation became notorious within Boston's under-world. He dumped bloodied corpses in the back alleys and on side-walks throughout Boston, including North Station, which adjoined the Boston Garden where the Celtics and Bruins played.

Martorano's description of three murders during a snowstorm in 1968 was particularly chilling. Herbert Smith had given Flemmi a beating, so Martorano decided to kill him. When he arranged to meet Smith alone, there were "shadows of three people" inside the car. Martorano testified: "I shot three times and killed three people. My ride didn't pick me up so I had to walk and wash up in the snow." The victims turned out to be Smith and two innocent teenagers: Elizabeth Dickson, age nineteen, and Douglas Barrett, age seventeen.

"I felt terrible," Martorano said. He didn't appear *that* sorry. We leaned forward and squinted for a closer look. *No tears.*

Another time, Martorano stabbed a guy multiple times because he wouldn't keep his mouth shut. He claimed he was going to bring the guy to the hospital, but ended up killing him and dumping the blood-ied corpse in the South End.

Whitey was neither involved in nor charged with Martorano's early murders.

In 1972, Martorano caught the attention of Howie Winter. They became co-owners of a popular restaurant and nightclub in the South End called Chandler's. Martorano met Whitey, who had been involved in the South Boston gang wars between the Mullens and the Killeens.

According to Martorano, Whitey had just murdered Donnie Killeen, and wanted Winter to arrange a meeting at Chandler's to call a truce. The government had not listed Killeen as one of the nineteen victims in the current case. We speculated there was not enough evidence to convict Whitey.

"Whitey surfaced as the leader over there," Martorano said. He suggested they team up with Winter and get into the gambling business. Martorano corroborated what the bookies had said. The Winter Hill Gang with Whitey on board soon gained control of the rackets. They went out and rounded up all the independent bookmakers and made them do business with Winter Hill. It was "not optional," Martorano said.

Jurors took vigorous notes as Martorano began ticking off the murders that Whitey was charged with. He started with the early ones from 1973 and worked forward in chronological order. Martorano explained that a gangland hit back in the old days involved loading up on military-style weapons, and using disguises and multiple cars. He defined terms such as "boiler," which is a stolen car containing the shooters. When they "broadside" somebody, it means they're pulling alongside the target car to shoot the occupants. They used "crash cars" to cause an accident and distract the police when necessary.

Several murders centered around the hunt for Alfred "Indian Al" Notorangeli. Under Count Two of the racketeering indictment, the government had listed in its first act: "Conspiracy to murder members of the Notorangeli group." Indian Al had killed Paulie Folino, a bookmaker who paid tribute to Mafia underboss Gennaro "Jerry" Angiulo in the North End. Angiulo provided him with protection in return, and was outraged over the murder. He asked Martorano to do the hit, calling Indian Al "a loose cannon." Martorano testified that Whitey, Howie Winter, Jimmy Sims, and Joe McDonald made a group decision to track Indian Al down and kill him. On March 8, 1973, the group gathered the equipment: machine guns, walkie-talkies, masks, and uniforms. Whitey drove the car behind the boiler. They followed the target as he drove away from a bar near North Station (Mother's) in a shiny brown Mercedes.

Martorano testified: "We pulled up alongside and gave it a broadside . . . both guns were shooting . . . myself and Winters was shooting." Martorano often referred to Winter as "Winters." After the gangland hit, he remembered Whitey saying, "It looked like the car exploded!"

"Wrong guy," Martorano said, without any emotion. It turned out that Michael Milano looked like Indian Al. They'd made a mistake and killed an innocent man. There were two other passengers in the car, Louis Lapiana and Diane Sussman. They were both hit with machine-gun fire. Lapiana became a paraplegic.

The search for Indian Al continued. On March 18, 1973, the group got word that he was in a Buick with three other people driving along Atlantic Avenue near the North End. They gathered the murder equipment and headed out for the kill. Whitey drove in the rear car and had to cut the Buick off as it came out of a side street. Martorano then pulled up in another car with the machine guns and "gave it another broadside . . . we spun around and started shooting out the back window . . . me and Howie Winters were the shooters that night." The occupants of the target car engaged them in a firefight. Bullets sailed right over Whitey's head; he thought he was going to get caught in the cross fire.

Once again, they had the wrong guy. It was Al Plummer who got killed, and two others were wounded. Why so many mistakes? we wondered. It sounded like the excitement over targeting Indian Al had gotten the best of them.

Several days later, we heard from Plummer's daughter, Nancy Ferrier. She was just thirteen years old when someone called from the hospital saying that her daddy had been shot in the face. When she became very upset, they said he'd be okay. Later that evening Nancy learned that he'd been dead on arrival.

Winter Hill became enraged with their mistakes and began targeting Indian Al's associates. On March 24, 1973, they hunted Indian Al associate William O'Brien. Martorano, Howie Winter, and Whitey followed the target car on Morrissey Boulevard. Whitey was driving.

"We passed the car and shot into it," Martorano said. "The driver, O'Brien, got killed and [Ralph] DeMasi got wounded." After that, they stocked up on six more machine guns from New York. Winter Hill Gang member Joe McDonald killed another Indian Al associate in Florida.

Joseph Notorangeli, shot and killed by John Martorano at the Pewter Pot restaurant in Medford on June 3, 1973. Martorano dressed in a meat cutter's disguise.

On June 3, 1973, Howie Winter arranged to speak with Joe Notorangeli, Indian Al's brother. Joe was afraid to meet in person, but provided the number of a pay phone. *Bad idea.* The phone company provided Martorano with the location of the phone: the Pewter Pot in Medford. Martorano disguised himself "in a long, white meat cutter's coat . . . and beard." He described the next step in a flat, careless tone: "I went in and shot him . . . Joe Notorangeli . . . shot him in the heart."

Indian Al had left town, but wanted to come back, so he reached out to Jerry Angiulo and asked for forgiveness over killing Folino in March of 1973. He offered to give money to the Folino family. Angiulo arranged for a meeting at Cafe Pompeii in the North End and agreed to settle the matter for fifty thousand dollars. Indian Al also promised to take care of Folino's widow for the rest of her life. Later on, after Angiulo received the money from Indian Al, he called Martorano and asked, "What's taking so long to kill Al?" Martorano and Winter arranged a meeting with Indian Al, who no longer considered himself a target. Whitey drove the car behind them.

"I shot him," Martorano said, in that businesslike, flat tone of his. They ended up leaving Indian Al's body in the trunk of a different car in Charlestown while Whitey burned the vehicle they killed him in. Kids stole the second car, and police recovered Indian Al's body.

"Was that the end of your involvement with the Notorangeli group?" Wyshak asked.

"Yes," Martorano said.

How many dead bodies had piled up in an effort to kill one guy? We counted five: Michael Milano, Al Plummer, William O'Brien, the

The car in which Al Plummer was killed.

unnamed guy down in Florida, and Joe Notorangeli. Indian Al, the original target, made six. All of them, except the guy from Florida, made up the members of the Notorangeli group. Jurors would have to decide whether Whitey participated in the conspiracy to murder them. In addition, the government listed each group member as victims in separate acts of murder under Count Two; thus, jurors would have to decide unanimously whether each murder allegedly committed by Whitey was "proven" or "unproven."

BEHIND THE SCENES

Juror Gusina Tremblay told us, "There was a lot of debate over that Indian Al group of murders. We kept going back to that chart . . . the Winter Hill Gang chart that they kept showing us with Bulger at the top, which was dated 1975. These murders occurred before 1975."[1]

Next, came the murder of James O'Toole in 1973. O'Toole had shot Stephen Flemmi's brother (Jimmy the Bear) eleven times. The Bear miraculously survived. O'Toole also told people he was going to kill

Howie Winter in retaliation for the old gang wars. The group decided to target O'Toole. They learned that he was drinking at Bulldogs, a bar owned by Eddie Connors. Martorano, Winter, and McDonald piled into one car, which Whitey drove. Pat Nee and several others got into the car behind. When the shooters pulled up, O'Toole shielded himself behind a big blue mailbox.

Martorano explained that he "reached over and shot him with a machine gun. Joe Mac then got out and put one or two more in him."

James Sousa was the next target in October of 1974. The Winter Hill Gang had swindled a dentist by selling him fake gold bullion, and Sousa was involved. When the dentist went to the police, the gang felt Sousa wouldn't stand up and decided to kill him.

Martorano made a point of saying, "Jim Bulger was part of that decision." They brought him to Marshal Motors in Somerville, and Martorano said, "I walked in and shot him." Again, no emotion. Joe McDonald and Jimmy Sims buried him. Whitey and Stevie cleaned up. According to Martorano, "The blood went everywhere."

It was getting close to the end of the day, so Wyshak switched from the topic of blood and guts to the unique relationship that Whitey had with FBI Special Agent John Connolly. Martorano explained that Winter Hill had been bribing a corrupt state trooper, Richard "Dick" Schneiderhan, for approximately a thousand dollars a month. He'd warn them about wiretaps and investigations in exchange for the cash. Whitey claimed he had discovered Agent Connolly, who could help them out in the same way. Martorano warned him to be a good listener but not to tell him anything. Whitey nicknamed the agent "Zip" because he lived in the same South Boston zip code as the Bulger family. They had grown up near each other, but Whitey was older. Connolly proved himself by tipping them off about an investigation, and they decided to use him as a source for information.

"We saw the potential," Martorano said. He added: "Whitey took care of him all the time . . . gave him money." Martorano claims he didn't know until 1997 that Whitey was an FBI informant for Connolly—a rat.

We wondered why Connolly was on neither the prosecution nor the defense witness lists. He was serving time in Florida for second-degree murder with a firearm. They could have subpoenaed him. What would he say?

Court recessed for the day. We watched members of the government's team as they escorted the hit man onto an elevator, and headed up to the U.S. Attorney's Office on the ninth floor. We wondered if they had filet mignon and lobster tails waiting for him. Martorano called the shots.

We crammed into a packed elevator headed down; no one said much. People looked overwhelmed. Just listening to the descriptions of murder after murder had been very sobering. It didn't seem to bother Martorano. He had more to tell us about, too.

It didn't look good for Whitey.

chapter

1|0

MORE MURDER BY
THE NUMBERS

We were up to our necks in murder.
—John Martorano, trial testimony

back on the witness stand. He displayed a photo of Whitey holding Martorano's son at the baby's baptism. Whitey was the proud godfather . . . he looked handsome in his suit . . . a wide smile. A good Catholic. Who would ever believe he was a killer?

Wyshak didn't waste much time on the "innocent" picture of Whitey. He jumped right back in with Martorano's body count. This time it was Edward Connors, owner of Bulldogs.

"Eddie Connors was talking about, bragging about, how he set up O'Toole," Martorano said. The word got back to Winter Hill, and they didn't like it.

Wyshak displayed his favorite Winter Hill organizational chart, circa 1975, as Martorano reminded jurors, "The six of us would discuss it and make a decision."

"What did you decide to do?" Wyshak asked.

"We decided to shoot him. Whitey devised a plan to go to South Boston and for us to . . ." Martorano hesitated and looked up at the ceiling. "Oh, this is a different one."

There were so many murders, he couldn't keep track of them all. We noticed a juror shaking her head with disgust. The family of Eddie Connors sat in the gallery . . . waiting.

Martorano suddenly remembered. They had arranged for Connors to receive a call at a target phone booth. He testified, "I went over to Southie, and I went in the main car this time with Whitey and Stevie Flemmi."

"What happened at that location?" Wyshak sounded relieved that his witness was back on track.

"Then I let them out, they went up the hill and walked to the phone booth and shot Eddie," Martorano said.

Wyshak couldn't help himself—he just had to flaunt that chart again: "Is it a fair and accurate depiction of the people who were part of Winter Hill and their associates during the time period 1975?"

"Yes."

Martorano then named his partners in crime in the top row: "Whitey,

Edward Connors's body in phone booth after gangland hit.

Stevie Flemmi, me, George Kaufman, Howie Winter, Jim Martorano, Jimmy Sims."

In November of 1975, Whitey wanted to get rid of Thomas King, who had been a rival member of the Mullens gang and had plotted to kill him at one point. According to Martorano, Whitey said, "Tommy's uncontrollable and he's going to kill some police detective and he's just not controllable."

"What did he ask you to do?" Wyshak asked.

"To kill Tommy, take him out."

They all decided in favor and devised a plan to tell Tommy they needed help killing a guy nicknamed "Suitcase Fiddler" who was "running his mouth" about Eddie Connors's murder in the phone booth. Tommy agreed. Howie Winter met Whitey on Carson Beach in South Boston. Flemmi greeted them with a bag of guns.

"And what did Mr. Bulger do with the guns?" Wyshak asked.

"He passed them out to the four of us."

"And was there anything special about these guns?"

"Tommy's had blanks in it."

Wyshak nodded. "Then what happened?"

"Then we were supposed to drive over and shoot Fiddler, and on the way, pretty much after we pulled out, I shot Tommy."

"Where did you shoot him?" Wyshak asked.

"In the head." He tapped his own head.

Martorano wasn't present when they buried Tommy's body, but he mentioned, "I was driving across Neponset bridge one day and Whitey said, 'Tip your hat, Tommy's over there.'" *And he was.* King's body was recovered in the year 2000 right next to that bridge.

On the same November night in 1975, they planned the murder of Francis "Buddy" Leonard. Martorano said, "It was part of his second, Plan B for the night. He [Whitey] was going to kill this other guy, Buddy Leonard, who they were going to make it look like Tommy King killed him . . . they left him in Tommy's car."

"Did Mr. Bulger tell you what happened to Mr. Leonard?" Wyshak asked.

"Yeah." Martorano glanced at Whitey. "He told me he shot him and left him in the car."

In the FBI file, Connolly made a notation that a "source" said King killed Leonard and fled Boston. This was clearly a fabrication from Whitey that made its way into the file. King was already dead. We wondered if Connolly knew the truth or had his suspicions at that point.

Wyshak shifted away from Buddy Leonard, and questioned Martorano about the next murder. We looked at each other in disbelief. We wanted to raise our hands, ask for a time-out, and tell Wyshak to go back. That was it? We wondered why Whitey wanted to kill Buddy Leonard. Were there any more details? Several jurors appeared perplexed as well. Were they wondering the same thing? Perhaps we would hear more about Leonard later on. Maybe Martorano simply didn't have any further information.

The relatives of King and Leonard testified a few days later. Margaret King, the widow of Tommy King, testified that the police came to her house looking for her husband on November 6, 1975. They told her that Buddy Leonard had been found dead in her husband's car. She never saw her husband again.

Later on, she spotted Whitey getting into a car outside Triple O's bar. She asked him if he knew what happened to her husband. He offered the widow an explanation: "He was probably in Canada robbing banks, that's what he originally wanted to do."

"What was his demeanor?" the prosecutor asked.

"I am sure he was a little agitated that I would even bother him," King recalled. "I was quite upset."

Joseph Leonard, Buddy's brother, came to court in a wheelchair. He had received a phone call in the middle of the night to go to the morgue and identify the body: "It was my brother, and he had been shot many times . . . his teeth were covered with his own blood."

The mood in the courtroom was somber. We felt for the victims' relatives. We felt for the victims who were never coming back. Their lives had been snuffed out years ago.

BEHIND THE SCENES

As it turned out, Juror Gusina Tremblay told us that during deliberations they were searching in their notebooks for more information on the Leonard murder. "I had six notebooks . . . I searched and searched but couldn't find much." The issue of whether the government had "proved" the Leonard murder became hotly contested. Gusina felt for the Leonard family; she wanted to bring them closure . . . and justice. What would the jury do?[1]

Next, Wyshak focused on the murder of FBI informant Richard Castucci, which followed the sweeping horse race fixing investigation going on at tracks both inside Massachusetts and out.

Martorano explained part of the scam: They'd "pay the jockeys to lose . . . he pulls the reins so the horse don't run so fast."

"How do you make money?" Wyshak asked.

"The long shots would win, so you'd clean out the whole pool," Martorano said. In addition, Howie Winter had a horse named Spread the Word. They "changed the numbers under the lip and phonied some of the paperwork . . . put a good horse in with inferior horses."

The feds targeted Winter Hill when Tony Ciulla got arrested for fixing races in New Jersey. Martorano claimed they learned about the grand jury investigation through Special Agent John "Zip" Connolly. Joe McDonald hid out in an apartment in Greenwich Village. When that location was compromised, they blamed Richard Castucci.

Martorano said, "Whitey came in and told us that 'Zip' told him that Richard Castucci went to the FBI and told them where Joe Mc-Donald was . . . so we all decided to take Richie out . . . me, Whitey, Howie, and Stevie." They instructed Castucci to go to Marshal Motors in Somerville, and specifically asked him to accompany Whitey in order to count money at an apartment down the street.

Wyshak paused for a moment. "And then what happened?"

"I waited for them to get down there. They were counting money at the table . . . him and Whitey . . . I walked around to the side of Castucci and shot him."

"Where?"

"In the temple." Martorano tapped the side of his head with two fingers. "Here." His voice sounded deep and firm.

Martorano continued, "After that, we had to clean it up. Stevie and Whitey had to clean it up. Leo McDonald [Joe's brother] got a sleeping

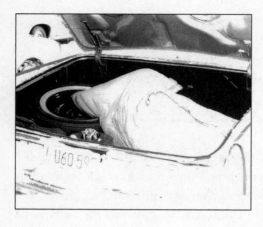

Body of FBI informant Richard Castucci, recovered in sleeping bag in trunk of car in December of 1976.

bag and we put him in the sleeping bag . . . put it in the trunk of his car."

We saw the photo of Castucci's big red car with snow on it, and then saw Castucci in the sleeping bag with the bullet wound in the side of his head. That made it real. According to Martorano, they had just murdered an FBI informant whose identity had been compromised via a tip from Special Agent Connolly.

Former FBI agent Tom Daly would testify later, and confirm that Castucci had been one of his top echelon informants. It was true that he had provided information about the location of the New York apartment, and was killed several days later. The FBI never investigated the murder.

The race fixing scheme heated up. Joe McDonald and Jimmy Sims became fugitives, and Martorano took off on the lam to Florida in 1978. Martorano claimed that Whitey and Stevie were left out of the indictment due to Connolly's influence. Howie Winter was arrested. Somebody forgot to tell Howie.

BEHIND THE SCENES

Howie Winter served two decades in prison for fixing horse races. He now believes Whitey may have been the one who ratted him out. He told Jon in an interview: "Evidently he had his own agenda there. I had known he had been talking with law en-

forcement but I always assumed he was getting information—
not giving it. I was wrong."[2]

While on the lam in Florida, the Winter Hill Gang helped Martorano with money they made by shaking down the bookies and drug dealers. They gave him about ten thousand dollars per month. "If they made a score, they would send me a piece of it," Martorano testified. He continued running his bookmaking business.

The next batch of murders dealt with Winter Hill's illegal activities over World Jai Alai in Miami, which was owned by businessman Roger Wheeler. Jai alai is a fast-paced Basque game where a ball is bounced off a walled space called a fronton. Players hurl the ball with baskets, similar to lacrosse sticks. People place bets on players.

Winter Hill had ties to World Jai Alai with retired and corrupt Boston FBI agent H. Paul Rico working as head of security at the Miami facility. John Callahan, who was an accountant from Boston, also became involved in the business and served as its president. Rico and Callahan devised a scheme for Winter Hill to skim up to ten thousand dollars a week from the parking lot and vending machines. They needed Winter Hill to protect them so the Mafia wouldn't bother them. Martorano described Callahan as a "high-priced accountant" during the day who wanted to "hang out with rogues at night."

"Did you ever hear the phrase 'wanna-be gangster'?" Wyshak asked. Martorano nodded. "That's what he was."

Roger Wheeler began investigating their illegal activities, so Callahan and Rico tried to convince Wheeler to sell the business to Callahan so they could control the skim. When he refused to sell, Winter Hill decided to "take him out" because they thought they'd have better luck convincing Wheeler's wife to sell.

Martorano received a call from Stevie Flemmi, claiming that he and Whitey were "on board" with the plan to murder Wheeler.

Rico asked Joe McDonald to help Martorano with the hit on Wheeler in Tulsa, Oklahoma. The former FBI agent had helped Winter Hill back in the day and they owed him a favor. Martorano said, "I arranged for Stevie to send me a package of equipment . . . machine guns, carbine, pistols, masks." He sent it from Boston in a suitcase "on a bus." Back then it was easy to pick something up at the bus station, and that's just what they did.

"So, equipment to murder someone?" Wyshak asked.

Martorano nodded. "And a dent puller to steal cars and stuff."

Neither McDonald nor Martorano knew what Wheeler looked like. They had flown into Oklahoma City, and rented a car for the drive to Tulsa. Rico provided them with a description and "gave his height and weight, like a ruddy description, a ruddy face," Martorano said. The former FBI agent also gave them Wheeler's home and business address and routine, along with a description of the car he drove. "It took four to six days of planning," Martorano testified.

Wheeler had a regular tee time every Wednesday at the Southern Hills Country Club. On Wednesday, May 27, 1981, the hit men stole a car from a mall parking lot and drove out to the club. They spotted a black Cadillac that appeared to be Wheeler's car, and waited in the club parking lot for a man fitting his description to return.

"Were you disguised?" Wyshak asked.

"Yes." Martorano described that he was wearing "sunglasses, beard, baseball cap."

A man fitting Wheeler's description came over a hill carrying a briefcase. He walked across the parking lot toward the Cadillac, and then "he opened the door and got in."

"And once he did that, what did you do?" Wyshak asked.

Martorano provided a simple, logical answer: "I opened the door and shot him."

"Where did you shoot him?"

"Between the eyes."

Wyshak grimaced and gazed at the jury. "And what happened to the gun at that time?"

"It exploded . . . blew open." Martorano was upset with Flemmi over the faulty gun. He still appeared agitated, displaying more emotion over the gun than the murder of Wheeler.

After shooting Wheeler, Martorano got rid of his clothes, the disguise, and "the boiler" (stolen car). They "sent the guns back on the bus to Florida . . . and got out of Oklahoma." They divided fifty thousand dollars they received from Callahan for the Wheeler hit three ways: twenty-five grand to Joe McDonald, and Martorano and Flemmi split the rest between them.

Wyshak moved on to the murder of John Callahan. Whitey and Stevie arranged for an emergency meeting with Martorano at LaGuardia Airport in New York. The meeting came on the heels of the Boston murders of Brian Halloran and Michael Donahue in May of 1982. Whitey had learned that Halloran had been cooperating with the FBI pertaining to the Wheeler murder, so they killed him in a gangland hit. Donahue had been giving him a ride home and also died.

Martorano testified: "Whitey was doing most of the talking" at the meeting. Whitey explained they had to kill Brian Halloran in Boston because Whitey learned from his friend "Zip" Connolly that "Halloran went to the FBI and told them that I killed Wheeler." Whitey said "that he did it for me." Whitey was also worried that investigators would "call Callahan in and put so much pressure on . . . he's gonna fold . . . if he does fold, we'll all go to jail for the rest of our lives."

Whitey and Stevie were nervous and wanted to take Callahan out. Martorano didn't like the idea, "I objected and told them Callahan was a friend of mine." They eventually convinced him that it had to be done and the hit should take place in Florida so they could have an alibi when it happened. They agreed to blame the Callahan murder on the Cubans. Whitey said he would ask Zip to put something in the FBI reports saying that Callahan was involved with drug deals involving Cubans in Miami.

"I felt lousy." Martorano frowned and wiped his brow. "We were up to our necks in murders already. . . . They just saved my life by killing Halloran, so I went back to Florida and met with Joe McDonald because he was in with the Wheeler murder . . . he agreed to help do it."

Martorano found out that Callahan was going to be flying into Fort Lauderdale airport in early August of 1982, so they stole a conversion van fitted with captain's chairs. McDonald followed behind him in another car . . . like a military maneuver. Martorano waited for Callahan at the curb, greeted him, and placed his luggage in the backseat. Callahan climbed in the front passenger's seat.

Martorano said, "I got in the back. I shot him in the head." He then placed Callahan's body in between the two captain's chairs and drove

John Callahan, former president of World Jai Alai, shot and killed by John Martorano in August of 1982 at age forty-five.

off. They had access to Callahan's garage at his apartment. When they moved Callahan's bloody body to the trunk of his own car, Martorano explained, "Joe thought he heard a moan and thought he was still alive, so we shot him again."

They spread Callahan's personal items around the Cuban section of Miami to throw off investigators.

Even after four murders (Wheeler, Halloran, Donahue, and Callahan), they were never able to reach their goal: Rico was unable to negotiate the sale of World Jai Alai.

Wyshak wrapped up his direct examination and sat down. His barrel chest heaved in and out as he drew a deep breath and exhaled. He looked exhausted. Martorano had been a key witness, and it had been up to Wyshak to make sure he'd left nothing out. That direct examination must have taken weeks if not months to prepare. The government was building its case against Whitey, brick by brick. Their legal strategy behind calling Martorano early on was to lay the foundation for murder and gangland violence dating back to the 1960s and to prove that Whitey was a "hands-on killer" and ruthless leader of the Winter Hill Gang. Listening to murder after murder had become numbing. Jurors appeared disgusted, some looked dazed.

Wyshak turned to his right to see which defense attorney would handle the cross. Hank Brennan.

It would be a bloodbath.

chapter

1|1

BATMAN

The priests and nuns I grew up with taught me that Judas is the worst person in the world.... Judas caused me to kill.
—John Martorano, trial testimony

WHAT GOES UP MUST COME DOWN. THE GOVERNMENT'S BRICKS CAME tumbling down as soon as Hank Brennan assumed the podium for cross-examination.

"Mr. Martorano, you are a mass murderer, are you not?" Brennan stared right through the hit man.

"I don't think so." Martorano sounded smug.

"You've killed for friends, right?"

"Correct."

"You've killed for family?"

"Correct."

"You've killed young, haven't you?"

"It was an accident."

Brennan narrowed his eyes to slits. "Have—you—killed—young, Mr. Martorano?" He slowed his delivery and emphasized each syllable.

"Yes."

"You've killed people that you know, true?"

"Correct."

"You've killed friends? Yes?"

"Correct."

"You've killed strangers?"

"Correct."

"You've killed innocent people, haven't you?"

"Correct."

"You don't like the term 'hit man,' do you, Mr. Martorano?" Brennan smirked and stressed "hit man."

"Not especially."

"Mr. Callahan gave you fifty thousand dollars after you killed Mr. Wheeler for him, didn't he?"

"Correct."

"You don't like the term 'hit man' because you think in some way it undermines your credibility, sir?"

"No, I wouldn't accept money to kill somebody." Martorano puckered his lips.

"So, there's a difference between what *you* did and someone who's a hit man?"

"I would think so."

"When you killed all these people, Mr. Martorano, rather than call yourself a mass murderer or rather than call yourself a hit man, how would you describe your conduct?"

"I don't know how to answer that." Martorano sounded dismissive.

Brennan cocked his head and stared at him for a moment. "Were you a serial killer?"

"No."

"You don't like that word?" Brennan's lips formed a pout.

"No."

"Okay, well, explain to the jury why you're not a serial murderer." Brennan extended his arm toward the jury box.

"Because I don't consider myself one, that's why. . . . A serial murderer kills for fun, they like it. I don't like it." Martorano glared at Brennan. "I never did like it."

He further explained that he "did it for free because I'm not a hit man."

"What about the fifty thousand dollars from Callahan?" Brennan cocked his head. Martorano had just testified on direct examination that he'd received money for the Wheeler murder. At least three jurors nodded.

Martorano claimed he would've done it anyway to help a friend.

"Callahan was your friend?" Brennan was quick to mention the friendship. He murdered that "friend."

Brennan continued firing questions, capitalizing on Martorano's defensive answers. He asked the hit man where he acquired his skills.

"Nobody taught me."

Brennan placed a finger to his lips in contemplation. "You just woke up one morning and started killing?"

Martorano huffed. "Family and friends come first." He explained that he'd learned to protect those who were close to him. "The priests and nuns I grew up with taught me that Judas is the worst person in the world. . . . Judas caused me to kill."

Judas? The man who betrayed Jesus? Brennan nailed him with that one by asking if Judas caused him to shoot Elizabeth Dickson, the teenaged girl in Herbert Smith's car.

Brennan continued the taunting. He informed jurors that Martorano bragged about being a vigilante during an interview on *60 Minutes.* Perhaps some of them had watched the episode. Whitey had probably watched while on the lam, too.

"Why that word?" Brennan asked.

Martorano explained that he called himself a vigilante because he killed people who deserved it, like Al Notorangeli, a bad guy who murdered others.

"Does that make you a vigilante?" Brennan cocked his head. "Like Batman?"

Everyone laughed. Brennan pulled Batman out of a hat. It was hard to picture Martorano donning that black suit and flying around Gotham City, fighting evil.

"I would rather be considered a vigilante than a serial killer," Martorano said.

"Is there any honor or integrity in what you did?"

"Yes."

"You're not exactly sure how many people you've killed?"

"I better be."

Brennan reminded him that he said on national TV that he wasn't sure of the exact number.

"If you got caught, couldn't you just tell people you were doing the right thing?" Brennan mocked him.

"I wish it never happened."

Brennan reviewed the chilling details of Martorano's early murders, reminding jurors that he was the triggerman, a heartless, stone-cold killer. He focused on the murders of the innocent teenagers, and John Banno, the man Martorano stabbed outside a restaurant while on a date.

"Was he screaming in the car?" Brennan asked.

"Yes, and I possibly stabbed him again."

"You weren't concerned about taking him to the hospital . . . you stabbed him again and again."

"Because he wouldn't shut up . . . that's when I had to keep stabbing him."

"Did you tell *60 Minutes* you wanted to be respected?" Brennan jumped back to the show.

"Who doesn't. . . . I always try to be a nice guy."

The audience laughed at that one. *A nice guy until somebody doesn't shut up. A nice guy unless you offend his brother. The nice guy who kills his friends.*

"When you decided to kill Mr. Wheeler, you didn't call Mr. Bulger, did you?"

"No."

"Mr. Bulger didn't call you?"

"No, I didn't speak to him."

Brennan glanced at the jury. He needed to create reasonable doubt about Whitey's involvement in the Wheeler and Callahan murders. That was a decent admission from Martorano, which could possibly distance Whitey from those out-of-state killings. Later, in a letter to us, Whitey was adamant that he was never involved in the Wheeler and Callahan murders.

Brennan skipped to the murder of Martorano's best friend, John Callahan.

"You selected a gun you were going to use to kill your friend?"

"I'm not sure of the gun. I think it was a twenty-two."

"You had to lie to your friend, Callahan, so he would have his guard down?"

"I didn't tell him that he was coming down to die."

"You had a smile on your face, you were trying to mislead him?"

"I just wanted to get him in the car."

"Did you look him in the eye?"

"I did."

"You made preparations to limit the mess?"

"I covered the floor and seats with plastic and towels so it wouldn't make a mess."

Brennan noted that he went for coffee after murdering his friend.

Martorano nodded. "To kill some time."

The answer received a few chuckles. It seemed like he was always out there killing something.

After hammering Martorano with more graphic details about various murders, he asked, "You didn't care about the suffering?"

"Yes, I did, but you can't change it."

Brennan spent a long time impeaching Martorano with prior inconsistent statements, making him out to be a liar, and claiming he changed details about some of the murders over the years. At times, there were too many details, and the jurors fidgeted. Whitey took notes without looking at Martorano.

BEHIND THE SCENES

Brennan explained to us later that Martorano was good at following the government's script. His legal strategy during cross-examination was to take Martorano "off script" as much as possible—that's when he floundered. Brennan said: "I practiced for months with imaginary witnesses. For example, I pretended Martorano was in the room with me, and I cross-examined him over and over, and came up with every possible follow-up question."[1]

Brennan noted that Martorano has never been called to testify about Pat Nee, Howie Winter, or his own brother Jimmy. They had participated in numerous murders. He didn't have to give up his friends or family. It didn't seem right. Those three were still out on the streets. Jurors must have been wondering why.

Brennan noted that the government did little favors for their star, including taking him to a special dentist when he had a toothache. Several jurors studied the prosecutors.

"It's good to have a partner in deals?" he asked.

"Yes."

Brennan gestured toward the prosecutors' table. "Your partner now is the federal government, isn't it?"

"Objection!" Wyshak jumped up.

"Sustained."

On redirect examination, Wyshak did his best to rehabilitate his star witness by shifting the focus away from Martorano and back to Whitey. He reminded jurors that this was Whitey's trial, not Martorano's.

"Were you and Mr. Bulger involved in the murder of Michael Milano?" Wyshak asked.

"Correct." Martorano relaxed back in his chair; he knew what was coming.

"Were you and Mr. Bulger involved in the murder of Al Plummer?"

"Correct."

"Were you and Mr. Bulger involved in the murder of William O'Brien?"

"Correct."

"Were you and Mr. Bulger involved in the murder of Al Notorangeli?"

"Correct."

"Were you and Mr. Bulger involved in the murder of Edward Connors?"

"Correct."

"Were you and Mr. Bulger involved in the murder of Tommy King?"

"Correct."

"Were you and Mr. Bulger involved in the murder of James O'Toole?"

"Correct."

"Were you and Mr. Bulger involved in the murder of James Sousa?"

"Correct."

"Were you and Mr. Bulger involved in the murder of Richard Castucci?"

"Correct."

"Were you and Mr. Bulger involved in the murder of Roger Wheeler?"

"Correct."

"Were you and Mr. Bulger involved in the murder of John Callahan?"

"Correct."

The questions and answers sounded rehearsed, yet the long list of murder victims could not be ignored. Jurors gazed at Whitey, which was Wyshak's goal.

He also let Martorano clarify what he meant when he referred to Judas.

"A Judas is a rat, it's a no-good guy, and I was always brought up that's the worst person in the world," Martorano said.

Overall, the cross-examination by Hank Brennan accomplished several defense goals. There's nothing more exciting than riveting "made-for-TV" drama, a verbal sword fight . . . blood drawn right there in the courtroom.

Brennan stole the jury's focus away from his client, and caused them to listen to his questions. The key to cross-examination is to control the witness with effective, leading questions. Martorano was no ordinary witness. He's a seasoned killer, who continues to instill fear in others, yet Brennan assumed complete control over Martorano. Effective cross-examination is a skill that takes years to master for most lawyers, and some never get it. Brennan had it down stone-cold.

BEHIND THE SCENES

We asked Brennan: "What is your secret to effective cross-examination?" He replied, "Devoid yourself of all emotion, suffocate and destroy every personal relationship you ever became involved in, and carry a small ball of hate when approaching the witness."[2]

1|2

REMEMBER US

Close to the apartment, we were at a stoplight, and all of a sudden
there was this noise, a continuous stream of noise, you know, gunfire, rocks throwing, and it was just nonstop. . . . In retrospect, it
was a machine gun, but whatever I heard was going on and on.
—*Diane Sussman, trial testimony*

THE MOOD CHANGED FROM ELECTRIC TO MELANCHOLY. THE PROSECU-
tion team knew the defense would score points during the cross-
examination of Martorano. It was inevitable. The case against Whitey
had too many land mines. They knew Carney and Brennan would capi-
talize on unholy alliances they'd had to make with killers like Martorano. Evidence of government corruption always hovered over the
courtroom like an ominous storm cloud, and sometimes that cloud let
loose. It poured when Brennan accused Martorano of being a mass murderer. When it got ugly, the prosecution team rescued itself with victims.

Zach Hafer called Sergeant Detective William Doogan from the
cold-case squad of the Boston Police. What better way to raise the dead
than with crime scene photographs?

Doogan identified people and places from the old crime scenes,
including Michael Milano's brand-new bullet-ridden Mercedes, the
mailbox O'Toole had been hiding behind, Al Plummer's bloody car,
and dead bodies on slabs at the morgue. The photo of Eddie Connors

with legs sprawled out in that blood-spattered phone booth was particularly gruesome. The receiver dangled on its silver cord, making it all too real. We could practically smell copper, car exhaust, and decay. The jurors appeared pensive. Their gazes shifted from the giant photographs to Whitey.

Remember us, the victims seemed to be saying.

The Donahue family sat up front when they displayed the photos of the blue Datsun that Michael Donahue had driven when he was machine gunned down with Brian Halloran, who had been cooperating with the FBI in the Wheeler investigation. The crime scene photographers had zoomed in on the bullet holes and bloodstains. Some of it was brain matter . . . on the headrest. Whitey and Kevin Weeks had secretly looked at the blood in the Datsun the following day. Did the photographs serve as a reminder for Whitey? Did he feel any remorse, especially with the Donahue family sitting a few feet away?

Pat Donahue, Michael's widow, looked away; seeing the car where her husband had been sitting when he was shot would have been too much.

We pulled tables together in the cafeteria during the morning recess. Close friendships had formed. The intimate group rallied around the Donahues that day. Words can't describe the emotion we all felt after seeing those shocking crime scene photographs. Tommy Donahue reminisced about the bloodstained blue Datsun that we had just seen where his father had been murdered: "I remember the Datsun. We had some good times in that car . . . us kids . . . we'd all pile in and go to the beach. We'd be hanging out the windows, nobody wore seatbelts in those days."

"The United States calls Diane Sussman de Tennen," Kelly said slowly. Diane marked the beginning of a string of witnesses who would tell their harrowing stories of having loved ones gunned down or strangled. Some would tell stories of survival. All would tell stories of perseverance.

When Diane raised her hand for the oath, the journey that began on March 8, 1973, was about to come full circle. She wore her chestnut brown hair short, and had chosen a conservative navy blazer with a crisp white shirt underneath. Back in 1973, Diane was a shy twenty-three-year-old who came to Boston from California for a dietetic internship. She immediately took an interest in a larger-than-life personality named Louis Lapiana.

Diane smiled briefly at Kelly and the jury, but appeared uncomfortable. She had to testify because the man she loved couldn't be there to speak for himself.

"Now, were you familiar with a place called Mother's?" Kelly asked.

Diane drew a deep breath. "Yes."

"And what was that?"

"It was . . . a bar by the Boston Gardens, where the hockey was played, ice hockey."

Louis Lapiana, Diane Sussman's boyfriend. Lapiana became a paraplegic following a gangland hit on March 8, 1973. The shooting involved a case of mistaken identity.

"So Louis was working at the bar called Mother's?"

"At that night." She nodded. "Yeah."

"You said he was working for Michael?" Kelly referred to Michael Milano, who had also worked there as a bartender.

"Yes, Michael asked Louis to cover for him that night," she said.

"Did you go outside?"

"Yeah, we went out and Michael had this brand-new car out front."

"What kind of car was it, do you know?"

"It was a Mercedes . . . he was very proud of it, showing it off." She smiled and sounded nostalgic. "I got the honor of sitting in the front passenger side, and, you know, getting to play with all the newness of the car."

"And did you drive away from the bar?" Kelly asked.

"Yes, we did."

"And what, in general, was being discussed in the car?"

"Louis and Mike . . . played chess together, and they were giving each other a hard time . . . who was going to win the game, and, you know, egging each other on."

Kelly glanced at the jurors. They appeared rapt with Diane's story. "Now, after a while with this drive, did something highly unusual happen?"

"Yes." She bit her lower lip. "Close to the apartment, we were at a stoplight, and all of a sudden there was this noise, a continuous stream of noise, you know, gunfire, rocks throwing, and it was just nonstop. There was dozens and dozens of . . . whatever. In retrospect, it was a machine gun, but whatever I heard was going on and on. And the car was hit with machine-gun bullets. I ducked . . . that's probably the only reason I'm here."

The jurors were now sitting on the edge of their seats, wide-eyed and captivated.

Diane continued. "But after the noise, the shooting, the bullets stopped, I got up, and Michael Milano was, you know, forward in the steering wheel and I looked at him and I asked him if he was okay, and I got no response." Diane's voice cracked. She closed her eyes and paused for a moment. "I turned around to ask Louis how he was, and he was forward, and his eyes were, like, glazed, and he barely shook his head, and I got a very low noise of 'No.'"

Diane laid on the horn to get someone's attention. When the police arrived, they were concerned for her safety because they thought she might be a target if the gangsters considered her a witness. All she wanted to do was ride in the ambulance with Louis, and they wouldn't let her.

Michael Milano's new Mercedes in which Michael Milano was killed, and Louis Lapiana was left paralyzed after a gangland hit in March of 1973.

Kelly looked at Whitey and then addressed Diane. "And what happened to your boyfriend, Louis Lapiana?"

"They wouldn't let me see him for the first day, and when I finally saw him, he could not speak. He . . . he . . . they had—The only thing they saved—They had to shave his head because he had bullets all over him. They saved his mustache, and that was like . . . that was the only Louis at that point . . . he could not talk. He could not move . . . and he was on a breathing apparatus." Her voice cracked.

"So he was paralyzed?" Kelly asked, almost in a whisper.

She closed her eyes for a moment. "He was paralyzed."

A juror in the front row bowed her head and started weeping, but she wasn't the only one. Several people in our row wiped tears from the corners of their eyes. Whitey kept his head angled toward his table. Was he feeling remorse?

Diane returned to California, married, and had two children, but still cared for Louis.

"I am to this day emotionally connected to Louie," Dianne said. "Louie was part of my life the full twenty-eight years. He moved to Long Beach VA Hospital. My children grew up from infancy with Louie."

Louis Lapiana died in 2001.

BEHIND THE SCENES

"How did I know to duck so fast?" Diane said to us. "It was survival." The longer story of survival played out over the next three decades when Diane stayed by Louie's side through

most of his struggles. "When he would get down, it would destroy me. As long as Louie was down, so was I. He could've
died five times. If he would have closed his eyes and said, 'This
is it'—that would be it." She added, "I said good-bye to him
three times and he said after, 'I heard you.'" Even though Louis
was confined to a wheelchair, "his love of life kept him hanging
on."[2]

John Martorano testified that he was the man who fired into Milano's car by mistake. The real target was not Milano, but rather Alfred
"Indian Al" Notorangeli. This was no solace for Diane.

BEHIND THE SCENES

Diane did not want to testify but told us she did it to be a voice
for Louie. She didn't want the "bad guys" to be the only voice
in the courtroom. In 2011, when Diane found out Whitey
had been indicted for Milano's murder, she said she felt
Whitey was a killer and also a puppet: "He only existed because he had all the people behind him—including his family.
The government is just as much to blame. There is no justice
here."[3]

On cross-examination, Carney asked Diane if she witnessed who
fired into Milano's car. She said she could not answer without speculating; however, she regarded Whitey for a long moment and added,
"In my mind, I do know."

As Diane left the stand, she appeared to be staring blankly at the
back wall, as if she were in another place. Was she back in 1973 reliving
the shooting? Was she imagining a larger than life Louis before he
was shot, on their first date with the cowboy boots? When she looked
in our direction, we could see the pain in her eyes. She passed Whitey,
yet he didn't acknowledge her. Was he touched by her story of love?
Did he admire the woman for her sheer dedication and loyalty over all

those years? Did he think about how one night's mistake touched so many lives? Did he care?

The juror in the front row continued weeping and Judge Casper called a recess.

Juror Gusina Tremblay had been so touched by Diane's story that the press started calling her "the weeping juror." She later told us that the love story affected her. She couldn't stop thinking about Diane and her love and dedication for Louie for all those years. "It makes you think about what's important in life," Gusina said.[4]

"The United States calls Donald Milano." Kelly stood behind the podium and waited for an older man to walk past Whitey and take his seat behind the witness stand. Milano had short-cropped white hair, a white mustache, and came across quite fidgety and nervous. He described his family as "close-knit." His dad died when he was two weeks old, so his mother had to raise five boys by herself. Michael Milano was Donald's older brother who tended bar at Mother's with Louis Lapiana.

"Let me direct your attention to March 8, 1973," Kelly said. "Do you remember that day?"

"I do." Milano stiffened and nodded once.

"Okay." Kelly glanced into the audience where the Milano family sat. "What happened that day?"

"I was on my way to work, and on the radio—" He looked down for a moment. "—I heard my brother was killed."

"And when was the last time you saw your brother alive?"

"The day before."

"What was the occasion?"

"He brought his car over for me to see, new car." Milano gasped and sipped his water. "A new car."

"What kind?"

"A Mercedes-Benz."

"Did he take you for a ride?"

"Yes, he did." He forced a smiled and then pressed his lips together. "He was very proud of it." Milano broke down with emotion and apologized to Judge Casper.

Kelly displayed his brother's photograph, and asked if he had listened to the testimony where Martorano talked about the mistaken gangland hit on Milano's car.

"Yes." He gazed at Whitey, who did not look up. Milano joined his family back in the gallery. They were visibly upset, yet appeared relieved as if they had finally achieved some closure after all the years.

Laura Mello also looked at Whitey as she raised her right hand for the oath. She was only ten years old in December of 1973 when she heard the news that her father, James "Spike" O'Toole, had been shot and killed.

"I remember going to the memorial mass." She frowned and exhaled. Hafer displayed O'Toole's photograph on the big screen. She stared for a long moment at the man standing in the snow. That man seemed to be peering out at her: *Remember me?*

"Yes, that's my father," she continued staring at the man in the snow. Laura appeared to be momentarily lost in thought. We felt for her—losing her dad as a ten-year-old, the few memories had likely faded.

Deborah Scully took the stand after Laura. She grew up in the same Old Colony housing project as Whitey in South Boston. She remembered the Bulgers' house with the shamrocks in the windows—everyone knew it.

Deborah was in love with William O'Brien and nine months pregnant with his baby when she heard an eruption of sirens.

"Now, I want to direct your attention to a specific day in March, specifically a Friday, March 23, 1973," Kelly said. "Do you remember that day?"

"Yes, I do."

Deborah had taken a leisurely walk with her daughter after dinner when she witnessed the "police flying toward Morrissey Boulevard in every direction, all kinds of police."

"So what did you learn?" Kelly asked.

"That O'B was dead, that he was machine-gunned out on Morrissey Boulevard."

"Did you happen to go to the crime scene?"

"I did."

"And what did you see?"

"Just a lot of blood and the tire tracks that went into the field."

She gave birth to O'Brien's son, and missed his funeral. She identified O'Brien in a photograph, which was taken with his young daughter, Marie. Jurors stared at that photo. It looked like he would have made a loving father, and never had the chance to hold his son.

Tom Angeli took the oath, and relayed the story about coming home from school one day in April of 1973 to learn that his Uncle Joe Notorangeli had been murdered at the Pewter Pot restaurant in Medford. He was almost sixteen years old. His family could not attend the funeral because his father (Alfred "Indian Al" Notorangeli) "was in fear for our safety," he said.

A year later in February of 1974, Tom learned that his father had also been murdered. He remembered attending the funeral.

Murder victim William O'Brien with his daughter, Marie. He was machine-gunned down on Morrissey Blvd. on March 23, 1973 as he drove back from the bakery after picking up his daughter's birthday cake.

Joseph Angeli (Tom's cousin) would testify later that he learned how his uncle was gunned down at the Pewter Pot on his fourteenth birthday. He came home and his mom was crying. They couldn't even attend the funeral—it was too dangerous. *What a thing for a kid to come home to . . . on his birthday.*

Each relative identified a murdered family member or close friend in an old photograph. Most victims had large smiles as they posed for the camera, having no idea that the particular moment captured in time would someday be displayed in Boston's federal court. *Murder? It can't happen to me,* they may have thought. These were living, breathing human beings whose lives had been cut short.

Remember us.

chapter

1|3

BAD VIBRATIONS

> Guys are walking the streets after they killed twenty people if they
> cooperated, and then you got . . . one person who kills somebody—
> they put him in the electric chair. That's the way the government
> works. You kill twenty people, go testify against somebody, you can
> walk.
>
> **—Ralph DeMasi Sr., trial testimony**

THE MOOD SWITCHED FROM SLOW AND PENSIVE TO PURE ENTERTAIN-
ment when Ralph DeMasi Sr. took the stand. If they make a movie,
DeMasi should play himself. He is the quintessential old-style gangster, a man of honor who had just been released from federal prison
after serving twenty-one and a half years. Guys like DeMasi added
color to the trial, providing jurors with an inside glimpse of "the
life."

"Were you served a subpoena to be here, sir?" Kelly asked.

"Yes, I was." DeMasi shouted every time he spoke, like he was hard
of hearing.

"A few years ago, did investigators try to talk to you when you were
in prison and you declined to talk to them?"

"Yes."

"In fact, before we began this proceeding today, did you refuse to
speak to me outside?" Kelly wanted to let the jury know that this witness

had not been prepped. What you see is what you get. He had been compelled, ordered to testify.

"Yes." DeMasi was old-school, where there were no gray areas between the good guys and the bad. He was a bad guy and would have nothing to do with the good guys, that is, cops and prosecutors.

"You've been convicted of multiple felonies over your lifetime, correct?"

"Yes, I have." DeMasi declared with authority. If prisons issued a service badge, DeMasi would have proudly displayed his.

"Do you know a man named William O'Brien?"

"I knew him for one day."

Kelly rubbed his chin. "Only one day, sir?" He had no clue what DeMasi would say on the stand.

He nodded. "One day only."

DeMasi admitted he knew Tommy King from prison.

"So let me direct your attention to a specific date in March of 1973. There was a shooting in South Boston. Do you remember that?"

"No, I don't." DeMasi pursed his lips and raised his chin.

Kelly stared at the witness for a moment. That was the most important part. How could he not remember the shooting? Judge Casper had granted DeMasi immunity from prosecution that morning. Was this guy toying with Kelly now? Would he suddenly get amnesia?

"Weren't you part of it?" Kelly asked.

"I don't know, tell me about it." DeMasi had all the control.

A man in the second row of the jury box smiled.

"Well, you're the witness, so you're supposed to answer the questions, okay?" Kelly sounded confrontational. This old-school ex-con had managed to crawl under his skin. "Were you with a man named Billy O'Brien that day?"

"Yes, I was."

Kelly must have been relieved; it was a start. "That was the one day you met him?"

"First day and last day."

"All right." Kelly exhaled loudly. "What happened that day?"

"You want the whole story or just a little bit of it?" DeMasi asked.

People in the gallery laughed, and Judge Casper smiled. Kelly gave him the floor and asked for the whole story.

Once DeMasi got on a roll, he couldn't stop talking. It was as if he'd been waiting his whole life to tell it, and now he had an audience. On the day of the shooting in March of 1973, he got a ride from Billy O'Brien so he could have coffee with Tommy King at Linda Mae's bakery in Dorchester. It wasn't clear why he couldn't drive himself.

O'Brien was getting a cake at the bakery for his daughter Marie's birthday. She was turning twelve. When they left, King got into a car with three other guys, and DeMasi drove with O'Brien. When they pulled out onto Morrissey Boulevard, he became nervous.

DeMasi testified: "I said, 'Billy, keep your eye on the rearview mirror, the side mirror. If a car comes up fast, hit the gas.' He started laughing, 'Ah, Ralph, you're—Ain't nobody going to hurt us, blah, blah, blah.'

"I said, 'Billy, pay attention, I got bad vibrations. Watch your mirrors, if a car comes up fast, hit the gas.' He keeps laughing."

Kelly let DeMasi ramble. He didn't know where the story was going. The jurors appeared riveted. Everyone likes a good storyteller. Even Whitey seemed to be enjoying it. He had stopped scribbling in his legal pad and cocked his head, listening.

DeMasi gestured wildly with his hands. "All of a sudden, a car pulls up, people start shooting at us. When it was over, Billy O'Brien was dead, I had eight bullets in me. We—he hit the gas—he said, 'What the fuck'—hit the gas, hit the brake, the car started fishtailing. He must have died instantly."

"What did you do?" Kelly asked when DeMasi came up for air.

"What did I do?" DeMasi shouted. He'd become overly animated, as if he'd been reliving the moment. "I got hit and I got thrown forward, and just instinct made me go down as low as I could near the floorboards. . . . The car hit the guardrail . . . boom!" He demonstrated by slapping his palm on the witness stand.

"My adrenaline was going." He spoke rapidly. "I didn't have a gun, but I had a stiletto. I opened the door, jumped out of the car. The cars that were shooting at us stopped about thirty yards up ahead. The two shooters was getting out. I ran towards them, hoping that I could stab one of them and get a gun from him . . . when they saw me coming, one of them yelled, 'Here he comes!' And they jumped back in the car and burned rubber." My adrenaline is going," he repeated. "I start running after him—"

MDC (Metropolitan District Commission) police officer inspecting body of murder victim William O'Brien on Morrissey Boulevard in Boston, March 1973.

Kelly extended his palm. "Now, wait a minute. You were shot eight times and you were running at guys with guns with a knife?"

Great question. The story was almost too good to be true, like something out of Hollywood. On the other hand, this guy was such a character. We wouldn't put it past him.

"So after I realize I'm a nitwit running after a car that's burning rubber," DeMasi continued, "I stop. . . . I walked back to the car. . . . I yell, 'Billy, Billy!' . . . The whole side of his face was blood. It's obvious he was dead."

DeMasi received treatment at the hospital for his gunshot wounds. He was proud of them and likely showed them off in prison. *Eight more badges.*

Several days later, DeMasi went to O'Brien's funeral and "got arrested coming out of the church for getting shot." We learned that he was arrested on a parole violation.

"The bottom line is, sir, you don't know who actually shot you, do you?" Kelly asked.

"No, I don't," DeMasi declared, with conviction.

Kelly must have known he wouldn't get that out of DeMasi. No way. DeMasi likely knew exactly who did it. When we saw the photograph of O'Brien's car with the windows blown out, we wondered if the box on the floor in the passenger's side had contained his daughter's birthday cake. Lieutenant Steve Johnson later confirmed it.

"Nothing further." Kelly gathered his papers and sat down.

Jay Carney rose for cross-examination. He didn't know what DeMasi would say either. Carney had been around long enough; he knew how to "wing it."

The vehicle Ralph DeMasi Sr. had been riding in when they machine-gunned William O'Brien on Morrissey Boulevard in Boston, March 1973. The box containing O'Brien's daughter's birthday cake can be seen on the floor.

Carney began with DeMasi's recent prison stint. He had served twenty-one and a half years for conspiracy to rob an armored car.

"Did the government put any money in your canteen account?" Carney asked.

DeMasi laughed. "Not that I know of."

"When you got out on March 1 this year, did the government give you twenty thousand dollars to help you resettle your life?"

"No, they gave me sixteen dollars. . . . I think about ten of it was mine."

"Did you kill anyone or hurt anyone in that conspiracy to rob an armored car?"

"No, I didn't."

Carney made his point and sat down. The comparison to Martorano's twenty thousand dollar start-up fund provided by the government was obvious.

Kelly rose for redirect. "You never cooperated with the government, did you, sir?" he asked.

"No, never will," DeMasi said with conviction.

"But you're an experienced criminal, aren't you, sir?"

"No, I'm retired."

"Well, okay." Kelly smiled. "Glad to hear that. In fact, when people refuse to cooperate, cases don't get made. Isn't that right?"

He shrugged. "I don't know."

Carney took one last shot with him on re-cross. "During your time in prison, you learned that people sometimes cooperate with the government and become a witness, right?"

"That's pretty obvious," DeMasi shouted. "Been going on for years."

"And people know they can get extraordinary benefits if they agree to be a cooperating witness. Isn't that true?" Carney emphasized the word "extraordinary." It was his favorite word.

"Absolutely."

"And is it fair to say that people won't hesitate to lie about their testimony if they think that will get them a benefit?"

"Objection," Kelly said.

"Sustained."

"Absolutely." DeMasi answered anyway. Judge Casper had to instruct him not to.

"Were the benefits of cooperating generally well known among the inmates?" Carney asked.

Kelly jumped up again. "Objection!"

"I'll allow that question. Overruled."

"Yeah. Guys are walking the streets after they killed twenty people if they cooperated, and then you got other—one person who kills somebody—they put him in the electric chair. That's the way the government works. You kill twenty people, go testify against somebody, you can walk."

Great answer. It was just what Carney had been looking for. He thanked the witness and sat down.

In hindsight, the government lost points by calling DeMasi. He didn't implicate Whitey in anything. He claimed he didn't know who shot at them and killed O'Brien. Carney used him to make his point about the all-powerful government giving "extraordinary" deals to some while they buried others. DeMasi made it real by putting it in his own words, plain and simple. He connected with the jury.

Kelly watched DeMasi hightail it down the aisle and out the door. It had to be a challenge for prosecutors to deal with the old-school gangsters, especially for the Whitey trial. Many, like DeMasi, would rather serve time than make any kind of deal—that's why murders went unsolved.

chapter

1|4

THE THROAT OF
THE DRAGON

My hand went into his neck where his head should've been.
—Frank Capizzi, trial testimony

EXPOSE THE SAVAGERY, HEAD ON. THAT WAS THE GOVERNMENT'S LE-
gal strategy in calling two more gangsters, Charles Raso and Frank
Capizzi.

Raso was a former bookie and colorful character from the bygone
streets of Boston. He did more damage to Whitey than DeMasi by
adding behind-the-scenes information about the Indian Al group of
murders. He knew the Notorangeli family growing up, and became
partners in the bookmaking and bar business with Joe Notorangeli.
Raso described Indian Al as "a roughneck. He liked to get in trouble. . . .
Hothead."

Raso owned Mother's, the bar where Michael Milano worked as
manager and Louie Lapiana was a bartender before Milano was killed
and Lapiana paralyzed in a case of mistaken identity. "Michael liked
Al. He tried to copy him. The long hair, the long coat. He even got a
Mercedes. Sad to say," Raso testified. When he learned that Milano
had been killed, he reflected, "Words can't explain it. I couldn't understand it."

Raso explained the origins of the Al Notorangeli hit. When Indian

Al got out of prison, he hooked up with Al Plummer. "They were ter-rorizing bookmakers who were connected," Raso said.

"You mean the Mafia?"

"There's no such thing." Raso grinned and added, "They were con-nected. In town. Mr. Angiulo."

When Raso heard that Al Plummer had been murdered on Com-mercial Street, he left town due to his association with the Notorangeli family. He figured he could be next on the hit list. When he learned it was safe to come back, Raso met with Johnny Martorano, Howie Win-ter, Joe McDonald, and Jim Bulger.

In court, he identified Whitey as "the gentleman in the green sweater."

Gentleman? That received a chuckle. Whitey smiled.

The Winter Hill group claimed they wanted to "sit down and make a meet" with Joe Notorangeli. Joe wanted to disassociate himself from his brother Al, and had told this to Sal Sperlinga (a close friend of Howie Winter).

The "meet" turned into murder. Joe got killed when Martorano dressed up as a meat cutter and opened fire at the Pewter Pot in Medford.

Raso fled town. "I felt in fear of my own life," he said.

After that, Raso went into the bookmaking business with Mar-torano and Winter, and his business grew. Were they doing him a favor? we wondered. Did Raso leave something out? One day he's in fear for his life and the next thing you know he's partners with them? It didn't add up. Did he possibly help set up the Joe Notorangeli hit? Would ju-rors read between the lines? Raso ultimately paid a thousand dollars per month in rent to Winter Hill when they decided to get out of the sports book business.

In 1995, Raso went to prison for eighteen months and a day for contempt. He was with Martorano when he got arrested in Florida and worried that others would think he "brought the law to him."

Suddenly, out of the blue, Raso pointed to the defense table and shouted: "Why do you keep staring at me?" He turned to Judge Casper. "Why is that lawyer staring at me?" He appeared to be point-ing at defense attorney Hank Brennan.

The judge explained that everyone in the courtroom was staring at him because he was testifying.

Later, we asked Brennan about Raso's outburst, and whether he had been doing anything out of the ordinary. Brennan admitted that he had been staring the witness down. He said, "I concentrated on the government witnesses, especially if I had to cross-examine them. I studied their body language, facial expressions, I looked into their eyes. I could tell when they became uncomfortable when it came to certain areas of their testimony. If they looked nervous, it could mean they were hiding something or lying, so I would explore those areas on cross."[1]

Hank Brennan grinned at the witness as he walked to the podium. "Mr. Raso, my name is Hank Brennan."

"Pleasure, sir." He smirked.

"The pleasure is mine," Brennan presented him with a knowing smile.

He questioned Raso about his friendship with Johnny Martorano, and accused him of laundering money by buying a house in his name for the former hit man. "You know the word 'money laundering,' don't you, sir? You know there's certain ways to hide money?"

Raso claimed it was a rental arrangement.

Brennan also suggested that perhaps Raso helped set up the hit on Joe Notorangeli. He denied it, but Brennan had planted the seed.

"Were you afraid of Mr. Martorano?" Brennan asked, referring to Raso's refusal to testify.

"I was scared because I thought I brought the law to him," he said again.

Overall, there wasn't much Brennan could do with Raso, but attack his credibility by highlighting his close ties with Martorano. If jurors read between the lines, they may have wondered why Raso was out walking the streets, especially if he had set up the Notorangeli hit and laundered money. This subtly played into the defense theory that if you cooperated with the government, you'd get special benefits.

Before calling the next gangster, the government shuffled the deck again and called Michael Coleman, a firearms ID specialist from the state police, and Kenneth Mason, an ATF agent. Coleman examined and test-fired Whitey's arsenal of weapons that came into evidence through Colonel Foley, and testified they were all in working order and "operated as designed." Mason explained that machine guns are heavily regulated and they sell for about twenty thousand dollars. He did a database search for James Bulger, Kevin Weeks, and Stephen Flemmi. There were no weapons registered under those names.

The law enforcement witnesses were a mundane, yet necessary small piece of the puzzle for the government to prove the weapons charges against Whitey. In a criminal case, each element of the offense must be proven beyond a reasonable doubt. Without the firearms experts, the defense could have argued that the government hadn't met its burden of proof.

"How do we know these weren't extraordinarily real-looking toy guns?" Carney would've said.

During the firearms testimony, heads twisted and turned toward the back of the courtroom. There was news of a celebrity in attendance. Jurors and spectators began whispering and pointing.

"Quiet in the courtroom!" our favorite marshal said a number of times.

Robert Duvall sat in the back of the gallery. He had been filming a movie in Boston, and wanted to catch Whitey's infamous gangster trial.

Hafer called Frank Capizzi, adding another splash of color, especially with his black suit and bright red pocket scarf. The seventy-nine-year-old painted and wrote screenplays, but there was a time when he hung with the gangster crowd. He grew up in a cold-water flat in the North End, and called himself a professional gambler back in the day. He knew Indian Al and at one point had purchased a ski lodge with him.

On March 19, 1973, Capizzi described riding in a car with Bud (the nickname for Al Plummer) and a guy named Hugh Shields on Commercial Street in the North End.

We braced for what was coming next. Bad things tended to happen when people took random car rides in Whitey's world.

"Did something unusual happen?" Hafer asked.

"Unusual?" Capizzi gasped. "A firing squad hit us!" He became animated. "Multiply that by about a hundred! For two and a half minutes about a hundred slugs hit the automobile and it imploded. I was behind the driver; Hugh was in the front seat next to Bud Plummer. It seemed like a day and a half but it was probably only a couple of minutes. It sounded and felt like two automatic weapons and a couple of rifles and pistols."

Hafer raised a finger. "What did you do when the shooting stopped?"

"I'd been hit in the head and could feel warm blood running down my neck. I said, 'Let's get the fuck out of this car.'"

Capizzi recalled the condition of one of the guys riding with him: "My hand went into his neck where his head should've been." *What an image.* He examined his hand. We could almost feel the stickiness, and the coppery smell of blood seemed to waft in the air.

Al Plummer was killed, as Martorano had testified. They had been gunning for Indian Al Notorangeli.

Capizzi described his condition: "I was embedded with twenty-five to thirty pellets, glass, and metal. . . . I have one slug millimeters from my heart." Eleven slugs were removed during a four-hour operation. He still had slugs in his back. After the shooting, a terrified Capizzi left Boston: "My wife and children were living in the throat of the dragon for forty years without any help from anyone," he shouted and glared at Whitey. He was lucky he lived to testify about it.

Overall, the gangsters drew the curtain back on Whitey's world. It was a complicated chess game back then. If you made the wrong move and crossed the wrong person, as Indian Al had done, it became a deadly game. If you happened to be riding in the wrong car on an unlucky night, it could spell the end, as it had for Plummer. The gangsters were credible witnesses for the government.

chapter

1|5

A RAT'S FILE

He [Whitey] was an informant who corrupted his handler!
 —*Assistant U.S. Attorney Fred Wyshak, arguing at trial hearing*

Just because there's a card with his name on it doesn't mean he's a
registered informant.
 —*Defense attorney Hank Brennan, arguing at trial hearing*

THE GOVERNMENT PLAYED A MURKY ROLE IN THE SORDID HISTORY OF
Whitey Bulger. We were about to learn much more about the secret
world of the FBI and its Top Echelon Informant Program through the
next witness.

Special Agent James Marra scurried to the stand. He was a clean-
cut, young-looking attorney who worked for the Inspector General's
Office, which is part of the Department of Justice. He appeared wide-
eyed and ready to testify. He had short dark hair and a slightly receding hairline. Marra usually sat in the government's section of the
gallery or in the back of the courtroom along the wall. Throughout the
trial, he milled about in the hallway, and often huddled with the prosecution team. He seemed to notice everything going on around him.
He smiled a lot, and came across as a pleasant man. Marra was the

Whitey Bulger's FBI informant card.

face behind the Department of Justice. The defense strategy was to vilify the DOJ for its long history of government cover-ups. We know Marra had a difficult task ahead of him.

Marra explained how the FBI organized Whitey's seven-hundred-page informant file. It revealed who was handling him, his criminal history, teletypes, insert files, memo, and quarterly reports, which were sent throughout the year to FBI headquarters to provide an update about the informant's productivity.

"If an informant is unproductive, they would be closed," Marra said.

When an agent meets with an informant, they prepare "209 reports" to document information on an insert for the file. They are required to document a negative contact, too, when the informant fails to produce.

Through Marra, Wyshak displayed document after document on the monitor for the jury to observe the special relationship Whitey had with the FBI over the years. This relationship paved the way for Whitey's long-running criminal enterprise. Wyshak wanted to show that Whitey had manipulated the system.

BEHIND THE SCENES

Wyshak later described the daunting job they had gathering documents and preparing for Marra's testimony: "It was a very complicated set of documents, which made it difficult. The FBI has the most byzantine system for keeping records."[1]

We learned that Whitey's informant number was BS 1544-OC (OC means "organized crime"). He was eventually upgraded to BS 1544-TE (TE means "top echelon informant"). Whitey was first opened as an informant in May of 1971 by Special Agent Dennis Condon for a few months, and closed due to lack of productivity. Special Agent John Connolly reopened Whitey as an informant again in September of 1975. He was closed in 1978 due to his status as a potential prosecution target in the race fix case. Connolly reopened and handled Whitey again in the spring of 1979. That informant/agent relationship continued for eleven years. According to the file, Whitey was an informant for fifteen years altogether. Marra read reports authored by Connolly and several FBI supervisors that described a range of criminal activity by others that Whitey told Connolly about, including a $25 million bank heist, drug dealing, and murder.

Marra also testified about the informant status of Stephen Flemmi, who was first handled by Special Agent H. Paul Rico back in the 1960s, and later by Connolly.

Marra said: "They frequently met together as a team. John Connolly would meet with Mr. Flemmi and Mr. Bulger together."

Henry Tameleo (center), former Mafia underboss of Patriarca crime family, escorted by FBI Agent H. Paul Rico (left) and his partner, Dennis Condon (right).

The documents revealed bits and pieces of information that Whitey secretly provided about members of the Italian Mafia, gangsters in Charlestown, and even criminals from South Boston. Whitey scowled as he listened to the testimony and viewed the exhibits. When the lawyers argued at sidebar, he mumbled, "I'm not a fucking informant."

Reports revealed that Whitey and Connolly grew up in the same neighborhood and shared "mutual childhood problems" along with a "deep hatred" of the Italian Mafia.

The numerous references in the file pertaining to the murders of Roger Wheeler, John Callahan, and Brian Halloran were particularly disturbing. We knew Halloran was an FBI informant who had been providing information about the World Jai Alai scheme and the murder of Wheeler in Oklahoma. Whitey gunned him down as a result of information leaked about the investigation from the FBI. He also killed Michael Donahue, who gave Halloran a ride home that night. As Marra read the reports, it appeared as if Whitey attempted to throw the FBI off the Halloran murder investigation. According to the documents, Whitey claimed that Halloran had lots of people gunning for him.

Prior to the Halloran and Donahue murders, Whitey reported that the Mafia wanted Halloran "hit in the head." Another report stated that "George Pappas was murdered by Brian Halloran." Next, Whitey told Connolly that Mafia gangster Jackie Salemme "was the person who shot Pappas and the Mafia was hiding him out." Then, as documented in the file, Whitey said: "Halloran allegedly confronted the Mafia and wanted to know why they wanted to hit him. They were dumbfounded and worried that he might be wired up." Whitey reported, "The outfit is worried about Halloran making a deal with the government against Jackie Salemme. They think he's weak," Whitey often referred to the Mafia as "the outfit." He also described Halloran as a drunk and a drug user.

In May of 1982, when they killed Halloran in the gangland-style hit along with Donahue, Whitey used a disguise that made him look like another guy, named Jimmy Flynn. Luckily for Whitey, Halloran made a dying declaration saying that it was Flynn who opened fire on him. But was it really luck? Many have questioned that dying declaration allegedly made by Halloran.

After that date, Whitey provided the FBI with further information that Jimmy Flynn killed Halloran and Donahue. It obviously worked to his advantage.

Police arrested Jimmy Flynn and brought him to trial for the murders of Brian Halloran and Michael Donahue. Pat Donahue attended Flynn's murder trial. She also believed Flynn was responsible for killing her husband back then. When he won at trial, Pat said, "I just figured he had a good lawyer." She often wonders how many others were responsible for the cover-up back then. "Can you believe they let another innocent man stand trial for a murder he didn't commit? What if he had been convicted?" She frowned. "Whitey was just so powerful. He had so many cops and FBI agents in his back pocket. Shame on the government."[2]

Wyshak cleared his throat, then looked at the jury as if to grab their attention. He addressed Marra, this time in a louder voice: "Based upon your review, is there any doubt in your mind that Mr. Bulger was an FBI informant?" He pointed at Whitey.

"Objection!" Brennan jumped out of his chair. Judge Casper gave jurors a quick break; she knew the informant issue was a hot one.

Brennan argued that Marra could not render an opinion regarding Bulger's informant status; he claimed Marra had no direct knowledge that Whitey was an informant, and that the sordid relationship with Bulger "goes all the way up to the DOJ."

Wyshak countered: "It's not like we have one report or two reports, but fifteen years of reports. The defendant doesn't like being called an informant. . . . All these agents got together to fabricate this file . . . absurd."

Brennan brought up convicted agent John Connolly and why the court shouldn't rely on his word from the FBI file that Whitey was in fact an informant. They "can't have it both ways, saying on the one hand he's a fraud and on the other he's to be believed now." Thus, based on the file alone, Marra should not be allowed to render an opinion that Whitey was an informant. There was still no solid proof. "If he's going to give that opinion that Bulger was an informant," Brennan gestured toward the witness stand, "I'm going to ask him about Barboza and the whole history."

Wyshak spread his arms and then pointed at Whitey. "He was an informant who corrupted his handler!"

BEHIND THE SCENES

We asked retired Massachusetts State Police Colonel Tom Foley what he thought about Whitey's claim that he was not an informant. He said: "That was ridiculous. It was typical of him how he tries to manipulate everything. We had file cabinets of evidence, a lot that didn't come out during trial that we could have used. Once again, it was Whitey trying to manipulate the system and public opinion saying he wasn't an informant. Whitey made a comment to his brother Billy on one of those prison tapes saying, 'Now I know why Martorano and those guys are bullshit at me. Look at all the stuff in the files . . . no wonder they're mad at me.' There were four huge folders of inserts. There might have been a few self-serving documents that Connolly threw in, but there's an overwhelming amount of stuff where Bulger gave information that would better himself in Boston's criminal community. There was just too much stuff there."[3]

Brennan continued with his argument that Whitey was not an informant: "Just because there's a card with his name on it doesn't mean he's a registered informant."

Judge Casper didn't buy it. Brennan lost and Marra was allowed to answer that Whitey was in fact an FBI informant. In Whitey's world, it's called a rat.

Overall, Wyshak's legal strategy was to educate the jury about Whitey's longstanding partnership with the FBI, which enabled him to operate a vast criminal empire for decades. He used the documents to show how Whitey manipulated the system, and pinned the blame for certain murders on others. Jurors would be able to sift through the documents during deliberations and see for themselves.

chapter

1|6

NOT A RAT

> And, the way this program worked, this top echelon program, is
> that the federal government would essentially get into bed with or-
> ganized crime figures. Isn't that fair to say?
> —*Defense attorney Hank Brennan,*
> *cross-examination of James Marra*

ON CROSS-EXAMINATION, BRENNAN HAMMERED MARRA HARD AND
fast, casting doubt on Whitey's status as a rat despite the government's
seven-hundred-page file to the contrary. He advanced the defense theory that Connolly opened an informant file on Whitey to cover up his
own payoffs and bribes, then padded and fabricated the file to make it
look like Whitey was a valuable informant. Whitey wasn't working the
system, it was the other way around: Whitey was the one being manipulated by the government.

Brennan emphasized that there was so much pressure from the
Department of Justice on agents to develop top echelon informants.
"And part of the Department of Justice's program during this time
when they characterized people as top echelon, the program was the
attack on the Mafia. Isn't that true?" he asked.

"Yes," Marra said.

"Because the Mafia was seen by Hoover as the biggest domestic
risk," Brennan said, raising his voice. "Isn't that fair to say?"

"Yes, the Mafia was a priority in the FBI at the time." Marra came across edgy.

"And the way this program worked, this top echelon program, is that the federal government would essentially get into bed with organized crime figures. Isn't that fair to say?" Brennan asked.

Wyshak nearly knocked his chair over when he jumped up. "Object to the characterizations, Your Honor."

"Sustained."

"And a top echelon informant would be seen as very different than a regular informant, correct?" Brennan said.

Marra nodded. "A top echelon informant would have access to the decision-making level."

"Somebody who was high enough in organized crime that they were involved in policy-making decisions?"

"Yes."

"Would it be fair to say that the development of informants in this program was important to the ratings and evaluations that members of the FBI got from their superiors?"

"Yes."

Brennan used Marra to paint a tainted image of the FBI and its informant program during Whitey's reign of power. He revealed that agents and supervisors received more money and recognition for cultivating special relationships with top echelon informants, and that the government would often go out of its way to protect these informants, which caused people to get killed out on the streets. Brennan noted that Connolly had received letters of commendation, incentives, and financial benefits for developing his informants, who included Whitey and Stephen Flemmi.

Brennan also suggested Whitey's informant file was padded with information from many other sources to make him appear useful, so that Agent Connolly and his supervisor John Morris could keep him open.

"There was a pattern in this file where there were absences of contacts?" Brennan asked, referring to unreported meetings between Connolly, Morris, and Whitey and Flemmi.

"Yes, they were not reporting their own criminal activity," Marra said, referring to the agents.

Marra admitted that FBI agents were not following protocol when handling informants and documenting files. At times, he came across as defensive and sounded like he didn't know what he was talking about. He had to admit he wasn't present when the file was created.

"So about ninety-five percent of that file was comprised by Mr. Connolly?" Brennan asked.

"The vast majority of it was authored by Mr. Connolly."

"In any of those pages in that file, were you there for any conversations that occurred?"

Marra scratched his neck. "No."

"Can you confirm that Mr. Bulger gave any information firsthand on any of those pages?"

"Well . . ." Marra hesitated. "Not firsthand."

Brennan hammered home the concept that Connolly was getting paid huge sums of money by Whitey; thus, Connolly would do anything to protect him.

In a letter to us, Whitey vehemently denied being an informant: "I never . . . gave info to anyone. I bought info," he wrote.

"Were you at all concerned with the legitimacy of information in the Bulger file?" Brennan asked.

Marra admitted that Connolly "fabricated some reports" but said he had "no reason to believe that Mr. Connolly fabricated all of the reports that were in that file." He also said that Connolly spoke of Whitey as "one of the most valuable informants in the battle against LCN," the Mafia.

Brennan's goal was to create reasonable doubt and show that most of the file was predicated on fabrication, omissions, and unverified reports. Through aggressive cross-examination, the defense advanced its theory that corrupt FBI agents fabricated the voluminous informant file to make it look like Whitey was a valuable informant, in order to cover up their illegal activities. In his opening statement, Carney made a promise to jurors that the FBI informant file was trumped up by agents Connolly and Morris to justify keeping Whitey open because they were getting paid off. Both Morris and Connolly had expensive tastes and enjoyed the lavish lifestyle according to the defense. That's why Brennan spent so much time on Marra's cross-examination. The legal strategy was to go for jury nullification: to make jurors lose faith in the justice system, and, ultimately, punish the government with "not guilty" verdicts against Whitey.

Even if some of the file was fabricated, should the whole thing be discounted? All seven hundred pages? Would jurors buy into the defense theory of government corruption? Brennan's cross was effective, but lasted too long. Jurors looked at the giant clock much too often. A woman in the back row kept dozing off, and the guy next to her nudged her awake again and again.

chapter

1|7

BLOOD MONEY

I knew that I was clearly compromised in my responsibilities having anything to do with Bulger or Flemmi.
—Former FBI supervisor John Morris, trial testimony

JOHN MORRIS MUST HAVE BEEN EMBARRASSED WHEN HE RAISED HIS right hand for the oath in Boston. He'd worked in the FBI's Boston office in the 1970s and 1980s, and supervised the C-3 organized crime squad for six years. The white-haired sixty-seven-year-old former agent was now living as far away as possible in California, working as a wine consultant. We shook our heads when we heard that, remembering that Whitey and Flemmi had given him the nickname "Vino."

Morris looked uncomfortable in that courtroom. He knew that he'd be questioned about his acceptance of bribes from Whitey, and his leaks of top secret information. We noticed he couldn't even make eye contact with FBI agents in the hallway. He was a disgrace to the badge. Of course, the government gave Morris immunity; he never spent a day in jail. He was allowed to retire and keep his pension. Former agent John Connolly, who worked under Morris, is currently serving time in Florida for second-degree murder with a firearm. In 2002, a federal jury in Boston convicted Connolly of racketeering and obstruction of justice

Morris testified that he had been a supervisor in Boston's C-3 organized crime unit, and knew Whitey as one of the core members of the

Winter Hill Gang and an as informant for John Connolly. Connolly was an agent on the squad, who became Morris's best friend. In 1978, Morris met socially with Whitey and Connolly at his home in Lexington, Massachusetts, where he hosted dinner. Morris testified that Connolly wanted the meeting to occur in "pleasant surroundings . . . he wanted James Bulger to be comfortable." Connolly also wanted Whitey "to be handled in a manner that informants aren't typically handled." This was "not standard, pretty rare," Morris recalled.

Morris praised Connolly as bright, glib, and extremely knowledgeable with the Boston landscape, people, and culture. "John Connolly's forte was always informants," Morris said. He had exceptional connections with the Boston police. Morris explained that in the 1970s and 1980s, the Mafia was the major focus for the FBI—the most significant by far, more than the Winter Hill group, the Hell's Angels, or the Asian groups. Morris met with Connolly, Whitey, and Flemmi to gather information about the Mafia. He described Flemmi as quiet, while Whitey was the dominant person who did most of the talking. Flemmi was close to the Mafia, and at one point they wanted him to be a "made" guy.

Morris described the help that Whitey and Flemmi provided with respect to planting listening devices at 98 Prince Street, the headquarters of Gennaro Angiulo, the underboss of New England's Patriarca crime family. He and Special Agent Ed Quinn met with Whitey and Flemmi in a parking lot at the Lechmere store in Cambridge in 1981. They provided the agents with a schematic of the interior of 98 Prince Street to use when they placed the bugs inside. The FBI ultimately recorded Angiulo, his brothers, and other Mafia associates talking about their criminal activities, which led to federal racketeering charges. Angiulo and his brothers were convicted at trial in 1986. Angiulo was sentenced to forty-five years in prison, and served twenty-four years until released in 2007. He died in 2009.

"Did you ever ask what they wanted in return?" Kelly asked, suggesting that Whitey and Flemmi must have wanted some benefit in return for providing information about the headquarters of Angiulo at 98 Prince Street.

"According to Connolly, they wanted a head start if they were going to be indicted, charged, arrested . . . tip them off so they could flee," Morris said. They never wanted their identities disclosed, especially to a judge.

Kelly cocked his head. "Would that be appropriate to give them a head start?"

Morris looked into his lap. "No, it would not."

In 1978, the feds were about to indict a number of Winter Hill gangsters, including Howie Winter, for fixing horse races, and Connolly wanted to intercede on Whitey's and Flemmi's behalf, according to Morris. Morris and Connolly contacted Jeremiah O'Sullivan, the prosecutor on the race fix case, and asked if he'd consider not indicting Whitey and Flemmi. Morris explained to O'Sullivan that they "needed them in their highest-priority case against the Mafia. There was a package deal—that's what the entire relationship was with Bulger and Flemmi," Morris recalled. O'Sullivan took it under consideration and decided not to prosecute the two "partners."

When the state police wiretap at the Lancaster Street garage became compromised, the FBI worried that the secret informant status pertaining to Whitey and Flemmi was also compromised. The FBI's SAC, Lawrence Sarhatt (the top guy in the Boston office), demanded a justification memo as to why they should continue to use the pair as informants.

Morris supported their continued use. The justification memo concluded that "Bulger is one of the highest-valued informants we have." Morris admitted to "some puffery in there by Connolly . . . I didn't correct it. I should have . . . I wanted to support Connolly in any way that I could."

Morris talked about the gifts he received from Whitey and Flemmi, which ranged from cash to expensive bottles of wine and a silver-plated ice bucket. One time he received a case of wine that Connolly had in his car. When Morris said he didn't want to take it, Connolly remarked, "They'll think that you don't trust them. If you want to give it back, you do it. I'm not going to do it." Morris's shoulders sagged as he testified. "I was his supervisor and his best friend. It was in violation of FBI regulations," he said.

When the FBI in Oklahoma opened an investigation into the Roger Wheeler murder in 1981 and asked Boston for help, the case was assigned to Connolly. The jury had just heard testimony from John Martorano that he shot Wheeler "between the eyes" because he refused to sell Miami-based World Jai Alai to the Winter Hill gangsters. According to Martorano, the Bulger group had arranged to skim ten thousand dollars per week from the business and needed to get rid of Wheeler.

Morris clarified that the Oklahoma FBI asked for a criminal check on John Callahan, an accountant and former president of World Jai Alai. Connolly contacted Whitey and Flemmi, and claimed they provided no information of value because Callahan had lost influence with Winter Hill after Howie Winter's arrest. The Boston agents interviewed Callahan and concluded that Callahan never even met Wheeler and had had no contact with World Jai Alai for five years. They closed the investigation in Boston, and forwarded the Callahan interview to Oklahoma. This was clearly a ruse.

"It must've been the cooperation of Edward 'Brian' Halloran that caused this investigation to be reopened," Morris said. Halloran was the subject of several investigations, and he was under indictment for murder and in contact with FBI Special Agent Montanari. Agents Brunnick and Montanari asked Morris for his assessment of Halloran as an informant. They set up a meeting between Halloran and Callahan, and requested that Morris go with them.

Morris testified: "Halloran was wearing a recording device to gain any evidence connecting Callahan and others with the murder of Wheeler."

Witness security was under Morris's supervision. He performed a threat assessment regarding Halloran's safety as an informant, and recommended that he be placed in the program.

At that point, Morris made a decision that got two people killed and would haunt him for the rest of his life. According to Morris, he compromised Halloran's status as an informant against Whitey and Flemmi when he posed a vague, hypothetical question alluding to Halloran's cooperation with the FBI to Connolly.

Morris testified that Connolly picked up on it and said, "They'd never trust Brian Halloran to do anything for them." Then Connolly asked Morris why he had asked the question. Morris spilled the beans by telling Connolly that Halloran was cooperating regarding the Wheeler murder and was in protective custody. Halloran claimed that Whitey and Stevie offered him the contract to kill Wheeler, but Halloran declined it. This could ultimately lead investigators to Winter Hill.

Within a day or so, Morris testified that he saw Connolly again and Connolly told him that Whitey and Stevie Flemmi already knew about Halloran's cooperation. They claimed that Halloran had reached out to them, and had offered not to cooperate with the FBI in exchange for money. Morris said he knew this was a lie. He realized he had exercised "bad judgment" when he leaked this top secret information and had placed Halloran, the informant, in extreme danger.

Morris reddened on the witness stand. He admitted he "was embarrassed" about what he had done, and he did nothing to correct the situation.

On May 11, 1982, Morris learned that Brian Halloran and Michael Donahue had been murdered. Donahue, an innocent victim, had simply been giving Halloran a ride home.

Several jurors frowned and regarded Morris with disgust. Some shook their heads. The Donahue family whispered to each other.

"Quiet in the courtroom!" the marshal said.

On the courtroom monitor, Kelly displayed an FBI memo written by Connolly regarding the Halloran and Donahue murders: "Source pointed out that no one knew Halloran was cooperating."

A male juror in the front row appeared angry when he read it. There it was for all to see, a blatant lie, a cover-up in black and white, which resulted in murder.

Morris read the words on the monitor, and admitted the document was false: "This was not true, *a lie*." He frowned and exhaled deeply. He did not have Connolly correct it, and allowed the continuation of the lie.

"If an informant is lying to you, you'd probably close it?" Kelly asked.

"Yes."

Morris admitted that the FBI file contained more disinformation about the Halloran and Donahue murders. At one point a document in the file blamed the state police for leaking the story about Halloran's cooperation. Jimmy Flynn became a prime suspect because Whitey had disguised himself to look like Flynn when he executed Halloran. Morris kept his mouth shut even if it meant an innocent man could be convicted and sent to prison. He *knew* Flynn was innocent, and did nothing when the man was arrested and tried for murder.

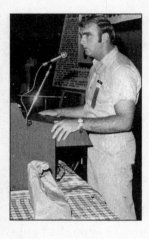

FBI informant Brian Halloran, who was gunned down in a gangland hit in May of 1982 on the South Boston waterfront.

Approximately a month after the Halloran and Donahue murders, Morris attended FBI training in Georgia. He had been cheating on his wife with his secretary, Debbie Noseworthy. She was now his second wife, and had accompanied him to court that day. Back then, he had called and asked Connolly if Whitey and Flemmi "would spring for an airline ticket" to bring her down to Georgia. Morris remembered that Connolly had said, "These guys really like you . . . if there's anything you ever wanted or needed, just ask." Morris needed a thousand-dollar round-trip plane ticket—he desperately wanted a few days of pleasure with his lover. Morris testified that Connolly got the cash from Whitey and Flemmi, and placed it in Morris's desk drawer for Noseworthy to use to purchase her ticket. Morris had his fun in Georgia.

"What was your state of mind?" Kelly asked.

"I knew that I was clearly compromised in my responsibilities having anything to do with Bulger or Flemmi," Morris said. He gazed into the gallery. It was hard to believe he and Noseworthy were still together. What was she thinking? Was she now ashamed that she had collected this blood money? Did she feel for Pat Donahue—woman to woman?

We wondered if Morris thought about the women who'd lost their husbands back in Boston as he enjoyed his lurid affair in Georgia. It was blood money, plain and simple. What was Whitey thinking as he listened to the testimony? He had apparently awarded Morris with a thousand dollars for leaking the information about Halloran and for steering investigators away from him on the Wheeler, Donahue, and Halloran murders. What a deal: one thousand dollars for derailing three murder investigations—Whitey got off cheap.

The Wheeler murder investigation in Oklahoma continued, and John Callahan became a target. According to Morris, Connolly told Whitey and Flemmi about their focus on Callahan. Morris admitted that "it was inappropriate for law enforcement to ask the targets of a murder investigation where a key witness was—that's what John Connolly did."

Martorano killed Callahan in Miami and memos in the FBI file made it look like a Cuban group did it. Still, Whitey was not closed as an informant even though he had now become a suspect in several murders. When asked why he steered investigators away from Whitey, Morris said: "As an accommodation to John Connolly, I did it. I didn't feel like challenging him on it. . . . I was compromised and went along with whatever John requested."

Morris pointed out that Connolly's lifestyle had changed by the early 1980s. He was showy, wore more jewelry, and had purchased homes in South Boston and on Cape Cod. He owned "a good-sized boat, and seemed like he was living beyond his means." Connolly aspired to be the Boston police commissioner, and he wanted Morris to be his "number two" guy. Morris claimed that Connolly had powerful political connections in Boston.

In 1988, Morris supervised an FBI investigation into a scandal involving Whitey's brother William (Billy) Bulger, a powerful politician in Massachusetts. The newspapers claimed he received questionable payments from a prominent developer for a high-rise at 75 State Street. While the investigation was under way, Morris accepted a five-thousand-dollar bribe that Whitey handed to him in an envelope after Morris had him over for dinner at his home. Morris closed the FBI investigation concerning Billy Bulger. The investigation was reopened briefly, assigned to Connolly, and closed again.

Finally, a reporter for the *Boston Globe* Spotlight series called and asked Morris to confirm that Whitey and Flemmi were in fact FBI informants. Pressure had been mounting, so Morris confirmed it, hoping "if their identities were surfaced they'd finally be closed and what had happened to me wouldn't happen to other agents." Morris had dug himself in so deep by that point, he felt he had no choice. This ended his relationship with Whitey, Flemmi, and John Connolly. Whitey despised him for naming them as informants, and still does.

While Whitey was on the lam, Morris received a bone-chilling call at his office: "Use your Machiavellian mind and contact your sources at the *Globe* to retract the story about me being an informant." Morris recognized Whitey's voice. Whitey also told Morris that "if he went to jail, I was coming with him" and to "remember the box." "The box" was a reference to the polygraph machine. After that, Morris became so distraught and stressed that his health deteriorated. He wound up in the hospital with heart problems.

In 1995, when the police finally arrested Flemmi, Morris feared that the truth about what he had done would come out. "I was worried about everything surfacing. I certainly did not want my bad behavior known in any way, shape, or form." Morris also lied to investigators, and they placed him on probation for a year without pay.

We watched Kelly take his seat upon wrapping up his direct examination. He knew there was a storm brewing in that courtroom. Morris was fodder for the defense, and he knew they would put the government on trial at every opportunity. Kelly undoubtedly wished he didn't have to use a corrupt, lying FBI supervisor as a key witness. What would jurors think about Morris's immunity deal? If someone on that panel didn't trust the government, they could create havoc during deliberations and cause a hung jury. Kelly had to make this case all about Whitey and his criminal empire. Whitey was the guy in the defendant's chair, not Morris, not the government. Like it or not, Morris served as an important brick in the government's foundation. Prosecutors had to connect the dots from Morris's FBI leak—to Whitey—to murders. They used Morris to prove that Whitey had corrupted his handlers. Whitey used people to accomplish his agenda. Whitey was always one step ahead, and that's how he ran such a successful criminal enterprise.

We knew the government would stress in closing arguments that jurors don't have to like Morris or the government, but they should *believe* him as a witness against Whitey.

Hank Brennan rose for cross-examination. He marched to the podium with a purpose; his facial muscles appeared taut, determined. This was going to be good. Brennan would make mincemeat out of Morris.

chapter

1|8

DOUBLE LIE

Not a day goes by that I don't pray that God gives you blessing and comfort for the pain. I do want to express my sincere apology for things I did, and didn't do. I do not ask for forgiveness—that's too much. But I do acknowledge it publicly.
—John Morris, trial testimony

LIAR! LIAR! LIAR! LIAR!

That's what the jackhammer sounded like in courtroom 11 during Hank Brennan's cross-examination of John Morris.

"Mr. Morris, *you* lied." Brennan cut right to the chase.

"Yes."

"You lied to your wife about your secretary?" Brennan asked.

"Yes."

"You lied to your secretary about money?"

"Yes." Morris peered into the spectators' section, possibly searching for his former secretary/lover and now wife.

"You had to commit a second lie to cover up your first lie?" Brennan widened his eyes.

"Yes."

"You wrote a ten-page report and lied about your first lie?" He blinked several times. "A double lie?"

"Yes."

"When it's a benefit to you, you lie?"

"It was to my benefit to lie," Morris admitted. He must have been squirming inside.

"You put your name to things you knew were a lie?" Brennan asked. Morris agreed.

Brennan regarded the witness. "You're a convincing liar."

"You're a fucking liar," Whitey interjected, loud enough for some to hear. He couldn't resist.

Kelly heard the expletive and complained as soon as the jurors left for lunch. He asked the judge to make Whitey "keep his little remarks to himself when the witness is testifying." He glared at the defendant. "I know he spent his whole life trying to intimidate people, but he should not be doing that here in federal court in the midst of trial." Spit flew from Kelly's mouth. It must have been tough for prosecutors to sit there and put up with Brennan's cross.

Judge Casper addressed Whitey and told him he was "well served" by his lawyers and they would speak for him in the courtroom. "Do you understand that, sir?"

"Yes, sir," Whitey replied. Had he addressed her with "sir" on purpose? Whitey was known to do everything for a reason. Why stop then?

Brennan hammered Morris to show jurors why they shouldn't believe him, now or ever. He forced Morris to admit that he often misled people, and was corrupt before he ever met John Connolly. Morris planted a fake bomb under a guy's car in his family's driveway "to scare him to death" so he would cooperate, and then called in the bomb to police.

"I knew it would scare him . . . his family would be upset," Morris recalled. Two male jurors in the front row exchanged eye contact, a small shake of the head, and frowns.

Brennan pointed out that the fire department had to rush to the scene. They didn't know the FBI had planted a fake bomb. Morris said he hadn't considered whether his actions would be dangerous to the public as emergency vehicles sped down city streets.

"Is that protocol?" Brennan wrinkled his brow and glanced at the jury. "Don't worry." He mocked. "I was only kidding?"

"No." Morris raised his voice, sounding defensive.

"All you thought about was what was in it for *you*?" Brennan pointed at him, while Morris nodded in acknowledgement.

"You took an oath to protect the public?" Brennan gestured toward the spectators' gallery.

"Yes."

"You were being paid by our federal government?" He eyed the government's table.

"That's correct."

"Your job is to protect the citizens?" Brennan nodded toward the jury box.

"Yes."

"Now, Mr. Morris." Brennan adjusted his glasses. "When you learned that Mr. Flemmi and other people were indicted, you were concerned, weren't you?"

Morris sighed. "Yes."

"In fact, you were worried that your secrets would no longer be secret?" Brennan stretched out the word "secret."

"That's correct."

"You had hidden your lies up to that point pretty successfully, hadn't you?"

"I had hidden my lies—most of my lies were disbelieved, and that's how I ended up getting punished." Morris folded his arms across his chest.

"I want to ask about your answer." Brennan paused. "You said most of your lies were disbelieved. Before you gave a proffer to the government, who did you tell about your impropriety and bribes that was disbelieved?"

"When I lied to the Office of Professional Responsibility, I was disbelieved, cited for lack of candor, and disciplined."

"Because you lied—"

"And that was prior, because I lied, that's correct. I did not admit that, but I was disciplined."

"I want to talk about your *bribes*." Brennan often jumped around to keep it fresh. The jurors' gazes oscillated from Brennan to the witness. They were paying attention. "Mr. Morris, did you tell anybody before your proffer in law enforcement about the bribes you had taken?"

"No." Morris curled his fingers around his opposite wrist.

"When you learned about these indictments, would it be fair to say you were a bit panicked?" Brennan asked.

"Yes."

"You knew you could get in trouble for obstruction of justice?"

Morris cocked his head and nodded. "Conceivably."

"Well, conceivably, were you worried about it, sir?"

"I was worried about everything surfacing, whether or not I could be prosecuted at the time. I think there were statute of limitations issues, but I certainly did not want my bad behavior known in any way, shape, or form."

Brennan rubbed his chin. "Is there a statute of limitations on conspiracy to commit murder?" He looked back at the Donahue family.

Morris followed Brennan's gaze and quickly looked down. "There is not."

"That crossed your mind, didn't it, sir?" Brennan blinked several times.

Morris hesitated. "It did."

"Was it an area of concern, those other reports you spoke about yesterday, that you signed, that you knew were false?" Brennan flattened his tie against his chest. "Was that a worry?"

"I really didn't think about those." Morris licked his lower lip. "What I thought about was accepting the money . . . my primary concern."

"You certainly were concerned with the fact that you told Mr. Connolly about Mr. Halloran, weren't you?"

"Yes, I was very concerned about that."

"That was probably the biggest concern you had?"

"That was one of the biggest concerns," Morris said softly. "Yes."

Brennan paused as he watched jurors taking notes. He likely hoped that they'd picked up on the concept that Morris worried more about the bribes he had taken than his role in the Halloran and Donahue murders and the subsequent cover-up.

"And Mr. Flemmi had said that you had promised that he wouldn't be prosecuted for his crimes?" Brennan looked at Whitey when he asked the question.

"Words to—along that line." Morris bit his upper lip. "Yes."

Brennan slipped the immunity issue in whenever he could. Would jurors make the leap to his client? Would they wonder if Morris or another government official had extended Whitey the same promise that he wouldn't be prosecuted for his crimes? Had the government gone back on its promise?

Brennan's next line of questioning focused on the proffer Morris made with the government in exchange for his "truthful" testimony.

"Did you tell them about the bribes you took from other people?"

"I told them about the bribes or money that I took from Mr. Bulger and Mr. Flemmi. I excluded one person, another informant that I had received a loan from. I held that back until they asked the question."

Brennan pounced on Morris for withholding the whole truth by not admitting that he took a five-thousand-dollar "loan" from another informant, which was against the rules. He never paid that loan back, either. Morris didn't think anyone would find out about it. How many loans and bribes were there altogether? we wondered. How many did Morris get away with? What other secrets would this man take to the grave with him?

When reviewing the various meetings Morris had with informants, Brennan kept asking, "Did you have anything extra in your pockets when you left?" We wondered if Whitey knew about more bribes and secrets. Everyone hoped Whitey would take the stand and "tell all." He continued giving Morris that icy stare. It was evident Whitey hated him.

Brennan noted that Morris often disparaged the state police, and hampered their investigations into the Winter Hill Gang. He focused on the importance of the Top Echelon Informant Program, and the FBI's goal to take down the Italian Mafia at all costs. The "costs" meant giving Whitey a free pass, and allowing pandemonium on the streets of Boston.

"It was a burning goal of yours to bug the Mafia headquarters, wasn't it?" Brennan asked.

"Absolutely." Morris raised his voice.

"And as a burning goal that you held at such a high priority, you would give the same fervor and effort you did in other investigations, right?"

"I think I put more fervor and effort into that investigation than any investigation," Morris said.

Brennan remembered Whitey's favorite topic of his *not* being labeled a rat. He wanted to drive home the point that Whitey was not an informant because he paid Morris seven thousand dollars in bribes for information. The government wanted jurors to believe the opposite: that Whitey was a valuable top echelon informant who ended up corrupting his handlers, got tipped about investigations, and committed multiple murders.

"You didn't say to him, 'You're an informant.' Did you?" Brennan asked.

"No."

Whitey perked up and stared hard at Morris.

"When you get an informant or cultivate an informant, you don't tell him that they're an informant?" Brennan squinted.

"I don't think we come out and say it in that sense, that you are now a card-carrying informant, and we're opening a file, and we're going to document everything that you say."

Several people laughed, and Morris smiled as if proud of his joke.

Brennan switched gears to Morris's leak that resulted in the murders of Halloran and Donahue. "You were hiding information relative to a murder?"

Morris closed his eyes for a moment. "This is really stupid that I allowed this to happen . . . I deceived headquarters."

"How much money did it cost to do something like this?" Brennan shook his head in disgust. "This involves a citizen's life?"

Morris lowered his gaze; he appeared defeated.

"How much is that bottle of wine worth, Mr. Morris?" Brennan pressed.

Morris closed his eyes. "I knew that I was clearly compromised."

Brennan questioned Morris further about his close relationship with John Connolly. He also mentioned that Whitey had said "use your Machiavellian mind." For some reason, Morris laughed on the stand. We couldn't figure out why he would be laughing. No one else laughed with him, which made the awkward situation worse. Was it nerves?

Brennan attacked. "Does it bring back good memories?"

"No." Morris's face turned bright red with embarrassment.

"You prosecuted cops for taking gifts?" Brennan referred to Morris's later assignment combating public corruption for the FBI. *Of all the possible jobs.*

"Yes, and it made me sick," he said.

Brennan segued back to the Halloran and Donahue murders. "You knew when Halloran became an informant, it shouldn't get into the hands of organized crime?"

"It was spontaneous," Morris said. "It just happened and I wish it hadn't."

"You knew when you were giving Mr. Connolly this information, you were signing his [Halloran's] death warrant?"

Morris drew a deep breath and exhaled. "I thought it was safe."

"We pay you to help victims' families?" Brennan opened his arm in a wide arc toward the spectators' section.

Morris admitted it.

"Do you know those people had families, Mr. Morris?" Brennan kept pointing into the gallery.

Morris admitted that when the police arrested Jimmy Flynn due to Halloran's alleged dying declaration, he was relieved.

"You kept that exculpatory information about Flynn secret?" Brennan asked.

"Yes."

Brennan puckered his lips and stared at him with a look of dismay. Morris was so concerned about himself that he allowed an innocent man to stand trial for a crime he didn't commit.

"Did you ask forgiveness from the Donahue and Halloran families?" Brennan pivoted toward the victims' relatives.

Morris paused for a long moment and gazed into the gallery, right at Pat Donahue. "Not a day goes by that I don't pray that God gives you blessing and comfort for the pain. I do want to express my sincere apology for things I did, and didn't do. I do not ask for forgiveness—that's too much. But I do acknowledge it publicly."

BEHIND THE SCENES

Pat Donahue did not accept the public apology. She said, "Morris looked straight at me as he was making his confession of guilt. I believe in my heart that the man does have a conscience, and the guilt that he has to live with for the rest of his life is his punishment. He is the definition of a wimp. Did he

really think that me and my family were going to forgive him? I
mean, really?"[1]

"Were you ever prosecuted for perjury?" Brennan raised his eyes at
the government's table.

"No."

"Who decides whether you're worthy of prosecution for perjury?"

"The government."

Brennan smirked. It was a strong answer to end on. This was the
government's game.

Brennan scored big during the cross-examination of Morris. Most
jurors frowned or appeared stoic. His questions drew out the worst in
Morris. This man had leaked information that got two men killed on
the waterfront, not far from where we all sat that day. Outside in the
heat, we watched Morris ignore the reporters who shoved microphones
up to his mouth. He'd be boarding a flight to California, and would possibly never return to Massachusetts. Was Morris evil to the core? We
didn't think so. He had dug himself into an abyss during the Whitey
years, and hoped he'd never get caught.

Brennan's piercing questions made most trial watchers contem-
plate the bigger picture, which involved trust. Why should jurors trust
testimony from a guy like Morris? Why should they trust a contami-
nated informant file? Why should anyone trust the government?

chapter

| 1 | 9 |

THE GREAT PROTECTOR

Mr. Bulger was well known and well feared. If you were with Mr. Bulger you didn't need the police.
—Joseph Tower, trial testimony

"THE UNITED STATES CALLS JOSEPH TOWER." KELLY LOOKED BACK AS the courtroom doors flew open.

Tower hightailed it to the witness stand. The fifty-nine-year-old wore a slimming navy blue suit and matching tie, but he still looked like he'd just stepped out of central casting to play the role of a washed-up cocaine dealer . . . and that's just what he was. Everything about him was fast. Judge Casper had to ask him to slow down on several occasions. His hands moved all over the place when he spoke in his thick Boston accent.

Tower made custom guitars for a living, and used to play in a rock 'n' roll band back in the 1980s.

"Did you ever play at a place called Triple O's?" Kelly asked.

Tower smiled. "Yes, I did."

"While at Triple O's, did you ever meet a guy named James Bulger?"

He nodded at Whitey. "Yes, I have."

In addition to being a popular musician, Tower was a successful cocaine and marijuana dealer. At one point, Tommy Nee began shaking down drug dealers.

Triple O's Lounge in South Boston, where Whitey committed a number of extortions.

Kelly rubbed his chin. "You were concerned that Tom Nee and his crew were going to get you?"

"Yes."

Kevin O'Neil, a part owner of Triple O's, suggested that Tower talk to Whitey about the problem. He met with Whitey, who told him to team up with Billy Shea and "you will not be bothered."

At that point, Kelly asked Tower to identify the defendant.

He grinned at Whitey. "How yah doin', Jim?"

Whitey smiled back. It looked like they could have been sitting across from each other in a Southie bar as opposed to the courtroom, chatting about the good ol' days when the drug money had been flowing in.

Tower worked with Billy Shea and taught Whitey's organization all about the cocaine business. He drove around with Shea and introduced him to the dealers in his fold, as well as customers. They would no longer have problems selling cocaine. They bought wholesale from various suppliers, including the Medellin Cartel in Columbia. Whitey didn't deal directly with drug dealers, but he received "his take."

"Why would Mr. Bulger be paid?" Kelly asked.

"He was the protection," Tower said.

In the drug business, protection was paramount. Tower relayed a story about a problem he had with a guy in Wakefield, Massachusetts, who was delinquent and wouldn't pay his drug debt. When Tower sent his brother up to collect, they kidnapped him. The "kidnappers" called Tower and said, "We hear you're with Boots and Rifleman." Boots was one of Whitey's nicknames, because he often wore cowboy boots.

Tower immediately called Shea and told him they had dropped Whitey's nickname. Whitey took care of the situation and informed Tower that his brother was coming home. As Whitey listened to the story in court, he chuckled.

In 1983, Tower got caught trafficking in cocaine and went to prison. His wife received one thousand dollars a week from Whitey's organization, but when Tower got out, the payments stopped, and Whitey forced him out of the business. They didn't need him anymore; he was expendable.

Carney handled the cross-examination, and pointed out that Tower was a successful drug dealer long before he met Whitey. Tower agreed, and talked about his supplier in Florida: "I would meet a person down there all the time, he was the photographer for the Patriots Cheerleaders."

People laughed and murmured, and we all received another: "Quiet in the courtroom!"

They would transport the cocaine back north in film containers. Tower would not reveal the photographer's name. "What would be a high week in terms of the amount of profit you would make?" Carney asked.

Tower pursed his lips. "Ten thousand."

"And you indicated that there was a power of suggestion that you join Mr. Shea?"

"Yes." Tower nodded several times.

"And that way you would have protection, correct?" Carney said.

"That is correct."

"Now, you were relieved, weren't you, that you were going to now be able to get protection if you hooked up with Billy Shea?"

"Yes."

Carney stated the obvious, but he was subtly suggesting that Tower sought protection from Whitey—that it was all Tower's idea. Was he trying to paint his client as the "great protector" now? The good guy in all of this? The irony was that back in the '80s, Whitey spread a rumor that he was responsible for keeping the drugs out of South Boston, that he protected the community from the drug dealers. Many believed it. Now we learned it was the other way around: Whitey had been protecting the dealers who were polluting South Boston. And he made lots of money doing it.

"By 1980, you and Billy Shea were moving multiple kilos a week, weren't you?" Carney asked.

"Yes."

Tower made it sound simple: "We would buy the piece, the kilo, and then we would, so called, cut it and double the amount we had purchased. Now we would have, instead of two point two pounds, you would have, you know, four point four."

"How much of a profit did you make on the sale of each ounce?"

Tower studied the ceiling. "Early on . . . three hundred dollars an ounce."

"Profit?"

"My end."

Carney rubbed his beard. "So, a kilo contains thirty-five ounces. Is that right?"

"It's more like thirty-six, but they were always overweight."

"Okay." Carney grabbed a square object from his table and walked back to the podium. "I'm using a calculator."

"Sure."

Wyshak and Kelly exchanged a smile, knowing that Carney would somehow screw up the math. Lawyers, in general, do not make good mathematicians.

"Thirty-six times three equals one hundred and eight." Carney pressed the tiny buttons on his old-fashioned-looking calculator. "It would be thirty-six ounces in a kilo doubled, when you cut it . . ." He pressed more buttons. "Makes seventy-two. And then times three for three kilos . . . I'm at two hundred and sixteen." He looked up at the witness. "Is that the number?"

Tower extended his palms. "I'm not doing the math, sir."

People laughed.

Carney went back to pressing buttons. "And two hundred and sixteen times three hundred. So in a given week, you and Mr. Shea would, on average, get sixty-four thousand dollars, give or take?"

"Not correct," Tower said forcefully.

Carney appeared startled. "Why not?"

"Because we didn't move that whole kilo that was doubled in one week."

When Carney continued with more math, Tower blurted, "Can I interrupt?"

"Only to go to the bathroom or take a drink of water," Carney said.

More laughter and wisecracks. And, right on cue, another "Quiet in the courtroom!"

The mood had become lighthearted. In another hour or so the Fourth of July vacation would start. It was Tuesday and the court would be in recess for the rest of the week.

Judge Casper advised Tower to stick with the questions and answers.

"You viewed yourself as a businessman?" Carney asked.

"Yes."

"You kept detailed records?"

"I kept limited records."

"And you called muscle in if necessary?"

"Yes."

Tower also made money on an after-hours club. He admitted to paying off a Boston police sergeant "a couple hundred a week" to stay in business.

"You didn't have a problem bribing a Boston police officer?" Carney asked.

"No."

Carney questioned Tower about the kidnapping of his brother, and how they threatened to kill him. "This had to be a terrifying situation for your brother, don't you think?"

"Positively."

When he realized his brother could be killed, Carney asked: "Did you call Boston police?"

"No."

"Did you call Lynn police?"

"No."

"Did you call the state police?"

"No."

Carney pointed out that Billy Shea was the person he called, and Whitey saved the day.

"I assumed one hundred percent that Mr. Bulger saved my brother from a problem he was having," Tower said.

"That's what you were paying for?" Carney asked.

"Yup."

Carney couldn't resist picking up his calculator again. He wanted to show how much they made in the drug business. They finally came up with four thousand to five thousand a week for five years. He then came up with another figure of $1 million. We weren't sure what that was for. The bottom line: they made a lot of money selling drugs. The jury seemed to grasp that part.

On redirect examination, Kelly made the point that selling cocaine was not a legitimate business. He asked Tower whom he relied upon as a criminal?

"Mr. Bulger—he was well known and well feared."

Next, Kelly called former drug dealer William Shea, who started by apologizing to everyone that his voice sounded like "Kermit the Frog." Laughter erupted in the courtroom several times, especially when Shea referred to Whitey as "the young-looking man over there." It had been thirty years since they'd last seen each other.

Kelly asked Shea about the first time he met Whitey:

He smiled. "First time I saw him we didn't speak. . . . Right beside Jim, it was Steve Flemmi . . . he heard good things about me . . . gave me an envelope with five hundred dollars in it because he said the holidays was coming up."

Flemmi explained to Shea they'd been having tension with the Fifth Street crew and could use some help. The relationship flourished after that.

Jurors appeared fascinated with the economics behind the drug trade. They listened to Shea reminisce about their infamous "dog and pony show" where he and other thugs rounded up drug dealers in Southie and forced them to work for Whitey's enterprise. He talked about the lousy "gangster grass" and the switch to the better-quality "Columbian Gold" marijuana. Shea smiled as he reminisced, "We sold a lot of pot in the early eighties."

Jurors learned about terms like "the chop," which is gangster language for one's weekly take of the profits. The dealers purchased at least two kilos of cocaine every week from Columbians, diluted the product, and resold it to mid-level drug dealers for huge profits.

Later on during the trial, jurors would hear from other dealers such as Paul "Polecat" Moore and Anthony Attardo, who would corroborate Shea's testimony. Moore paid approximately five thousand dollars per week in tribute to Whitey, and had to buy drugs wholesale through Shea. One time he was fined ten thousand dollars for not buying through Whitey's organization. If he failed to abide by Whitey's rules, "he'd end up in a body bag." Attardo moved large amounts of cocaine, and had to pay Whitey eighty thousand dollars or risk his life: "Everybody knew his reputation. Very dangerous. He meant what he said." They all needed Whitey's permission to operate in Southie, and Whitey got a nice piece of the action.

Shea testified that he didn't mind working with Whitey: "You could reason with Jim," he said.

"Could you deal cocaine without Jim Bulger?" Kelly asked.

"Probably not."

The real problem Shea had was when he wanted to get out of the drug business in 1986. He asked Whitey if he could retire down in Florida with his young family: "I told him I'm not looking for a pension plan. I put my ass, my butt, on that street for six or seven years. It was time for me to cash in."

Whitey told him, "It wouldn't run without you, Bill."

Shea went to Florida anyway and Whitey summoned him back up and threatened him at Triple O's:

"I could tell there were signs he was getting aggravated. He makes it very, very clear I cannot leave," Shea said. "Now I'm back, I listen to the riot act."

Whitey sat him down and told him: "You remember what happened to Bucky Barrett?"

According to Shea, this meant, "Do what I say, or I'll whack you."

Jurors had just heard Martorano testify about how Whitey chained Barrett to a chair, tortured, and then shot him. It was a serious threat.

At the time, Shea knew Barrett was missing and assumed dead. He recalled, "I took it as Bucky Barrett is among the missing. I took it as a threat. It was the first time he ever did it and it changed my perception of Jim just like that."

Shea looked right at Whitey sitting at the defense table and said: "I don't know if you remember it, but I do."

The last incident Shea experienced with Whitey was the most terrifying. He still insisted on getting out of the drug business, so Whitey took him to an area of the South Boston projects under construction, into a dark cellar that resembled a coffin. Shea thought he was going to die; he kept watching Whitey's hands, knowing that he kept a knife in his boot. Flemmi and criminal associate Kevin Weeks stood guard outside. The wide-eyed jurors sat on the edge of their seats. What were the chances of making it out alive given the situation?

Shea convinced Whitey that he could be trusted if he left the business. That's what it was all about.

Shea testified, "I'm down there . . . my heart's beating a little bit. All of a sudden he relaxed and the tension went out of his face. He said, 'Let's get the hell out of here.'"

After that, Whitey permitted Shea to retire. The defense did not cross-examine Shea.

BEHIND THE SCENES

Later, Assistant U.S. Attorney Zachary Hafer told us that Shea's testimony represented a high-point or most memorable moment of the trial for him." His testimony made an impact, especially when Shea turned to Whitey and addressed him directly like an old friend. I couldn't believe the defense didn't cross-examine him. That was a mistake."[1] Defense attorney Hank Brennan responded: "That is why they are prosecutors and not Bulger's attorney. They had their hands full trying to hide the government's complicity in the deaths of the dozens of victims over that thirty-year period. I wouldn't expect them to be able to comprehend the defense strategy."[2]

Why bother with the parade of drug dealers when the defense conceded during opening statements that Whitey was involved in the drug trade? The government's legal strategy was to grab the jurors' attention through good storytellers and hit them with important facts central to finding Whitey guilty on the sweeping racketeering indictment.

Prosecutors hoped jurors would reflect on the horror-movie image of Shea with Whitey in the dark cellar. This paints Whitey as that "hands-on killer" and fearsome leader of a vast criminal enterprise—exactly what the government set out to prove.

chapter

2|0

JUST JOKING

Pa-pa-pa-pa-pow.
—*James Bulger, recorded jailhouse conversation*

IT'S NOT THE AMOUNT OF TIME A WITNESS IS ON THE STAND THAT DIC-
tates her importance in a trial. Such was the case when the government called Karen Smith. Her father, Edward Connors, was brutally
gunned down in 1975 in that Dorchester phone booth: "They walked
to the phone booth and shot Eddie," Martorano already had testified.
Whitey killed him because he had bragged about helping with a
murder.

Eddie Connors was known by a different name to Karen; he wasn't
just one of Whitey's victims, he was simply "Dad." As she gingerly
made her way past Whitey to the witness stand, we wondered what she
would remember.

Smith informed jurors that her father had owned two bars in 1975:
Bulldogs and Connors' Tavern.

"How old were you on the day your father died?" Hafer asked.

"I was seven."

Smith recalled on June 12, 1975, she had dinner with her father.
Later, when she was in her pajamas ready to go to bed, someone called
the house phone and she answered. There was a man's voice on the

LEFT: Edward Connors, owner of Bulldogs and Connors' Tavern. He was gunned down on June 12, 1975.

RIGHT: Crime scene photograph showing the phone booth where Edward Connors was killed by machine-gun fire.

other end. Her father picked up and said he had it. When she asked if she could go with him, he said no.

Her dad walked past her bedroom on his way out, and that was the last time she saw him alive.

"What happened next?" Hafer asked.

"I was woken up in the middle of the night by a man in a suit who carried me out of my home," she said. The next day she saw the photograph of her dad lying dead in the phone booth.

"Was there a funeral?

"Yes."

"Did you go?"

"No, I was too young."

Hafer displayed a photograph of Connors in a bartender apron.

Smith identified her father and cried. We imagined her as a heartbroken little girl crying herself to sleep every night, missing her daddy.

Another family member doubled over and sobbed in the gallery. Jurors noticed . . . jurors notice everything.

"The United States calls Ken Brady," Kelly said. The timing for the next witness was clearly orchestrated, for Eddie Connors would be mentioned again, but this time by Whitey.

We knew that prosecutors had planned to introduce recorded jail-house conversations between Whitey and relatives. This would be the first time the jury would hear the sound of Whitey's voice. What would he say? Could it be that incriminating? Didn't Whitey realize that anything he said could be used against him?

Brady would be the person to verify the authenticity of the recordings and to testify that the voice on the tape belonged to Whitey. He was an investigator with the Plymouth County sheriff's office who had spoken with Whitey more than one hundred times at the Plymouth County Correctional Facility where Whitey had been held since they brought him back from California. The jail housed nearly seventeen hundred male inmates, making it the largest correctional facility under one roof in New England. The inmates included a mix of those who stand accused and those convicted. Many awaiting trials scheduled in federal court were held there.

Brady explained that phone calls and visitations with inmates are monitored. At that point, Judge Casper handed out transcripts of the recorded conversations to jurors. She explained that the audio recordings were the evidence, not the transcript.

The first recorded conversation took place between Whitey and his brother John as the two talked about an incident in which Whitey pulled a shotgun on a group of suspicious African-American kids in Rotary Liquors.

Whitey said, "So, I'm picking up a shotgun and I'm aiming it at them. . . . I put one in the chamber. . . . Stevie had a .45." Whitey laughed. "We would've had to tell the kids who worked there . . . you've gotta say you shot these bastards."

"Whose voice is on the tape?"

"The defendant, Mr. Bulger," Brady said.

Another recorded conversation occurred between Whitey and his brother John about cash he sent to either John Martorano or Kevin Weeks.

The most significant moment was when Brady testified about a recorded conversation between Whitey and William Bulger Jr., his nephew. It was a conversation that the Connors family would never forget.

Once again, the clerk hit the Play button. The courtroom was silent for a moment until the sound of Whitey's voice filled the empty air. They were talking about a bar: "And Bulldogs was Eddie Connors's . . . that guy in the phone booth . . . pa-pa-pa-pa-pow. . . . Somebody threw my name in the mix, as usual." Whitey repeated the machine-gun sound: "Pa-pa-pa-pa-pow."

We glanced at Karen Smith, Eddie's daughter who had just testified. Her blank look showed she was holding back tears. It had been thirty-eight years since her father's murder, and she had to sit there and listen to Whitey making a joke out of it. His other daughter, Cheryl, sat silent.

The primary legal strategy in calling Brady was for jurors to hear Whitey talk about the Connors murder with the family sitting right there. Whitey didn't admit to the killing on the tape, but he made light of it.

When the government finished playing the tapes, Carney took over. It was a solemn moment. Jurors seemed to be studying Whitey and looking into the gallery at the Connors family. What could Carney possibly do to rectify the situation? We half expected him to turn around and explain that his client had been merely joking—no harm intended. Instead, he changed the subject and got the jury thinking about something else.

"Now, by being in solitary, it means that two days a week he remains in his cell twenty-four hours, right?"

"Correct."

"And the other five days a week he's allowed out one hour a day."

"Correct."

"Now, at the outset of his being there, he was strip-searched, wasn't he?"

"Yes, sir."

"And strip-searched by you personally, right?"

"Yes, sir."

"And he was strip-searched sometimes five to eight times every day; isn't that correct?"

Mr. Brady hesitated.

"Any contraband ever found?"

"No."

"You are aware the strip searches only ended when I intervened?" Carney said.

In a handwritten letter to us, Whitey said: "I'm in solitary cell 23 hours a day 5 days a week plus on Tuesday and Thursday 24 hours a day—little human contact and after long trial little sleep 3–4 hours a day at the most—kind of weary."

Jurors frowned when they listened to the testimony about the excessive strip searches. Why would they harass an old man like that? What's the point when he's under twenty-four-hour surveillance? Carney's legal strategy: attack the government whenever possible. He wanted to infuriate jurors about harsh prison conditions in a government facility. Perhaps they'd start to think along the lines of Gitmo and waterboarding.

When court ended later that day, lawyers, spectators, and jurors scattered for the Fourth of July holiday week. The trial had become part of us by then. At barbecues and beach parties people wanted to know every detail, as if the trial had followed us out. They longed for the little stories that came out; they wanted to hear about characters like Ralph DiMasi, who lived by that infamous code of silence but couldn't resist telling his part in the Whitey saga—how he chased the guys with machine guns down Morrissey Boulevard with a stiletto. There was Billy Shea alone with Whitey in the tiny, dark, coffinlike basement—would he make it out alive? Others wanted to hear all about the cross-examination of Morris and his public apology.

Some stories couldn't be told—you had to be there to "feel" them. Diane Sussman caring for Louie all those years in his wheelchair is one. Another would be the image of Karen Smith as a little seven-year-old girl waking up at night, crying, and missing her daddy.

chapter

2|1

ON THE WATERFRONT

*Jim Bulger just started shooting at him—his body was bouncing
along the ground.... I drove by and I could see the bodies.*
—Kevin Weeks, trial testimony

SPECTATORS ARRIVED EXTRA EARLY THAT MONDAY MORNING, JULY 8,
2013, to snatch a seat. We were back from the holiday week, and anxious to get started. We knew the government was about to call a star
witness, someone with intimate insight into Whitey's world of extortion and murder.

"The United States calls Kevin Weeks."

Weeks had a somewhat bowlegged fat man's stride as he walked
past Whitey and took his seat on the witness stand. His dark, curly
hair came down in a V on his round forehead. He had saggy jowls and
looked permanently angry. We listened for a low snarl—it had to be
there beneath the surface. He wore a black blazer and tan T-shirt.

Kelly began the direct examination by bringing out the terms of
Weeks's sweetheart deal with the government. In July of 2000, he pled
guilty to aiding and abetting in five murders and extortion in exchange
for truthful cooperation. He received only six years.

Weeks explained, "These charges related to the remnants of the
criminal enterprise of the Winter Hill Gang. Bulger, Steve Flemmi,
and myself. We committed many crimes together."

Whitey Bulger (left) and Kevin Weeks (right) in an FBI surveillance photo in South Boston.

Weeks met Whitey while he was a bouncer at Triple O's bar in South Boston. Over time they became closer, and he eventually went to work as Whitey's muscle man. At first, Weeks picked up envelopes of money from bookmakers, and "beat people up."

He described a typical day: "Usually Jimmy would come out around three thirty in the afternoon. We never talked on the phone or in enclosed areas. . . . Jim liked to walk for the fresh air and exercise at Castle Island, or through the projects, where they would discuss business. We walked around the Sugar Bowl, an area in Castle Island that juts out toward the water. We talked outside so we wouldn't be intercepted by law enforcement."

Kelly displayed multiple photographs of Weeks with Whitey and Stevie sitting on lawn chairs in a South Boston park, and walking around the Sugar Bowl in Castle Island. They weren't engaged in any criminal activity, yet the array established an association between the three.

Next, Weeks identified the guns on the clerk's table and those in the photos as belonging to Whitey. He described how they stored the weapons in various "hides" so they wouldn't be discovered. One hide was located at Flemmi's mother's house in South Boston, and another at George Kaufman's home. They had to insert a putty knife into a space, which created an electrical contact for the wall to slide open and reveal a secret room for their machine guns, silencers, and handguns. It was something right out of a James Bond film.

Kaufman was a member of the group and the liaison with the bookies. When Kaufman sold his house, all the guns had to be moved on a dark, rainy night to Flemmi's mother's house. To accommodate

Stephen Flemmi (left), Kevin Weeks (center), and Whitey Bulger (right) in an FBI surveillance photo.

their growing arsenal, there were additional hides in the basement of Pat Nee's South Boston home, and Weeks's mother's house.

Weeks testified, "The guns, magazines, handcuffs, knives . . . they were all part of the kit that Jim Bulger wanted. We always carried knives for intimidation."

Kelly picked up an M-16 and it fell apart in several pieces and landed on the floor. The gallery fell silent at first, stunned, and then everyone laughed. Of all people, Kelly broke the gun? They had carefully stored all those weapons for decades, and leave it to the organized and articulate prosecutor to fumble at the worst possible moment—in open court for all to see.

He gathered the pieces, and placed the big gun gently back on the table. "That's the last demo I'm going to do, Your Honor," he said. Judge Casper nodded with relief. We laughed again.

Murder came next on Kelly's agenda. Weeks claimed he wasn't involved in any murders until May of 1982, when Michael Donahue and Brian Halloran were killed. Weeks said they'd received word that Halloran was cooperating with the FBI regarding the Wheeler murder, and Whitey wanted to kill him. Someone spotted Halloran talking on a pay phone near the waterfront, and informed Whitey. This was their opportunity, so Weeks drove around Southie looking for Stevie Flemmi, but couldn't find him. The hit had to go down, so Whitey retrieved the souped-up car and moved forward with the execution without Stevie.

Weeks testified, "Bulger was in 'the tow truck,' a '75 Malibu, which was a stolen car used to intercept law enforcement." It was "equipped with a smoke screen, oil slick." Whitey wore a floppy mustache and a wig that made him look like another gangster, Jimmy Flynn. They also had a police scanner and two-way radio.

We had already heard testimony about Whitey wearing the disguise. This was the type of corroboration that the government needed.

Weeks met Whitey at Jimmy's Harborside, which was located right up the street from the federal courthouse. Whitey gave him a two-way radio and instructed him to be the "lookout." Weeks described "a guy with a ski mask" who accompanied Whitey, but he didn't know who that was. Many speculated it was Pat Nee, which Flemmi would confirm later. We knew they had been close friends. It appeared that Weeks was still protecting Nee. The jurors wouldn't know that unless the defense got him to admit it on cross.

Weeks testified: "I pulled into the parking lot at Anthony's Pier 4. I could see him sitting there in the restaurant [the Pier] and when he got up to leave I radioed to Bulger and his crew and said, 'The balloon's rising.' When he left the restaurant, I said, 'The balloon's in the air.'" They nicknamed Halloran "balloon head" due to his big head and his heavy cocaine use.

"What happened next?" Kelly asked.

"A blue Datsun pulled up, and Brian Halloran got in the passenger's side. Jim Bulger slid across the seat and yelled out, 'Brian' and he started shooting. When Jim Bulger started shooting, people were screaming, diving to get out of the way."

Michael Donahue drove the blue Datsun, and it drifted across the road and hit something while they were shooting at it. Weeks said, "Bulger made a U-turn. Brian Halloran had exited the vehicle. He was still alive and walking, so Jim Bulger just started shooting at him—his body was bouncing along the ground. . . . I drove by and I could see the bodies." Weeks also saw the "guy with the ski mask" shooting at the Datsun from the backseat.

BEHIND THE SCENES

Patricia Donahue learned from witnesses that her husband Michael kept ducking to avoid being hit. "I've always wondered what was going through his mind," she said. "Did he know he was going to die? What were his last thoughts? Was he thinking of me and the kids? God, he loved those kids. He must've been terrified."[1]

After the shooting, Weeks contacted Whitey, who told him to go eat something. How could anyone eat after that massacre? we wondered. Whitey went to Teresa Stanley's house for dinner. Later on, Whitey and Weeks drove back to the murder scene because the hubcap had fallen off the hit car (the tow truck). They somehow found it before the police did, and drove to Flemmi's mother's house, where they discussed the shooting. Whitey had so many cops on the take back then, we wondered if somebody gave him a "heads up" about the hubcap.

Weeks said, "Jim Bulger and Stevie Flemmi sat at the kitchen table and they were discussing the day's events. . . . He described how he was shooting Brian, and it was all about him at that time. Stevie Flemmi was upset that he wasn't there." Whitey stopped writing in his notebook; he cocked his head and appeared to be listening. Did he remember other details that weren't brought out? The smell of gunfire and blood? Something cooking in the kitchen? He never denied those murders like he had some of the others. *Whitey remained silent.*

The next morning at breakfast, Jimmy Mantville joined them and Whitey said, "We finally got him."

"A couple days later," Weeks recalled, "Jim Bulger, myself, and Stevie Flemmi looked at the Datsun in the South Boston tow lot." He remembered Whitey saying, "Let's get out of here before someone spots us." Whitey then instructed him to dispose of the weapons, take the stock off the carbine, and throw the guns into the ocean at Marina Bay because they were used in a murder.

Weeks glanced at the jury and shifted in his chair. "I knew I was involved in a double homicide."

Weeks provided jurors with a summary of the Wheeler, Halloran, and Callahan murders, and explained how they were "all connected." First, Wheeler had been investigating the Winter Hill Gang's money skimming scam at World Jai Alai. Whitey and Stevie were afraid he was politically connected and they wouldn't survive prosecution if caught. Thus, Johnny Martorano killed Wheeler. Later, John Connolly told Whitey that Halloran had been arrested for the Pappas murder,

Roger Wheeler, Tulsa businessman and owner of World Jai Alai who was murdered at his country club on May 27, 1981.

and he was cutting a deal with the FBI. Halloran claimed that Whitey had originally asked him to do the Wheeler hit. Therefore, Halloran had to go. Finally, Whitey and Stevie worried that John Callahan "would never stand up." They worried that he'd cave when questioned by the FBI about the World Jai Alai scam and the Wheeler murder. Thus, "John Callahan was killed."

We observed most jurors taking vigorous notes. Kelly had been watching them, too. He paused as if giving them a chance to catch up. They'd already heard testimony about the World Jai Alai group of murders from Morris and Martorano. *Four dead.* Weeks linked together more pieces of the puzzle from a different perspective. He provided a view as Whitey's right-hand man. The jurors had to piece it all together. The government was doing its best to "package" the testimony and make it easy for jurors to convict.

Weeks had more to say as the extortions and murder count increased. After that first double homicide back in 1982, there was no turning back.

chapter

2|2

WARM BLOOD,
COLD WATER

Her eyes had rolled up and her lips were blue.
—Kevin Weeks, trial testimony

WHEN THE JURORS STOPPED TAKING NOTES ABOUT THE WORLD JAI
Alai murders and looked up, Kelly focused on Whitey's counts of extortion, which must have been terrifying for the victims.

Weeks relayed the story about the extortion of Michael Solimando, which occurred in the fall of 1982, shortly after the Callahan murder in Florida. It was brazen and opportunistic. Solimando wasn't a gangster—he was involved in real estate, and had been buddies with Callahan. Weeks sat him down in a chair as Whitey stuck a machine gun to his chest, and concocted a lie about Callahan having Winter Hill's money tied up in a building in downtown Boston. According to Weeks, Whitey told Solimando, "Your muscles aren't going to do you any good now." They demanded six hundred thousand dollars and Solimando ended up paying four hundred and eighty thousand. He made payments to George Kaufman. Weeks got eighty thousand.

"It was a crime of opportunity—it was BS," Weeks admitted.

They extorted Richard Buccheri, a real estate developer, who simply rendered an opinion about moving a fence on Weeks's property line. The opinion was not favorable to Weeks, so Whitey and Stevie

The *Valhalla*, the fishing boat on which Whitey and others shipped tons of weapons to the IRA.

told Buccheri he should've kept his mouth shut, and demanded two hundred thousand dollars just for getting involved. Weeks received fifty thousand from Whitey for that extortion. *Easy money.*

In 1988, Ray Slinger owed money to Kevin O'Neil, so he was summoned down to Triple O's. Weeks described the scene: "Jim Bulger was sitting down, and started talking to him. Slinger moved . . . he had a gun in his waistband, and he yelled at Slinger and kicked him in the shin." According to Weeks, Whitey said, "I can kill yah now, be no blood, no one will know." Then Whitey lied and said that he had been offered money to kill Slinger. He then shook him down for twenty-five thousand dollars. Weeks received money from that shakedown as well.

Weeks described the 1994 extortion of Kevin Hayes, who came into the Rotary Variety Store and offered to place a bet for Weeks, not knowing who he was. How could he not know? we wondered. Weeks informed Whitey that he wanted to shake Hayes down for operating in their territory. Whitey replied, "See what you can do." Weeks took him to Pat Nee's brother's house, where they had killed three other people and buried them in the basement. He chastised Hayes for operating in their territory and claimed, "I was going to kill him." Hayes agreed to pay over twenty-five thousand dollars and then pay monthly rent for the next year and a half. Weeks received twenty-five hundred for the Hayes extortion.

The extortion of Stephen "Stippo" Rakes and his wife Julie, involving the sale of their liquor store, called Stippo's, came next. There were many different versions of the story over the years. We were looking forward to hearing what Weeks had to say. Stippo had been with us every day at the courthouse. During breaks, he'd often stand while he ate lunch in the cafeteria or pace in the hallway. He seemed anxious.

Weeks explained that the organization needed "a good source of legitimate income." Mary O'Malley, Stippo's sister, spoke with Whitey and informed him that Stippo wanted to sell the liquor store.

"I don't trust this guy—he's a piece of garbage," Weeks sneered, and scanned the gallery until he found Stippo sitting in the victims' section. Stippo crossed his arms and stared back.

Weeks and Kevin O'Neil went to Stippo's house to discuss the sale and look at the books for the business. "Jim Bulger, Stevie, and myself agreed on one hundred thousand dollars for the price. . . . Jim Bulger brings thirty thousand. . . . I brought money and we put it in a paper bag and took it to Stippo's and told him to count it." As Whitey bounced Stippo's little girl on his knee, Stippo started asking for more money. "He was trying to shake us down. . . . I pulled a gun out and put it on the table and the little girl reached for the gun." Weeks had informed Stippo that they had a deal. He became visibly red-faced and angry as he testified and reminded everyone that Stippo "came to us to buy the store. It wasn't our regular extortion." Weeks raised his voice. "I don't like Stippo."

The animosity between the two was obvious. Stippo Rakes sat in the gallery, seething.

BEHIND THE SCENES

During the break that day, Stippo said he couldn't wait to take the stand and tell the truth about the forced sale of his liquor store. "We had no choice there. None. They forced us to sell—it was not for sale at all. Never. Kevin's a liar, *a liar*. Just wait till I get up there."[1]

Weeks said that after the liquor store sale went through "there were all kinds of rumors—that we stuck a gun in his daughter's mouth . . . that we killed him." Stippo took a vacation with his family, and the rumors floating around South Boston intensified. "We made him come up and stand in front of the store to show he was alive." Whitey

South Boston Liquor Mart, formerly "Stippo's." Steve "Stippo" Rakes and his wife, Julie, claimed that Whitey and Kevin Weeks extorted them out of their liquor store by forcing them to sell at gunpoint.

and Stevie were the true owners now, but no one knew. They changed the name to Rotary Liquors.

Drug dealers were easy targets for extortion. What could they do about it? Complain to the cops that Whitey stole their drug proceeds? In addition, no one knew which ones were on the take. Weeks explained how Whitey and his gang made an extraordinary amount of money extorting drug dealers over the years.

First, Weeks explained that Billy Shea recognized a potential, and suggested that Whitey grab all the marijuana dealers and put them under one umbrella. Whitey readily agreed. Shea collected from the dealers and made regular payments to Whitey in cash envelopes containing fifty-two hundred to fifty-four hundred dollars.

Retirement from a lucrative criminal activity like drug dealing was not an option unless you were willing to pay Whitey a handsome severance package. One successful drug dealer had to pay five hundred grand.

"Jim and I cut up the money . . . I ended up with ninety thousand dollars," Weeks said.

Whitey also extorted a man in the amount of $250,000 because he called the Italians "guineas." He'd use just about any excuse when he perceived weakness and saw an opportunity to capitalize. Whitey and Stevie would make up stories for drug dealers about how they were going to get killed by someone else, and that they needed to pay a premium for "special protection."

Frank Lepere, who shipped tons of marijuana into the area, had to pay Whitey for permission. They shook him down for fifty-five thousand dollars, and told him they were looking to kill his brother. Weeks said they extorted Red Shea for fifteen thousand dollars with a replica Uzi from FBI Agent John Connolly.

Weeks described the special "Ex-Fund," which was a large pool of money set aside for operational expenses such as bribing law enforcement. Whitey's payroll included FBI agents, members of the state police, and Boston police officers.

Kelly shifted papers and peered at the jury. They were still with him. Weeks came across as a credible witness pertaining to the profit and loss side of Whitey's business. The truth came through in the details.

Kelly's gaze rested on Weeks again. His lips stretched across his face into a slight smile; he appeared satisfied. It was time for another dose of murder. The 1983 execution of Arthur "Bucky" Barrett was the first one he had highlighted in his opening statement. It was cruel—they tortured the man for hours before killing him.

Theresa Barrett Bond and her sons huddled together in the victims' section. Theresa is an attractive mother of five with long blond hair. She was a young girl when Bucky, her father, was killed. We knew this next bit of testimony would be tough for her to get through.

Barrett was a skilled criminal: an expert safecracker and bank robber. So, why kill him? we wondered. Every organization needs a good safecracker. We listened as Weeks provided the background: "Bucky had robbed the Medford Trust [a $ 1.5 million heist] and Jim Bulger and Stevie Flemmi tried to shake him down, but he ran to Mafia leader Frank Salemme," he said. They had to "back off" and "they didn't like it."

Later, after Whitey ran into Barrett by chance, he came up with a plan to suck him in and shake him down. They invited him to 799 East Third Street in South Boston to look at some stolen diamonds, and Barrett fell for it.

"John Martorano brought him to the house," Weeks explained. "Jim Bulger pointed a machine gun at him and said, 'Bucky Barrett, freeze' and he did. Stevie chained and manacled him to a chair." They told Bucky they were upset that he had gone to Frankie Salemme, but he could buy his way out of the situation. They made Bucky call his wife to get her and the kids out of the house so they could go in and take all his cash.

Out in the gallery, Barrett's daughter Theresa buried her face in her hands. Did she remember that day? Had her mother sensed the fear in her husband's voice? Did she have the ominous feeling she'd never see him again?

Weeks and Pat Nee had guarded the chained and manacled Barrett as Whitey and Stevie left and stole forty-seven thousand dollars from his house. They grabbed another ten thousand at a bar in Faneuil Hall. Whitey made Bucky call drug kingpin Joe Murray, who was from Charlestown, for more money, but Murray swore at him and hung up. Murray ran a lucrative drug business, and was shot to death by his wife in 1992.

Weeks testified: "Later, Whitey said, 'Bucky's got to go downstairs and lay down for a while.' He put a MAC-10 to the back of his head, pulled the trigger, and nothing happened. Jim Bulger had to put his glasses on because the safety was on."

"What happened next?" Kelly asked.

"He shot him in the back of the head."

Out in the gallery, Theresa bowed her head, and her sons consoled her. Several jurors looked in her direction. Seeing the distraught family members of victims had a visible impact on jurors and the people in the gallery. It raised the dead in a way, and accentuated the finality of the murders. After Whitey turned the safety off on that gun, Bucky would never see his family again.

Kelly turned around, gazed at Theresa, and paused before moving on. He must have realized that the family and others needed time for reflection. How many people in that courtroom were thinking of Bucky and the terror he must have been feeling when Whitey pulled the trigger the first time and nothing happened? *Click*. Weeks later added that "Bucky was saying his prayers." *He knew he was going to die.*

After Whitey killed Barrett, Weeks said, "Jim Bulger went up and laid down on the couch while we cleaned up. . . . Cold water helps congeal the blood, helps with the cleanup." Weeks gazed into the gallery for a moment before continuing. His testimony sounded truthful, especially the morbid detail about the cold water congealing the blood. Bucky's blood and brain matter must have been everywhere.

"Pat Nee helped dig the hole, and he was upset because it was his brother's house." Weeks concentrated on the ceiling as if trying to recount everything. "Stevie prepared the body. Phil Costa brought lime, which helped with the decomposition. We took the clothing, Stevie pulled his teeth. We smashed up his gold chain and gold cross."

Out in the gallery, Bucky's daughter wiped tears from her eyes. Weeks's description of the basement burial process came across as degrading and cold. The courtroom took on a somber mood. We could almost hear the scrape of shovels and smell the dank basement.

Kelly paused before moving on to the next victim. The murder of John McIntyre, a simple fisherman and boat engineer, involved more deception and torture. Whitey supported the Irish Republican Army, and had a plan to smuggle guns to Ireland aboard the *Valhalla,* a fishing trawler from Gloucester. They loaded it with seven tons of weapons and ammunition, which was one of the largest illegal arms shipments to the IRA. At sea, the crew transported the arms to an Irish ship, the *Marita Ann,* which was intercepted by Irish authorities. As a result, U.S. Customs officials interviewed McIntyre and the *Valhalla*'s captain when the boat arrived back in Boston. Later, authorities stopped the *Ramsland,* Joe Murray's boat, and seized forty tons of marijuana in a "hide" in the ballast. "We were getting a piece of that," Weeks testified. Whitey wasn't happy.

"We were suspicious," Weeks said, especially when Whitey received information from FBI agent John Connolly that "we were going to get arrested." Due to Connolly's leaks about McIntyre's status as an informant, Weeks testified, Whitey came up with a plot for McIntyre to invest money, and receive ten times the amount back. He fell for it, and met with Pat Nee, who took McIntyre's twenty thousand dollars to be "invested." The next day, Nee invited him to a party at 799 East Third Street, where they had killed Barrett.

Weeks described exactly what happened at the party: "McIntyre came in with a case of beer. . . . I grabbed him by the neck and threw him down to the ground. . . . He was chained and manacled to a chair. . . . Pat Nee had another party to go to." Weeks quickly threw the part about Nee in, and it sounded contrived and rehearsed. *How convenient.* Was Weeks covering for his friend again? Would the jury see through it? Did prosecutors have their doubts, too? What is the ethical obligation if a lawyer suspects his witness is lying or covering for someone? Kelly moved on, perhaps a bit too fast.

Weeks continued testifying about McIntyre's intense fear after they chained him up. Whitey told him to calm down, and they'd figure out what to tell the grand jury. McIntyre likely thought he'd be spared by a benevolent Whitey. "He felt a little better," Weeks said. Whitey drilled McIntyre about Joe Murray, seeking details about his lucrative drug business. "Jim Bulger was looking for the next score," Weeks said.

Finally, after Whitey received all the information he could out of McIntyre, he decided to strangle him. He took out a rope, but "it was too thick and he started vomiting, so he shot him in the back of the head." Weeks glanced at Whitey, who did not look up.

"McIntyre was still alive," Weeks continued, so Whitey "shot him four to five more times in the face. Stevie Flemmi pulled his teeth and we buried him. . . . Bucky Barrett was on one side of a support column, and John McIntyre was on the other side. . . . Jim Bulger was upstairs lying on the couch."

Kelly exchanged eye contact with several jurors, who appeared disgusted. Some studied Whitey with arms crossed. Were they thinking about a man getting shot five times in the face at close range? We imagined Whitey using all his strength to yank that rope tight around the neck . . . McIntyre struggling, chained to that chair, turning blue . . . the smell of vomit . . . the fear of death.

While the bitter taste of the McIntyre murder lingered, Kelly pushed forward with the sad story of Deborah Hussey. Deborah was Flemmi's stepdaughter. He had a long-term live-in relationship with her mother, Marion, who Flemmi considered his common-law wife. He had raised Deborah since she was a small child.

Weeks described a day in January of 1985 when he and Whitey drove up to the murder house at 799 East Third Street. He knew Stevie had planned to meet them with his twenty-six-year-old stepdaughter, Deborah. "She wasn't a criminal, she wasn't involved with us," he recalled. "I didn't think anything was going to happen to her." Stevie had been out buying her a coat.

The young woman had allegedly turned to drugs and prostitution in her early twenties. She would show up at Triple O's and use Whitey's name. She had become an embarrassment for Whitey and Flemmi. Perhaps she knew too much? We had seen only one photograph of

Deborah, in her large sunglasses and a colorful sweater with a starched white shirt underneath. She fashioned her brown hair in a 1970s shag haircut, which may have been out of style when someone snapped the picture.

Weeks testified: "I didn't think anything was going to come of it. . . . I heard a thud. . . . Jim Bulger had her on the ground, choking her."

"How long did it take?" Kelly asked.

"Maybe four minutes; her eyes had rolled up and her lips were blue. . . ." Stevie thought she was still alive, so he "put a rope around her neck with a stick and wrapped it tight," Weeks said. Flemmi pulled his stepdaughter's teeth, and buried her in the basement. After that, Whitey occasionally called him "Dr. Mengele" because he seemed to enjoy the killing.

We knew we'd be hearing from Flemmi later on about the Hussey murder. What would he say? How could he help kill a young woman who he raised? Who buys somebody a coat before killing her? We wanted to hear more from Flemmi about the motive behind Deborah's murder. We couldn't look at that picture again without imagining the rolled-up eyes and blue lips. Did jurors visualize the same thing? How long did it take to pull her teeth? We could almost detect a scent of sulphur.

Next, Kelly asked Weeks for details surrounding the pending sale of the murder house at 799 East Third Street. Nee's brother insisted on selling, so they had to scramble and get the bodies out. A new owner might refinish the basement and dig up a few skeletons. On

Deborah Hussey, Stephen Flemmi's stepdaughter. She was twenty-six years old when Flemmi brought her to a home in South Boston to be strangled.

The remains of Arthur "Bucky" Barrett, unearthed in 2000 across from Florian Hall, Dorchester .

Halloween weekend of 1985, Weeks, Flemmi, and Pat Nee exhumed the bodies of Barrett, McIntyre, and Hussey. The stench of rotted corpses must have been overwhelming. They placed them in plastic bags, and transported them in an old station wagon. They had dug the holes the night before, across from Florian Hall in Dorchester. Whitey placed a twenty-dollar bill on top of the disguised holes the night before so they'd know if the site had been compromised.

Weeks testified: "Jim backed the station wagon in, pulled the body bags out . . . emptied the bodies, and we covered them with dirt." Whitey stood guard with "a grease gun . . . a machine gun." At one point, a car pulled up and a young man relieved himself. There was a Halloween party going on across the street that night.

Weeks glanced up at Judge Casper, who was just a few feet away from him. He indicated that the man stood as close as the judge was to him. After the partygoer drove away, Whitey said, "We should've shot him . . . we had plenty of room in the hole. You let him get too close."

That man had no idea that real monsters loomed so close in the bushes on that Halloween weekend night.

Kelly briefly touched upon murders in which Weeks was not an eyewitness, but had learned details through Whitey. He claimed he didn't know whether Whitey or Flemmi strangled Debra Davis (Flemmi's girlfriend). Weeks learned that Whitey and Flemmi wrapped duct tape around Debra's mouth at Flemmi's mother's house. He recalled that Stevie gave her a kiss and "then she was strangled so I don't know who strangled her." We would have to wait for the details from Flemmi.

Weeks recounted learning from Agent Connolly about the secret grand jury investigation and pending racketeering indictments against Whitey and Flemmi in December of 1994. Weeks warned both of them. Whitey fled, while Flemmi hung around too long and got arrested.

Weeks later aided Whitey with IDs while he was on the lam. He also picked up Theresa Stanley, Whitey's common-law wife, when she became homesick, and swapped her out for Whitey's other girlfriend, Catherine Greig.

BEHIND THE SCENES

"He was preparing for a long time away because he always knew the outcome of everything," Theresa Stanley said in a 2008 interview with Jon, one of her last before she died. Theresa was Whitey's common-law wife of twenty-nine years. Whitey initially took Theresa with him when he fled in 1994. "I wanted to go home and very calmly he said, 'I will take you home.' I never saw him again."[2]

Kelly gathered his papers and walked back to the defense table. He rubbed his eyes, and looked drained. Jurors sat still. Many stared at Whitey and appeared deep in thought, similar to how they looked after hearing testimony from hit man John Martorano. The details behind the murders had been sobering . . . a body bouncing across the ground, a man saying his prayers before getting shot in the head, Flemmi using a stick to twist the rope around Deborah Hussey's neck.

Weeks had been a solid witness for the government. He painted a grim, detailed portrait of Whitey Bulger, fearsome leader and killer.

Veteran defense attorney Jay Carney rose for cross-examination. What would he do? How would he tear into Weeks?

chapter

2|3

TWO RATS

I said, "I'm a criminal and I lie." We all lie. All criminals lie. That's why we're criminals, you know. I'm not going to tell the truth to law enforcement if they come up and ask me something.
—*Kevin Weeks, trial testimony*

FOLLOWING SUCH VIVID TESTIMONY ABOUT GRUESOME MURDERS AND extortion, up close and personal, the defense faced an uphill battle. Weeks had testified at least five times before, which made him a seasoned witness and tough to shake.

Carney positioned himself behind the podium. He had to attack Weeks's credibility and make the jury despise him by the end. He had to expose Weeks for what he was: a self-serving, lying criminal. The kind who should not be believed.

"How much do you think you made in your entire career working with Mr. Bulger? What would you estimate?" Carney asked.

Weeks cocked his head. "I don't know, over a million, maybe two million."

Weeks confirmed he was employed full time in all manners of crime, including extortion, loan sharking, money laundering, and crimes of violence. Carney invited him to come down from the witness stand and physically show the jury how to load and fire machine guns. Weeks picked up several of the big guns from the clerk's table and provided an excellent demonstration. The marshals stood guard close by, obviously uncomfortable with it. Carney wanted to sear the image of Weeks as a menacing criminal in the minds of the jury.

Carney's strategy worked for Juror Gusina Tremblay: "Kevin Weeks handled those guns like a pro, like he really knew what he was doing."[1]

Carney used Weeks to present jurors with a different side of Whitey. He emphasized that Whitey was a father figure and mentor for Weeks. For instance, he'd tell Weeks not to drink, to stay away from drugs, and remain physically fit. He'd often give the younger Weeks advice about life and business on their long walks. Perhaps jurors would envision Whitey as a wise philosopher—a modern-day Aristotle. It was all about softening his client's image before the jury. Possibly they'd think of the old man and his young prodigy from *The Karate Kid*.

Carney shifted gears. There was only so much he could do with Whitey's image. He zeroed in on his favorite theme, government corruption, and the number of FBI agents on the take. Jurors had already witnessed the ugliness firsthand when Morris testified. The defense had scored with an apology. Now, Carney wanted to show how the corruption went way beyond Morris and Connolly.

"In fact, he had a whole group of FBI agents who would provide him with information. Isn't that correct?" Carney asked.

Weeks nodded. "He claimed he had six FBI agents up there that he had corrupted."

"In fact, didn't Jim have an expression that Christmas—"

"For kids and cops." Weeks cut him off and grinned.

"How much did Agent John Connolly get in cash, usually?" Carney asked.

"The one time I gave John Connolly two envelopes, one had five thousand in it, the other had one thousand in it, that one was for 'Agent Orange,' John Newton."

Christmas must have been a very busy time for the organization. Weeks recalled he'd go out shopping with Whitey, and buy all kinds of presents for law enforcement, including figurines and crystal clocks. Some preferred gifts over cash. Weeks said he'd give gifts to John Connolly to distribute to his fellow agents. During Christmas they'd have to hand out over thirty envelopes stuffed with cash. Some received five thousand dollars, others more. Flemmi gave Trooper Schneiderhan ten thousand.

In return for cash and gifts, Carney pointed out that Whitey would receive tips on wiretaps and police investigations. In other words, he paid for information; he didn't provide any in return. This was important to Whitey. Weeks acknowledged that Whitey was never "charged with any crime in Boston until 1995." That was Carney's way of flirting with the immunity argument, since Whitey was not allowed to present evidence before the jury in order to show that the government had promised him immunity to commit crimes. Carney hoped they'd be able to read between the lines. If Whitey had been promised immunity, he shouldn't be seated in the defendant's chair. Carney reminded Weeks that Flemmi told him the same thing—that the government had promised him immunity, too.

"In your dealings on a daily basis for decades with Jim Bulger, you learned that what he hated above all else was informants, didn't you?" Carney jumped to his client's favorite topic.

Weeks licked his lips. "We *killed* people for being informants."

"In fact, you and he called them 'rats,' right?" Carney spat out "rats" like it was a dirty word.

"It wasn't just us, I mean, everybody in Boston . . . called them rats." Weeks leaned forward and explained the code of silence: "You don't rat on your friends, you don't rat on your enemies; if you have a problem, you take it to the street and deal with it."

Carney reminded Weeks that he never heard Whitey providing any information to law enforcement officials. Further, part of Whitey's absolute code was that "you never be an informant to law enforcement— that's what he preached!" Carney declared as he extended an arm toward his client.

Weeks scowled. Carney knew how to get under Weeks's skin: turn the tables and accuse him of being the only rat in the courtroom. After-all, Weeks had become quite skilled at testifying against people, while Whitey had never testified in court nor any type of legal proceeding. "It was your decision to become a *cooperating witness,* in 1995?" Carney asked. The question made Weeks bristle.

Carney dove right into Weeks's plea bargain, indicating that he would cooperate against anyone to save himself. When he mentioned the terms with the U.S. Attorney's Office, Weeks snapped, "You'd have to ask them!" He extended his arm toward the government's table.

Carney accused Weeks of changing his story about what happened with the Stippo Rakes extortion. We knew that Weeks had flunked a lie detector test, but Carney could not bring that up in front of the jury. Judge Casper would not allow it due to the unreliability of the polygraph.

Carney knew the mere mention of Rakes would upset him even more, especially with Stippo grinning from the gallery, witnessing his destruction on cross.

"So I don't like Stippo Rakes, so I lied," Weeks yelled.

"You told the investigators a lie because you didn't like Rakes?" Carney sounded incredulous.

"I've been lying my whole life. I'm a criminal," Weeks declared.

Carney paused for effect, or perhaps out of shock. Did Weeks really say that? *I've been lying my whole life.* If so, why should the jury believe anything from this witness? Carney had just succeeded in blowing Weeks's credibility to smithereens. That never happens. The prosecutors probably wanted to crawl under the table. Brennan must've wanted to break out his harmonica (he actually plays in a band). Would Carney sit down now and end on that beautiful note? He must have been tempted, but he kept going.

Carney knew he had Weeks in a vise; he was in control of the witness. Weeks was the one chained and manacled to a chair—psychological torture. Carney needled Weeks again over his plea deal, emphasizing how fast the government broke him down. This made him look weak in the criminal world. Weeks likely despised his nickname "Two Weeks," which is how long it took for him to agree to cooperate.

"I made a deal before Stevie did." Weeks spoke quickly, sounding defensive.

"Because that would be the way that you could get a better deal," Carney said. "Right?"

"That's how to avoid a life sentence, yes." He glared at Carney. "I would be a fool not to."

"You knew Martorano had his deal in place?"

"Correct."

"Now, when you were making a decision to provide information against Jim Bulger, you were concerned that *you* would be viewed as a *rat*, weren't you?" Carney loved that word. Whenever he used it, Weeks clenched his jaw. *We thought we detected a low snarl.*

"To a degree," Weeks said.

"You knew—"

"I was concerned that I was going to get lumped in with them as an informant." His face turned crimson. "That was my real concern."

"What was the expression you started using?" Carney asked.

"You can't rat on a rat." Weeks raised his voice and glared at Whitey.

"And what that means was if Jim Bulger was an informant, then your cooperating against him would not constitute you being an informant or a rat, right?"

"Correct." Weeks raised a nostril.

Carney suggested that Weeks should be afraid to walk the streets.

"I go to the North End, you know. The Mafia's over there. No one says nothing," Weeks said.

"No one calls you *a rat?*"

"No one." Weeks's face puffed up, like he was ready to explode.

"Because 'you can't rat on a rat,' according to you?" Carney mocked him.

"Maybe they don't have the balls to say it to my face," Weeks yelled. "They might say it behind my back, but no one's ever said it to me."

"Because what would you do if they said it to you?" Carney asked.

"Well, we'd have a problem."

"What kind of problem?"

"I'd go after them."

"In what way?"

"Physically!" Weeks made a fist. *He was tougher than the Mafia now.*

"What would you do?" Carney wouldn't let it go.

"Well, why don't you call me outside when it's just me and you and see what I do." Weeks's voice sounded garbled.

Carney let it all sink in. He had succeeded in wearing Weeks down to the point where he lashed out. The witness simply couldn't take it anymore. *That never happens.* We felt the raw tension, the heat of the moment.

"No," Carney said. "I'd like to hear you in front of this jury say what you would do."

Weeks leaned over the witness stand and scowled. "You just heard it."

Carney kept pressing; he was on a roll. "Do you ever go to Mirisola's?" he asked.

"All the time. It's right around the corner from my house."

Mirisola's is a small, family owned restaurant in South Boston. They have the best homemade chicken parmesan and fresh fish specials. It's also where Pat Nee goes regularly.

"Pat Nee, is he still a friend of yours?" Carney asked.

"Yes."

Carney suggested it was Pat Nee who wore the ski mask and shot at Michael Donahue and Brian Halloran from the backseat of the "tow truck." Weeks claimed he didn't know; he was obviously being evasive.

"Nee had brought John McIntyre to the house—"

"Correct."

"Pat Nee had stayed with you to guard Bucky Barrett while others went to get money off Bucky Barrett, right?"

"Correct."

"So Pat Nee had a lot to do with your criminal activities, didn't he?"

"He was active," Weeks admitted. "Yes."

Carney scratched his head. "Have you ever had to testify at a hearing against Pat Nee?"

Weeks shrugged. "He hasn't been charged with any of these crimes."

Carney glanced at the jury. He let those words sink in for a moment. Were they wondering why Nee had never been charged? So far, they'd heard quite a bit about Nee. He'd been on hand for several murders—he'd disposed of bodies. Why not prosecute him? Many spectators whispered about it in the hallways. How does the government pick and choose who gets prosecuted and who gets a free ticket? Carney wanted jurors to think about that.

"Now, you said, about fifteen minutes ago, that you've been a liar all your life?" Carney couldn't help himself.

Weeks rolled his eyes. "I said, 'I'm a criminal and I lie.' We all lie. All criminals lie. That's why we're criminals, you know. I'm not going to tell the truth to law enforcement if they come up and ask me something, you know."

The prosecutors looked like statues. They must have been ready to kill Weeks. Now, it seemed like their star witness would say anything, as if he had thrown in the towel.

"Why would you lie?" Carney asked.

"Why would I lie?" Weeks rubbed his fingers together.

"Yes."

"Criminal activity. I'm not going to tell the truth."

"If you get a benefit, you would lie?" Carney asked.

"Sure." He shrugged.

"Are you a good liar?"

"I'd invite people down to the store and say I had a job for them, and then I'd extort them."

"Who were some of the people you would lie to?" Carney pressed.

"I lied to my parents. I lied to my wife. I lie to girlfriends."

"What lies do you tell your wife?"

"I'm not cheating."

"Does she know you're lying?"

"We're divorced."

The sound of laughter filled the courtroom. Carney glanced at the chuckling jurors. They were clearly entertained. Drama and humor—a winning combination.

"Did she know you were lying?"

"Of course she did," Weeks replied.

"What lies do you tell your girlfriend?"

"I'm not cheating on them." Weeks hated testifying and added: "I was hoping he'd never get caught so we wouldn't be in this circus right now."

"You won against the system?" Carney said.

"What did I win?" Weeks gestured wildly with his hands. "What did I win?"

"You won five years—"

"Five people are dead." Weeks spread and raised five fingers. "Five people are dead."

Carney squinted. "Does that bother you at all?"

"Yeah, it bothers me."

"How does it bother you?"

"Because we killed people that were rats, and I had the two biggest rats right next to me. That's why it—"

Whitey yelled, "You suck!"

Weeks pointed at Whitey: "Fuck you, okay!"

"Fuck you, too!" Whitey yelled back.

"What do you want to do?" Weeks leaned over the stand.

"Hey!" Judge Casper extended her palms. "Mr. Bulger. Mr. Bulger, let your attorneys speak for you."

Carney thrived on conflict. He got the best of Weeks by chipping away, getting under his skin until he broke down and copped a tough-guy attitude. He did a superb job placing Weeks on the defensive and painting him as a liar, someone who couldn't be trusted. Carney scored points with the jury. Following the massacre, jurors appeared upbeat. It looked like they had enjoyed the show; he had them on the edge of their seats.

The high drama created by Carney's cross overshadowed the damaging testimony against Whitey. Some criticized Carney for not cross-examining Weeks about some of the other murders. A seasoned lawyer knows better than to go after the government's strengths—always attack the weaknesses. In addition, Carney didn't want damaging information repeated.

BEHIND THE SCENES

We congratulated a beaming Jay Carney outside the courthouse. "In all my years," Carney said, "I've never had a witness admit he's a liar and then threaten to 'take me outside.'" He set his briefcase down on the hot sidewalk. "And then, to have the victims' families come over and shake my hand? I'm a defense attorney." He shook his head with disbelief. "It's an extraordinary trial."[2]

It was extraordinary. The media recognized it, and couldn't get enough. They loved the threats and the exchange of expletives between Whitey and Weeks. Throngs of reporters scurried with microphones and cables to capture the mood live on camera. Additional media trucks lined Seaport Boulevard. A large public crowd had gathered on the sidewalk and spilled into the street. A helicopter hovered above.

Jay Carney could barely make it to his car. People just wanted an opportunity to shake his hand.

2|4

SKULLS SMILE

This body was tightly flexed in a fetal position and she was on her
side . . . rope wrapped around the long bones.
—Dr. Ann Marie Mires, *trial testimony*

THE SCIENCE OF MURDER IS GRISLY. TO THOSE WHO AREN'T USED TO
seeing images of stained skulls pierced with bullet holes and limbs
poking up through dirt in shallow graves, it can be a harrowing experience. We knew that when forensic anthropologist Dr. Ann Marie
Mires took the stand there would be plenty of wincing from the jury
box and the spectators' gallery. The defense battled to keep the photographs out, claiming they were highly inflammatory and prejudicial.
Judge Casper ruled in favor of admission, noting that jurors had already seen graphic pictures.

The government timed this forensic testimony to corroborate what
Weeks had said about removing the bodies of Barrett, McIntyre, and
Hussey from the burial site in the basement of 799 East Third Street
in South Boston to the unmarked graves across from Florian Hall in
Dorchester. Prosecutors also needed to replace the high drama created by Carney's cross with a sense of melancholy. It was time to turn
down the heat.

"It was cold, windy . . . snowing," Dr. Mires said, describing the scene
on January 13, 2000, when investigators called her out to a potential

burial site in Dorchester across from Florian Hall. Cars and trucks traveling along the Southeast Expressway roared from above. Weeks led investigators to an approximate location of where they had buried the bodies years ago.

It's one thing to know where the bodies are buried. It's quite another to have to dig them up and preserve them, particularly in the dead of winter. Dr. Mires described the grim task in detail. A tent and heaters had to be brought in to protect the team from the blustery wind and frigid temperatures. The excavation process lasted throughout the night. The team started with a large backhoe and small Bobcat to remove the "overburden," which is the soil over the burial pit. They noticed "mottled colors" and discoloration, which could indicate a change "depicting the top of the grave." They also used a soil probe to test the consistency. "Inside the pit it would be very soft," Dr. Mires said.

Eventually, the Bobcat "picked up some leg bones." Once they saw the bones, the crew stopped with the Bobcat, and dug by hand using rakes and screens.

"The bones take on the same color as the soil and develop a natural patina from being buried," she explained. They proceeded down in layers, and uncovered an orange-brown funeral-issue body bag at 12:50 A.M. At that point, the team "changed to a pedestal technique, where we excavate the soil around the remains, so the material would be plateaued." Dr. Mires addressed the jury sounding like a clinical professor. It appeared that the remains had been stacked on top of each other, making it clear that someone had moved them from another location. Mires showed the jury a photograph of a white chalky material, which appeared to be traces of garden lime. She speculated that someone used it to suppress the smell of decomposition. Weeks had testified about using lime during the burial of Bucky Barrett. This was the type of corroboration that the government needed.

Dr. Mires noted that roots growing through the remains indicated that the bodies had been there for quite some time. The forensic science morphed into a haunting reality when Wyshak displayed a photograph of Barrett's skull with the rest of his bones laid out on a table. We could see the gaping hole in the back of his head, and the empty sockets where the teeth should have been. *The last thing Barrett heard before he died—Whitey clicking the safety off.*

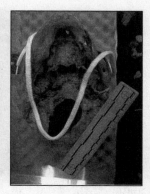

LEFT: Remains of murder victim Arthur "Bucky" Barrett after excavation near Florian Hall, Dorchester. CENTER: Skull of murder victim Arthur "Bucky" Barrett showing missing teeth. RIGHT: Bottom of skull of murder victim Arthur "Bucky" Barrett showing bullet hole at base of skull.

Deborah Hussey's skull gazed at us a few minutes later. Dr. Mires said she had a "gracile skull." Again, we noticed the missing teeth. "There was no evidence of blunt trauma, gunshot, or strangulation." Mires explained that less than 15 percent of deaths due to strangulations show any evidence of skeletal damage. As Weeks had testified, Deborah was a frail girl, and had probably been easy to strangle. The lack of blunt trauma made sense.

Mires also pointed out that the damage on Hussey's skeleton was consistent with a tool used to remove the body late in the decomposition period, which matched what Weeks had said about moving the bodies from the basement of the murder house.

The cause of death for Hussey was listed as "homicidal violence, cause unknown." Mires explained that she couldn't specify in scientific terms "the mechanism that stopped life."

We looked at Whitey. *A man's hands had stopped life.*

Next, John McIntyre revealed his gunshot wound on the big screen. *The one he begged for as opposed to being choked with the thick rope.* Again, no teeth. The round green circle on the inside of his skull was caused by copper from the jacket of the bullet. The copper had broken down, leaving residue behind.

Another excavation in September of 2000 unearthed Paul McGonagle at Tenean Beach in Dorchester. Dr. Mires testified that it was a

Murder victim Paul McGonagle's remains with leg bones protruding from platform shoes.

"difficult body recovery with collapsing of sand and rising of water. . . . His bones took on the color of the beach." And they did. We noticed he matched the sand exactly. McGonagle was murdered in 1974, but the coastal area preserved him. We saw his button-down shirt and belt, and his underwear still near the pelvic bones where it belonged. One of the most memorable images: McGonagle's leg bones still in his platform shoes. *Socks and all.* After all those years? We imagined the scent of low tide as they dug him up.

Paul McGonagle Jr. had testified earlier that he was just fourteen when his father went missing after he had dropped his ten-year-old brother off at hockey practice. "My dad always told me to take care of my mom and my brother if anything should happen." It was November of 1974. He remembered that his dad wore heels to appear taller and a gold Irish Claddagh ring. About a year later, Whitey "rolled up on me in his blue Chevrolet, aviator glasses, and said they had taken care of the guys who did what they did to my father."

Whitey had listened to McGonagle's son without making eye contact. Did he remember the encounter? Did he now feel guilty about lying to a fifteen-year-old about who murdered his dad?

Weeks had testified that Whitey would drive by the beach and say, "Drink up, Paulie!"

What was Whitey thinking as he looked at McGonagle's skeletal legs sticking out of his shoes? Was he feeling remorse at the ripe age of eighty-three? Was he conflicted by any of it? Did he think about his victims? Or an afterlife?

Mires presented a video showing how they scooped reddish brown material from McGonagle's skull, caused by hemorrhaging when the bullet entered. Jurors seemed both horrified and fascinated.

The next dig occurred in October of 2000, near the Neponset River Bridge in Quincy. It took two weeks of digging until the backhoe accidentally struck Tommy King's remains, which damaged them. We saw a clear view of King's skull with the bullet hole. Mires explained it was an entry wound due to inner beveling. King still wore his bulletproof vest. Martorano testified they had tricked him into thinking he was participating in a hit, but his gun had blanks. This served as further corroborating testimony for the government.

King's skeletal fingers wore driving gloves. He also wore a gold Claddagh ring. Which way was the heart on that Claddagh ring facing? It stood for love, loyalty, and friendship. If the heart faced in, it meant you were taken. Was the heart on McGonagle's ring facing in? Had he been in love with somebody when he died? These tiny details made us think about the importance of life. Did any of the jurors wear Claddagh rings? It was hard to tell from our vantage point.

The team continued digging and digging with the backhoes, searching for the body of Debra Davis, Flemmi's longtime girlfriend, who went missing in 1981. Weeks had not witnessed the murder, but believed that either Whitey or Flemmi had strangled her because she knew too much. We would learn more about Debra's murder during Flemmi's testimony. Weeks had guided investigators to the general area where he thought they buried her, but it didn't look promising. They searched for weeks, and were about to call it off when "the backhoe grabbed the rope in the dirt," Mires said. They recovered her skull in a plastic bag, and observed "rope wrapped around the long bones." Mires noted: "The knots are intact . . . the length of rope spirals around.

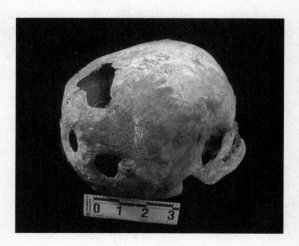

Skull of Debra Davis with lesions due to wave action.

Debra Davis, the girlfriend of Stephen Flemmi, who was strangled when she was twenty-six years old. Investigators recovered her remains in an unmarked grave in 2000.

"Forensically, knots are important because they can tell you something about who tied them . . . perhaps how the person died. Rope can also contain DNA samples," Mires explained. We saw the photographs of the rope wrapped around and around Debra's skeleton.

"This body was tightly flexed in a fetal position and she was on her side. . . . The hair was preserved due to the coastal environment." Mires pointed to three lesions on Debra's skull, which resulted from the knots in the rope due to wave action and the movement of the tide. We learned that Debra had been submerged twice a day.

Steve Davis listened from the gallery. He wiped tears from his eyes. That was his sister found in the fetal position with ropes tangled around her bones. Cause of death: "homicidal violence."

Wyshak displayed an enlarged image of Debra's skull. She had been a gorgeous twenty-six-year-old woman, full of life, with that Farrah Fawcett hair and beaming smile.

Now, her skull smiled back at us as it had in her picture.

chapter

2|5

WHY?

I don't understand why all these people that were involved in my husband's death are walking around like nothing ever happened. I don't think it's fair and I don't understand why the government lets that happen.

—*Patricia Donahue, trial testimony*

PAT DONAHUE MARCHED TO THE WITNESS STAND WITH CONFIDENCE, right past Whitey. On May 11, 1982, her three boys were thirteen, twelve, and eight years old. Her husband Michael worked for the Teamsters, Local 28. She remembered fixing his hair that day at her salon, and giving him a kiss good-bye. He smiled and told her he'd talk to her later. Michael had planned to pick up bait on the waterfront for the father-son fishing trip he was taking with Tommy for making his first communion. It was Mother's Day weekend, she recalled, sadly.

Pat said that Michael was coming home for dinner. "It was quarter of six, and he was on his way home, he had to drop somebody off. A news bulletin flashed across the TV screen reporting a gangland slaying." Pat continued to cook dinner, and when the six o'clock news came on, she recognized her father-in-law's car, and knew Michael had been driving it. She was confused and began hyperventilating. How could it be?

Pat testified: "I waited and waited for someone to call me and let me know where my husband was. . . . No one gave me information."

Michael Donahue, who was gunned down by Whitey Bulger in a gangland hit in May of 1982.

She knew "one was dead and one was alive." She called every hospital in the area and received no information. All she wanted was to find out where he was, so she could be with him. "I was thinking about all the things I could say to him if I could only get to where he was."

Around ten that night, the police finally came to take her to the hospital. "It was too late, he had already died."

Kelly displayed a picture of Michael Donahue in a wedding tuxedo. "That's my husband." The Donahue sons embraced each other.

Carney rose for the cross-examination of Pat Donahue. "Is there any other information about your husband that the jury should know?"

"Yes, what took law enforcement so long to come get me? Why did it take so long? Why couldn't I be with him after all that time? After he was killed, I was told someone else had killed him . . . other than Bulger. I learned later that Kevin Weeks was involved and James Bulger, and a person in the backseat with a machine gun."

"Do you now know that person's name is Patrick Nee?" Carney asked.

"Yes."

"How much interest have you seen from federal prosecutors going after Pat Nee?" Carney asked.

"Objection!" Kelly jumped up. His face appeared red and angry.

"Sustained."

"You saw that Kevin Weeks made a deal to cooperate?" Carney asked.

"Six years for five murders—it made me sick!" She addressed the government's table, looking right at Kelly.

"You learned about the role that John Morris played, and he agreed to be a cooperating witness. He was allowed to keep his pension, and received full immunity," Carney said. "Do you have feelings about that, Mrs. Donahue?"

"Objection!" Kelly stood again.

"Sustained."

"In 2001, you and your three sons filed a lawsuit against the government?"

"Tommy, Michael, and Shawn." Pat pointed to her three sons and Carney asked them to stand.

"Did the federal government and the FBI acknowledge their responsibility?"

"Objection!" Kelly yelled.

"Sustained."

"Did they ever apologize?"

"Objection!" Kelly yelled again.

"Sustained."

"I don't think it's fair, and I don't understand why the government lets that happen. I don't understand why all these people involved in my husband's death are still walking around and nothing has happened." Pat spoke with authority. Her disdain for the government came across loud and clear.

Carney sat down and Kelly rose for redirect.

"Are you aware that your husband's murder was never solved until Kevin Weeks came forward?" he asked. He sounded annoyed with her.

"Yes," Pat replied in a softer voice.

"Are you aware that the man accused of shooting your husband is right there?" Kelly pointed right at Whitey.

"Yes."

Kelly had no further questions for Pat; she rejoined her sons in the spectators section. Most jurors gazed at the family, appearing sympathetic.

Whitey never made eye contact with Pat during her testimony. Did he feel for her? We watched him whispering to Brennan behind his raised legal pad.

The next relative to take the stand was Steve Davis, a rugged-looking man with a full head of white hair and Fu Manchu. Steve

Interior of the blue Datsun that Michael Donahue had been driving when attacked with machine-gun fire. Whitey Bulger and Kevin Weeks snuck a peek at the blood and bits of brain matter within a day or so after the hit while the car sat in a tow lot.

made a point of getting to know everyone. He was friendly, outgoing, and full of life like his sister Debra had been. He attended the trial every day, and always spoke out at the press conferences. Steve and his sister were very close, just eighteen months apart. It was difficult for him to talk about her. On September 17, 1981, Debra went missing. Steve was twenty-four. He recalled seeing his sister a couple of days before she disappeared.

His mother called him, and said something was wrong, that Debra hadn't called her.

"I kept saying, she'll be all right, she'll be all right," Steve testified.

Steve recalled that his mother must've put a hundred calls in to a beeper that Stevie Flemmi had given Debra. Flemmi told the family that Debra must've simply taken off.

"Did you ever see her again?" Hafer asked.

"I never saw her again until yesterday." Steve broke down. He referred to the images of his sister's skeletal remains displayed in court by Dr. Mires.

In the fall of 2000, the investigators told him they were digging for bodies in Quincy. When they found Debra, the family scheduled a funeral.

Hafer displayed the beautiful picture of Debra. "Do you recognize this?"

"That's my sister." Steve's voice cracked again.

Carney rose for cross-examination. "How old was Debbie when she met Flemmi?" he asked.

"Seventeen."

"They began dating?"

Steve nodded. "He met her at the jewelry store."

Steve testified that Flemmi gave his sister expensive gifts ranging from jewelry to cars.

"Did Stevie Flemmi act in a possessive way toward Debbie?" Carney asked.

"All men did." Steve spoke with a soft voice. "She was his prize trophy."

Davis was aware of Flemmi's bad reputation, and knew that his sister wanted to end the relationship and had started seeing someone else. After her disappearance, Flemmi would still come around the house and say he was doing everything he could to try and find her.

"I never believed it from the beginning," Steve said. "It was all bullshit, it was a bunch of crap. She was a beautiful young woman and had no enemies except for two and she was full of life." Steve caught his breath. "She was my best friend growing up." He picked up a photo of Debra, and showed it to Whitey as he left the stand.

Whitey didn't look.

Carney's legal strategy during cross-examination was to suggest that Flemmi had the motive to murder Debbie. He was a jealous lover, and she had been his prize possession. During the Donahue cross, Carney pointed the finger at the government. Lawyers have to be very careful cross-examining victims, and he and Brennan chose not to question most of them. The key for lawyers is to cross-examine in areas where they will gain ground, not lose it.

BEHIND THE SCENES

Juror Gusina Tremblay told us that she knew the defense was there to play a role. The cross-examination of Pat Donahue by Carney bothered her. She felt the defense took advantage of her by advancing its case against the government. "I saw her being played. They were using Pat to take the focus away from their client, James Bulger. I liked Kelly's last question, when he asked Pat if she was aware that the man accused of killing her husband was sitting right there."[1]

chapter

2|6

THE SCIENCE OF MURDER

**So, you didn't pursue a claim by Halloran that Pat Nee set him up
for an attempted hit?**
—Defense attorney Hank Brennan, cross-examination

We didn't want to expose our operation.
—Former FBI agent Gerald Montanari

THE GOVERNMENT SHUFFLED THE DECK AGAIN. THEY CHANGED THINGS
by calling a forensics investigator, Martorano's former girlfriend, another former FBI agent, and extortion victims. It was an action-packed
two days. They ran on all cylinders.

Medical examiner Richard Evans testified about the cause and manner of death for each of the nineteen murder victims. Some of the gruesome testimony included details about Al Plummer, who died as a
result of "a gaping wound to the left side of his face." William O'Brien
had twenty gunshot wounds, Brian Halloran had twenty-two, Francis
"Buddy" Leonard had thirteen, Michael Donahue, four.

Roger Wheeler had only one gunshot wound, through his left eye.
"It's likely it went through a pair of glasses," Dr. Evans said.

The medical examiner's testimony dragged on a bit, but was necessary for the government to prove the cause of death and produce

death certificates. The medical examiner usually comes toward the end of a trial like this. It's testimony that bolsters the government's case—scientific evidence of murder.

Patty Carlson was next up. She was John Martorano's girlfriend for over twenty years, and she lived with him in Florida while he was a fugitive. They started dating when she was fifteen and he was thirty-five, and have one son together. Kelly displayed the baptism photograph depicting Whitey and her son.

Carlson admitted receiving cash payments for Martorano from Whitey and Flemmi while he was on the lam, and later lied to the grand jury about it.

Carlson seemed to help the defense because she painted Martorano in a bad light, as someone who took advantage of a vulnerable teenaged girl.

"You spent sixteen years in Florida with Martorano?" Brennan said on cross.

"Yes."

"You knew he was wanted?"

"Yes."

Brennan scratched his head, looking confused. "You made efforts to help him evade arrest?"

"Yes."

The defense would later point out that Carlson harbored a fugitive, and committed perjury, yet was neither arrested nor charged. Whitey's girlfriend, Catherine Greig, received an eight-year prison sentence. Again, Brennan suggested, the government favors some and crushes others.

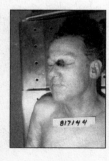

Autopsy photograph of prominent businessman Roger Wheeler after he was killed by hit man John Martorano at his golf club in Tulsa, Oklahoma, in May of 1981.

Whitey Bulger holding James Martorano, his godson, at the child's baptism. He is the son of John Martorano and Patty Carlson.

Former FBI agent Gerald Montanari testified about his meetings with informant Brian Halloran. He claimed that Halloran came to the FBI seeking protection because he wanted to get a deal on a murder charge. Halloran had been arrested for killing George Pappas at the Four Seas restaurant in Chinatown. He was willing to testify against Whitey regarding the Wheeler murder, which was significant.

"Did Mr. Halloran provide you with information about other murders in which Mr. Bulger was involved?" Wyshak asked.

"Yes, Louis Litif."

Litif was another FBI informant, who was killed at Triple O's. Whitey was never charged with his murder.

The FBI housed Halloran's family in a safe house on the Cape. It was surprising how much information Halloran possessed, and yet the FBI didn't do more to protect him. According to Halloran, Whitey had a contact in a cemetery in Boston and he'd bury bodies beneath the vaults. We wondered if investigators ever looked for them.

Brennan cross-examined Montanari about government leaks and compromises over Halloran's cooperation, which got him killed. At one point, he questioned Montanari about an attempted hit on Halloran's life by Pat Nee.

"So, you didn't pursue a claim by Halloran that Pat Nee set him up for an attempted hit?" Brennan asked.

"We didn't want to expose our operation." Montanari spoke in a deep, official-sounding voice.

"But you wanted your own case?" Brennan said.

"Yes."

"There was a lot of distrust among agents in the Boston FBI at the time, wasn't there?"

The agent looked surprised. "I'm not aware of that."

Montanari admitted he told John Morris, his supervisor, about Halloran's cooperation. He wanted an assessment of Halloran as a co-operating witness.

"But telling Morris about this was like letting the fox in the hen-house?" Brennan said.

Laughter erupted from the gallery.

"Objection!"

"Sustained."

Brennan hammered the former agent about the lack of FBI protection for this key informant.

"We afforded him with the opportunity to be safe, and we were not responsible for his daily activities." Montanari sounded defensive. He claimed Halloran had waffled. He also said he had no reason to distrust John Connolly. Montanari came across rigid and defensive. He was not the type to volunteer information. We could tell he didn't want to be there.

Retired State Trooper Barry Halloran took the stand after the former FBI agent. He was the brother of Brian Halloran, and before he died, Brian confided in him that he was cooperating with the FBI against Whitey and others. He worried they were going to set him up for mur-der just like they had done to Tommy King.

"Who's 'they'?"

"Whitey and Stevie," Halloran said.

Pam Wheeler traveled all the way from Oklahoma to testify, and provide a voice for her father, Roger Wheeler. She was an attractive and intelligent tax attorney. She described her father as good to his chil-dren, and a caring husband. He was a role model and successful busi-nessman, an investor, and an entrepreneur with multiple businesses. She had worked for her dad, doing his tax planning and accounting.

In 1978, her father acquired World Jai Alai, which operated fron-tons in Florida and Connecticut; it involved legalized gambling. He was happy with the acquisition at first and then became disillusioned

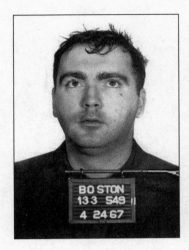 

LEFT: Brian Halloran was an FBI informant who had been cooperating with authorities about the murder of Roger Wheeler. He was shot twenty-two times in a gangland hit in May of 1982.

RIGHT: Murder victim Roger Wheeler after John Martorano shot him through the left eye at the Southern Hills Country Club in Tulsa, Oklahoma, on May 27, 1981.

with it; it was not performing as well as it should have. He wanted to get his money out, and they couldn't work out a deal to sell. That was on May 20, 1981.

On May 27, 1981, Pam learned from her secretary that her father had been shot and killed at the Southern Hills Country Club in Tulsa. The last time she spoke with her dad was at ten thirty that morning. "He always took Wednesday afternoons and played golf."

The crime scene photographs depicting Wheeler in his suit, tilted over on his side, dead, cast a pall over the courtroom. The man had just left the golf course. Like any other ordinary day. What were his last thoughts when he turned to see John Martorano shove a gun between his eyes? The government's legal strategy was to show how the violence originating from Whitey's criminal enterprise in Boston had killed an innocent businessman all the way out in Oklahoma.

chapter

2|7

TRIPLE O'S

Mr. Bulger was upset ... he put the gun back in my face. Weeks handed Mr. Bulger a machine gun. Mr. Bulger shoved it under the table. Pointed it at my stomach, my groin.
—Michael Solimando, trial testimony

KEVIN HAYES AND MICHAEL SOLIMANDO GAVE THE JURY AN INSIDE glimpse at just how ruthless and brazen Whitey had become when there was no one to stand in his way.

Hayes is a former bookmaker who got summoned to a meeting with Weeks and Whitey. "I had been taking sports action, and I wasn't paying rent, so I figured that's what it was all about," Hayes said.

"What if you didn't pay?" Kelly asked.

Hayes snickered. "I'd fear for my life."

Hayes described how Weeks brought him to the cellar of 799 East Third Street in South Boston (the murder house), and there was a large plastic tarp spread out on the ground. Tarps made for easier cleanup, and they could be used to roll up a body. *A bad sign.*

Weeks swore at him and said, "We should blow your brains out. You disrespect us . . . we should just take care of you right now." He then demanded one hundred thousand dollars. Another man said not to waste time with Hayes: "Just put a cap in him."

Hayes lived to tell about it, but had to pay one thousand dollars a week during football season and one thousand dollars per month during the off-season.

"Why didn't you go to the police?" Kelly asked.

"I was in fear for my life . . . I had five young kids at home."

On cross-examination, Carney laid the blame on Weeks.

"You never met Jim Bulger?" he asked.

"Correct."

Hayes admitted that Weeks never even mentioned Whitey's name. Carney scored for his client; maybe the jury would let him off on the extortion count involving Hayes. Piece by piece, the defense chipped away at the government's case.

The extortion of Michael Solimando occurred in the fall of 1982, shortly after John Callahan's murder in Florida. Solimando wasn't a gangster; he had no criminal record. He was a legitimate businessman with a civil engineering degree from Villanova University.

He testified that he met Jimmy Martorano and Stephen Flemmi back in the 1970s at Chandler's nightclub in the South End. He used to go jogging with Flemmi, who lived near Solimando's office in Milton.

Solimando developed a very close friendship with John Callahan at Chandler's. Eventually, he became aware of Callahan's involvement with World Jai Alai in Miami. In 1982, the two became partners in a real estate deal at 126 High Street in Boston. He invested one hundred and fifty thousand dollars in the project.

When Halloran got killed, Callahan informed Solimando that Halloran had been cooperating with the FBI, and advised him not to attend the funeral: "Law enforcement will take pictures."

Not long after that, Solimando saw Whitey and Callahan meeting at the Pier Restaurant in South Boston. He noticed a big change in his friend's demeanor after the meeting: "He'd shut off, he'd become sullen, very introspective," Solimando testified. Callahan had always been a jovial, happy-go-lucky type of guy.

Solimando asked Callahan what was wrong and he answered, "'Whitey and Stevie don't think I'm going to stand up.'" He didn't want to talk about it anymore or get into specifics. In July of 1982, Callahan had plans to go on a trip with Solimando to Germany, but changed his mind at the last minute and flew to Florida instead. Solimando thought

John Callahan was forty-five years old when John Martorano shot him in Florida. They worried he wouldn't stand up if authorities questioned him about the Roger Wheeler murder.

that was odd. A week later, Solimando heard a rumor that Callahan had been shot by Cubans in Miami.

A few weeks after Callahan's murder, Flemmi contacted Solimando out of the blue, and asked him to meet at Triple O's. Solimando went and sat at the end of the bar. "Out of the corner of my eye, I saw Mr. Bulger and another gentleman run upstairs," he said.

Flemmi brought him upstairs, where Whitey sat at a card table next to Weeks. Solimando recalled it was eerie up there; the shades were pulled down.

Solimando testified, "As I sat down, Mr. Bulger pulled out a revolver and stuck it in my face. 'We want our money,' he said." He didn't know what Whitey was talking about. *What money?*

Whitey demanded four hundred thousand dollars, claiming it was their money that Callahan had invested in the building at 126 High Street. It was a blatant lie, as Weeks had testified earlier.

Whitey pointed a revolver in his face and a machine gun in his groin and demanded the money. Solimando presented documents proving that Callahan didn't have their money invested in the real estate deal, but Bulger said, "Get us our money. We don't care about the mumbo jumbo legal papers." He warned Solimando that if he went to the authorities, they'd know about it. Ultimately, Solimando coughed up the money out of his own funds, and lied to a grand jury to save himself.

Brennan cross-examined Solimando about his close ties with Callahan, who had been very involved with World Jai Alai and the Winter Hill scam. He was trying to suggest that Solimando had to be a bit shady as well.

"You claimed you were surprised John Callahan was with organized crime figures?" Brennan shot him a look of disbelief. "You knew."

"No, I didn't."

Whether he knew or not, Solimando was still one of the most compelling witnesses. His story of terror resonated; jurors appeared riveted.

Another story of extortion was that of large-scale marijuana dealer David Lindholm. He took the stand and recalled, "The quality of marijuana coming out of Columbia was very good at the time, and there was an abundance . . . from shrimp boats. . . . We were doing some really good numbers then." Lindholm brought in 125 tons of marijuana in just one load with a barge and a tugboat. They had to rent two farms in Louisiana to bag it all and then truck it east. They made $72 million and owed the Columbians $40 million, but paid them off in six weeks.

In 1983, Whitey and three other men approached Lindholm at the Marconi Club in Roxbury. They wanted a piece of his drug business. Lindholm described how they threatened him with a gun to his head: "A bullet was put in the chamber and spun like Russian roulette, and the trigger was pulled."

Lindholm said Whitey demanded $1 million, but he was able to negotiate by bluffing about the scale of his drug business. He believes Whitey didn't know about the multimillion-dollar profit in the deal with the Columbians. He ended up paying Whitey two hundred fifty thousand dollars.

Lindholm sighed and recalled, "I was just glad to get myself out of there."

On cross-examination, Carney pointed out that he had been arrested and imprisoned for drug dealing later on. He focused on a deal that Lindholm had forged for himself with the government to testify in another case where a Boston police officer had been killed. Carney insinuated that Lindholm was self-serving, and would say anything to cut down on his prison sentence, just like many of the other witnesses the government had lined up against Whitey.

When court recessed that afternoon, we had one thing on our minds: Stephen "the Rifleman" Flemmi would be coming in the next day from a secret location. The city of Boston buzzed with anticipation.

chapter

2|8

SILENCED

Mr. Bulger was an FBI informant because he was giving information over a period of years . . . hundreds of times.
—*Stephen Flemmi, trial testimony*

"NO PARKING SPOTS THIS MORNING—NOT WITH FLEMMI TAKING THE
stand. Try the median strip. There's room behind me," the reporter said
to us. He must've noticed we'd been circling for a space along Seaport
Avenue. "They're not ticketing. And who cares? It's Whitey versus
Stevie Flemmi today." We drove right up over the curb and parked in
the middle of Seaport Boulevard—that never happens in Boston. We
didn't get a ticket and continued to park there throughout the remain-
der of the trial. It was an anomaly, but we realized by then that anything could happen: it was the summer of Whitey.

Nothing else seemed to matter. Not even the heat. Weathermen
had predicted a hundred-degree day for Thursday, July 18, 2013, day
twenty-four of the trial. It was already in the low nineties at eight fifteen in the morning.

Marshals had transported Stephen "the Rifleman" Flemmi from a
secret prison in the federal witness protection program to testify against
his former partner in crime. Flemmi was a ruthless career killer serving a life sentence, and a cooperating witness, *a rat*. Would he say anything the government wanted him to say? How did they flip him?

The usual traffic cop waved us across the street. "Betcha Stevie pins the two girls on Whitey," he said. "I'd love to be in there today. They'll go at each other good, I'm sure."

The United States Marshal stood in his usual spot outside the courthouse doors, wearing his dapper blue blazer. "Did you hear about Stippo Rakes?" he whispered.

"No. Traffic was backed up on the Pike. Took us forever," Margaret said. "Hope we still have seats up there with Flemmi going on. Can't imagine the lines at security—"

"Rakes is dead," the marshal whispered.

"What?" Jon nearly spilled his coffee.

"Dead," he repeated.

"Dead?"

"Dead."

Steve "Stippo" Rakes was a fixture at the courthouse. He was supposed to testify. He was our friend.

"It's under investigation, but keep it under wraps because the story hasn't broken yet." The marshal held the door for us.

Rakes had promised to drop a "bombshell."

Silenced.

The media room buzzed as news spread about the mysterious death of Stippo Rakes. Reporters scrambled to break the story. At one point there was a report of a dead body found floating somewhere in South Boston. News trucks fled to that location. *Not him.* The Bulger Twitter feeds went crazy. We could hardly pay attention as the lawyers finished questioning Lindholm, the last drug dealer, and it seemed like Carney was stalling on cross so they'd have the weekend to prepare for Flemmi. It was only Thursday, but they must've figured that Wyshak would spend a full day on Flemmi's direct examination.

Right before 11:00 A.M., news broke that a jogger found Rakes's body near a trail in the woods in Lincoln, Massachusetts. It was reported there was no identification found on or near the body, and no apparent signs of foul play.

We sat around our usual tables in the cafeteria for the morning break. The special was a ham and cheese panini that day—Stippo would've been right there with us, eating his yogurt. We speculated about what could have happened to him. It was a hot day, could he have had a heart attack? Dehydration? The timing seemed odd. He was about to testify in the trial of the century.

Steve Davis came over and mentioned that when Stippo left the courthouse the day before, he was very upset that prosecutors had told him he would not be testifying.

"What? Off the list?" Pat Donahue appeared surprised. "I never heard that."

"Yeah, they didn't need him, I guess." Steve shook his head. "It doesn't make sense. Poor Stippo."

Most of us hadn't heard that Stippo had been taken off the list. He was a victim in one of the extortion counts against Whitey, and he couldn't wait to get up there and tell his story, especially after Weeks had said how much he didn't like him.

"Maybe they didn't want Stippo contradicting their star witness," Tommy Donahue said. "I wouldn't put it past the government."

True. It wouldn't look good to have another prosecution witness contradicting Weeks. Weeks was one of their key witnesses, and Carney had already made him out to be a liar. Stippo had a different version of what had gone down over the sale of his South Boston liquor store. He claimed it was never for sale.

"Something's going on, for sure. Time to go back to court. She'll be starting up any minute." Tommy Donahue headed toward the elevators. "I hope they get to Flemmi soon."

"Me too." Pat balled up her napkin. "That Lindholm looks like he's still on something—right out of the eighties." She paused. "I can't get over Steve Rakes. Do you think it was suicide?"

We were leaning toward that possibility, especially if he was so upset about being removed from the witness list. We had to split up—all the elevators going up to the fifth floor were packed.

Back in court, we listened to more testimony from Lindholm, followed by a chemist from the state police confirming that the white substance buried with Barrett was lime. We continued to follow the Twitter feeds on Rakes. "This is ridiculous," a reporter leaned over and whispered. "They're not going to get to Flemmi today . . . a Carney delay tactic for sure."

We agreed, and our favorite marshal sprinted over. "Quiet in the courtroom!"

Around 12:30 P.M., they escorted Flemmi in, but it was too early. He sat there staring down Whitey—*if looks could kill*. Marshals had to take him back out for jurors began to notice the animosity between the two.

We kept checking our watches and the Twitter feed for news on Rakes. Many were leaning toward the suicide angle, but it didn't make sense. *Twenty minutes left. Come on.*

"The United States calls Stephen Flemmi," Wyshak announced at 12:45. *Finally.*

The seventy-nine-year-old graying gangster and decorated Korean War veteran took the stand. Flemmi earned his nickname "The Rifleman" during the Korean War, due to his skill as a marksman in the army. He wore a casual windbreaker with a dark green collared shirt underneath.

BEHIND THE SCENES

South Boston native Brian Burke described the following conversation with Stephen Flemmi back in the 1980s. "Flemmi told me about the first time he ever killed someone in the army: 'I was sick, I threw up,' Flemmi said. 'The dead boy I killed looked like he was about fourteen years old and a sergeant slapped me on the back later and told me I had done a good job.' Flemmi killed others who were just young boys. 'I had no grudge against those people and there I was congratulated for killing as many as possible. When I came back home from the war, I had to settle a problem for my brother Jimmy, and now I'm considered a murderer.'"[1]

The last time Flemmi saw Whitey was a week before Christmas in 1994. Wyshak asked him to identify the defendant, and he pointed at Whitey: "Right there at his table." He grinned, clearly mocking his old partner. Whitey sneered and ignored him.

"What was the nature of your relationship?" Wyshak asked.

"Strictly criminal." Flemmi leaned back in his chair; he had a cocky air about him.

"Was Mr. Bulger an informant?" Wyshak knew he'd irritate Whitey with that question.

Flemmi brightened. He appeared eager to declare that Whitey was an informant who had a "quid pro quo" relationship with the FBI: "Mr. Bulger was an FBI informant because he was giving information over a period of years . . . hundreds of times." They both provided information, primarily about the Mafia, to John Connolly and other agents. According to Flemmi, Whitey did most of the talking due to his overbearing, forceful personality. He even went on vacations with Connolly.

Whitey scowled and glared at Flemmi. He was likely having a tough time maintaining his composure.

Wyshak focused on Flemmi's sentence. He pled guilty to racketeering charges, and is serving a life sentence plus thirty years in the federal Witness Security Program with other cooperating witnesses. Wyshak listed ten names of victims that Flemmi pled guilty to killing.

At that point court recessed for the day. After the judge dismissed the jury, Whitey glared at Flemmi as he stood in the witness box. Flemmi put his hands on his hips and called him a "motherfucker." Whitey said something back, which none of us could hear.

Flemmi spread his arms. "Really?" Marshals cuffed him after that.

Reporters rushed out of the courtroom that afternoon to break stories on live television about Flemmi and the expletives flying back and forth, and the latest on Rakes. The outside temperatures were in the high nineties, yet emotions ran higher. The prosecution team huddled with the FBI and state police. They must have been discussing the impact that Rakes's mysterious death could potentially have on the trial. Would the jurors hear the news about the dead witness? Could it cause a mistrial if it was somehow related?

After the press conference, Whitey's entourage sped out onto Seaport Boulevard with sirens blaring.

Did Whitey order a hit on Rakes? People were speculating about Rakes on the sidewalk outside the courthouse. Maybe twenty years ago—he'd gone after witnesses in his heyday, but did he still have that power?

chapter

2|9

BURNT BLOOD

> He grabbed her around the throat and strangled her. He was holding her, strangling her all the way down to the basement. When we got into the basement, she was dead.
> —*Stephen Flemmi, trial testimony*

FRIDAY MORNING STARTED OFF AS ANOTHER SCORCHER, WITH TEMPeratures in the nineties and expected to reach one hundred. We parked on the median strip in the middle of Seaport Boulevard again. Heat wafted up from the pavement. The two-block walk to the courthouse felt like a five-mile run on hot coals.

"Any news on Stippo Rakes?" we asked the marshal who first broke the story to us.

"It doesn't look like suicide," he said.

The district attorney's office hadn't released much information. Overnight, we learned, Rakes's car had been located several miles away in another town, in a McDonald's parking lot. That sounded suspicious. Someone had to have transported him to the woods in Lincoln where his body had been recovered.

"I heard it was a hot shot," the marshal whispered.

Hot shot meant needle. The first thing that came to mind was heroin. Had someone given him a fatal dose? If so, who wanted him dead? Was someone worried about what he was going to testify about?

Did the killer not realize the prosecution had taken him off the list? There were so many unanswered questions. We felt sorry for Stippo.

Rakes and Flemmi—that's all anyone could talk about. People had formed a line outside the courthouse at 1:30 A.M. to get a seat for the Flemmi/Whitey showdown. Only ten seats were made available for the public in the courtroom. When the doors opened at 7:30 A.M., the crowd lined up to pass through security, and then sprinted for the elevators. You'd think they were running for free seats at a Rolling Stones concert. Tempers flared when a couple who had waited all night were turned away because they had to check their phones at the front desk and lost their place in line. Nearly 350 people ended up watching the Flemmi testimony in multiple overflow courtrooms with closed-circuit TV. The national media had descended upon Boston for a glimpse of Flemmi. The Rakes story added to the excitement. The marshals and the clerk's office did an outstanding job with crowd control that day.

Flemmi sat in the same spot behind the witness stand, and wore the same windbreaker. He looked right at Whitey, but his old partner ignored him that time. Flemmi leaned back and testified with ease about the beginnings of criminal life in the 1950s. He had his hands in all kinds of scores, including bookmaking, loan sharking, and murder. He participated in the gang wars between Somerville and Charlestown, and became aligned with various factions, including Howie Winter and the Mafia. He sounded like a veteran telling old war stories to his grandchildren as he boasted about committing gangland slayings. At one point he became partners with Edward "Wimpy" Bennett and his brother Walter. Flemmi ultimately killed the two brothers, along with the third brother, William, and took over their loan sharking business. Business trumped friendships back then. He talked about being partners with guys and then killing them because he or somebody else wanted them killed. It was simply part of the job, and he seemed to love that career.

At least sixty people were killed during the gang wars in Boston. Flemmi didn't kill them all, but he had his hands in a good number. He'd whack guys and dispose of the corpses here and there. We eventually lost track of his body count.

Flemmi came across as a no-nonsense, seasoned criminal with a carefree attitude about various murders: "We shot him with a carbine. . . . We just fired on him . . . oh, he was killed, yes." Flemmi casually sipped his water, and waited for the next question.

After one of the murders, there was way too much blood to clean up: "I lit a fire in the back room and burnt the blood," Flemmi recalled. We could practically smell that burnt blood. What vivid imagery. Who would make that up?

Where was Whitey during the gang wars? He had been serving time for bank robbery in federal prison, including Alcatraz, and got out in 1965.

Flemmi described his early relationship with corrupt FBI agent H. Paul Rico during the 1960s. It was "quid pro quo," he explained. "He was giving me information and I was giving him information." Rico was heavily involved in the murders of the McLaughlin brothers from Charlestown.

"Why did Rico do this?" Wyshak asked.

"He was friendly with the Bennetts." Flemmi adjusted his glasses. "He didn't like the McLaughlins."

We glanced at the jury; some looked confused. There were so many gangster names and nicknames during the gang wars. It was tough for anyone to follow who killed whom. Whitey must have been known to or heard of most. Some were legends.

Hank Brennan concentrated on Flemmi and took notes at the defense table. We figured he'd handle the cross-examination. He would certainly highlight the fact that FBI corruption in Boston went all the way back to the gang wars. It became a deadly game if the government took sides against you. Was the government still taking sides? The question lingered.

Flemmi also passed information to corrupt FBI Agent Rico about a plot to kill Edward Fitzgerald, Joe Barboza's lawyer. The Mafia hated Barboza, a notorious criminal and the first top echelon informant who cooperated against its leaders. In 1968, Mafia figure Frank Salemme and two others wired the lawyer's car to make it explode when Fitzgerald turned the key in the ignition. The FBI never stopped it, even though they knew about it. The bomb blew Fitzgerald's leg off, but he survived.

The photograph of Fitzgerald in the hospital with one leg torn off accentuated the brutality of the times. The story had been big news in Boston.

Rico warned Flemmi to flee before the indictment came down for the Fitzgerald attempted murder in 1969, so he did. In 1974, Rico cleared the way for Flemmi to come back. "The coast is clear," Rico had said.

Wyshak displayed his favorite Winter Hill organizational chart from 1975–1980 again, and had Flemmi point out the leaders: "Jim Bulger, myself, John Martorano, Howie Winter, Joe McDonald, Jimmy Sims." Flemmi explained the structure of the organization all the way down to the bookmakers.

"What type of criminal activities was this group involved in?" Wyshak asked.

"Gambling, bookmaking, extortion, money laundering." The crimes rolled off Flemmi's tongue.

"Murders?"

He smirked. "Definitely murders."

Wyshak finally got into the early murders listed as predicate acts in one of the racketeering counts against Whitey. During deliberations, the jury would have to decide whether each murder was "proven" or "not proven" by the government. Wyshak started with James O'Toole. Flemmi was on the lam, and had learned that O'Toole had shot his brother Jimmy, who survived. In 1973, Flemmi asked Howie Winter to kill O'Toole, and arranged for John Martorano to do it with his (Flemmi's) machine gun. Flemmi was not an eyewitness, but we had already heard from Martorano, who testified that he, Winter, and McDonald piled into a car and Whitey drove. Pat Nee and others got into the car behind. When the shooters pulled up, O'Toole shielded himself behind a mailbox, but was killed. The government would stress that Whitey was involved as a coconspirator in the premeditated murder even if he wasn't a shooter.

Flemmi was back in the Boston area, and present for the James Sousa murder in October of 1974, around the time he cemented his partnership with Whitey. Flemmi glanced at Whitey taking vigorous notes at the defense table, and described his old partner: "He didn't drink, he didn't smoke. He worked out a lot."

Flemmi explained that it was a Winter Hill group decision to kill Sousa, because he had been involved in a gold bullion scam involving a dentist. The police arrested Sousa, so the Winter Hill Gang worried he wouldn't stand up.

"How were decisions made?" Wyshak asked.

"We all decided, because we were a group . . . we all decided that if anything were to be accomplished we had to agree to it . . . six of us." They brought Sousa to the Marshall Street garage in Somerville and "Johnny shot him, he was bleeding, so I put a can under him to stop the blood." Whitey wasn't there that day, but Flemmi tried to implicate him by saying he was part of the group decision to kill Sousa. Jurors took notes, but would they have enough evidence against Whitey? They would really have to buy into the concept of the joint venture/coconspirator group murder theory, especially when Whitey wasn't present.

Jurors had already heard from Sousa's widow, Barbara, who recalled that her husband went missing in October of 1974. He told her he was going to meet with Billy Barnowski (a Winter Hill associate) and some lawyers. He didn't come back, and his remains were never found.

During that time period, Whitey informed Flemmi and the rest of the group that FBI agent John Connolly had approached him and wanted to set up a meeting. Connolly claimed the Mafia had their sources and "we can help you . . . if they want to play checkers, we can play chess." Whitey asked the group how they felt about it. They agreed that Whitey should meet with Connolly as a source for information.

According to Flemmi, Connolly came through with valuable information about a loan shark investigation in Quincy. Flemmi recalled they were warned about a place that had been "wired for sound." Connolly also warned them through Whitey about an investigation into the Melo-Tone vending machine scam. Winter Hill started its own vending machine company, and strong-armed bar owners into breaking contracts with Melo-Tone. Connolly convinced Melo-Tone to drop the complaints.

Flemmi first met Connolly at Whitey's mother's house on O'Callaghan Way in South Boston.

"You're not meeting him to talk about the Red Sox, right?" Wyshak asked.

"No." Flemmi cracked a smile. "Criminal activity."

Wyshak tapped his pen on the podium and moved on to the next Bulger-related murder. "What did Whitey tell you about Paul Mc-Gonagle?" he asked.

"He said he wanted to kill him."

Whitey asked Flemmi for help killing McGonagle, but ended up taking care of the situation himself, and burying him at Tenean Beach. Again, we wondered if this scant evidence would be enough for the jury to implicate Whitey. Flemmi added that Whitey shot and killed McGonagle's brother Don by mistake. The brothers looked alike. Due to lack of eyewitness testimony, prosecutors left Don McGonagle's murder out of the indictment.

Flemmi corroborated Martorano's testimony about the murder of Eddie Connors. Word had traveled around town that Connors had been bragging about how he set O'Toole up by calling Howie Winter when O'Toole left his bar. Flemmi met with Whitey to discuss the situation, and they decided to kill him. They set him up to receive a telephone call from Howie Winter at a designated phone booth on Morrissey Boulevard. Flemmi recalled: "We just fired on him. We emptied our pistols. I fired seven to eight shots."

"Was he killed?" Wyshak asked.

"He was killed." Flemmi nodded several times. "Yes."

Tommy King's murder came next. "Bulger was insistent upon it," Flemmi said, "because he was an overly aggressive person. . . . Tommy King was going to be killed." King had also been a rival of Whitey's in the South Boston gang wars.

In November of 1975, Flemmi explained how they concocted a story about why they needed King's help killing another gangster, Suitcase Fiddler. Whitey provided the weapons and gave Tommy a gun with blanks. Martorano shot King from behind while Whitey drove with King in the passenger's seat. Flemmi and Winter drove the backup car. Pat Nee and Jack Curran buried King in his bulletproof vest near the Neponset River Bridge in Quincy.

"Did you talk to Whitey about Buddy Leonard?" Wyshak asked.

"He said he wanted to kill him." Flemmi nodded toward Whitey.

Flemmi didn't add much to the Leonard murder. He simply noted that Whitey and Leonard had a previous history, so Whitey murdered

Leonard and put his corpse in Tommy King's car. Whitey wanted people to think that King killed Leonard and went on the lam. Flemmi was not present for the murder. The jury would likely struggle with this one too; there were no eyewitnesses.

It was time for the 11:00 A.M. break. Friday was clam chowder day, and the lines were long because Flemmi had attracted the crowds. We put three tables together in the cafeteria to accommodate everyone. A columnist for *The New York Times* joined us that day, so we teased him about how poorly the Yankees were doing. The Sox and the Yankees were scheduled to play at Fenway that evening in the heat. Sometimes we made small talk instead of discussing the emotionally draining trial.

"Any news on Rakes?" Pat asked.

"Nope. What else is new?" Tommy rolled his eyes. "It's probably another government cover-up."

We discussed some of the old murders and corrupt agent Paul Rico, and how he took sides in the gang wars.

"I can't wait until the defense cross-examines him about the FBI," Mike Donahue said. "Do you think it will be Hank or Carney?"

"I bet it's Hank." Margaret split her peanut butter cookie with Pat. "He loves putting the government on trial. He can bring a lot of corruption out with Flemmi."

"Like he did with Morris." Pat bit into her half of the cookie. "That was the best." We launched into a debate over which Brennan cross-examination we liked best.

As the break ended and we crammed onto the elevators again, it amazed us how much the victims rooted for the defense. They couldn't wait to see what damage the lawyers would do to the government's star witness.

Next, Wyshak asked questions about the sweeping horse race fixing case in which Howie Winter and most of the Winter Hill leadership ended up getting convicted and sent to prison in the late 1970s. Flemmi claimed that Connolly and Morris spared him and Whitey from the race fix indictment, as Morris had previously testified. When most of the gang got locked up, Flemmi moved their headquarters from the Marshall Street garage in Somerville to Lancaster Street. Wyshak had Flemmi identify people from the photographs taken by the state police.

Flemmi corroborated Martorano's testimony about the chain of events leading to the World Jai Alai murders. He recalled Whitey liking the idea of making ten thousand dollars a week on parking and concessions from World Jai Alai. Flemmi conferred with his old friend, former corrupt FBI Agent Paul Rico, who "wanted us on board." Rico was the head of security for World Jai Alai in Miami.

When the deal failed to go through as planned, Flemmi sent a package of equipment to Oklahoma on a Trailways bus to be used for the Wheeler murder. The package included "a grease gun, a slim jim, dent puller, and a pistol." He explained that a grease gun is a machine gun with a silencer. Flemmi testified about what he heard secondhand concerning the murders of Wheeler and Callahan.

Wyshak changed it up from murder to extortion, and Flemmi corroborated testimony from Weeks and Martorano about the brutal extortion techniques used against bookmakers, drug dealers, and regular businessmen. They made up to ten grand a week from the drug rings in South Boston, and received over a million dollars from marijuana dealer Frank Lepere.

Flemmi talked about the Ex-Fund used for buying guns and other supplies, and for paying off law enforcement. In addition to Connolly and Morris, Flemmi claimed they paid FBI agents Mike Buckley, John Newton, Nick Gianturco, and John Cloherty. Newton allegedly provided them with C-4 explosives. These agents, other than Morris, have publically denied the allegations.

According to Flemmi, they paid FBI agents Connolly and Morris thousands of dollars. Connolly dressed better than any other agent, had a nice car and boat, and a vacation home on the Cape. Flemmi figured they paid Connolly over two hundred and thirty thousand dollars, plus free vacations, over the years.

Wyshak glanced back at the wall clock; he had ten minutes to go before court recessed for the weekend. He knew he wouldn't finish his direct examination, but he must have figured it was best to end on a strong note.

"Did you know a woman named Debbie Davis?" he asked.

Flemmi stared back at him for a moment as if caught off guard. "Yes . . . a friend of mine, a girlfriend." He explained how they met in 1976, and started dating and then living together.

"Were you in love with her?" Wyshak asked.

"I loved her but I wasn't in love with her."

Wyshak seemed surprised; he'd probably expected Flemmi to answer in the affirmative. Instead, the statement came across cocky. Steve Davis mumbled something from the front row.

"Quiet in the courtroom!" the marshal said.

Wyshak cleared his throat. "How did this relationship impact your relationship with Jim Bulger?"

"He wasn't happy I had a relationship with her because it started to impact our business," Flemmi said. When he'd have to go out for meetings at night, Debra would complain. "She required a lot of attention; she was a young girl." Flemmi recalled one time at her birthday party, they had an argument about him having to leave. He told her he had to meet with Connolly. "I blurted it out," Flemmi said. "We have a connection—John Connolly and the FBI—I've got to leave."

After Debra's brother was killed in Walpole State Prison, the family wanted to know what happened. She asked Flemmi to speak with Connolly about who was responsible for her brother's death.

Flemmi told Whitey that Debra knew about their relationship with Connolly, and "he was not too happy about it." Neither was Connolly.

Whitey also felt that Debra's flashy lifestyle called attention to them. Flemmi had given her a Mercedes, and lots of money and jewelry. "It upset Bulger, because he was a low-key guy." He added that Debra's brother did drugs and they believed he was an informant.

"I wanted to send her away," Flemmi said, but Whitey disagreed. He wanted to kill Debra because he feared she would jeopardize the relationship they had with Connolly.

Flemmi lowered his head. "He wanted me to agree to kill her, and I eventually agreed, and it's affected me, and it will affect me until the day I die." He sounded remorseful, but it could have been an act. Again, Steve Davis mouthed something from the gallery.

Wyshak feigned a sympathetic look, and asked Flemmi to describe the circumstances surrounding Debra's murder.

"I bought a house in South Boston, and he said to bring her there." Flemmi looked right at Whitey. "We walked in the entrance there, and he grabbed her by the neck. I couldn't do it. He knew it. He told me, 'I'll take care of it.'"

"What happened next?" Wyshak asked.

"He grabbed her around the throat and strangled her. He was holding her, strangling her all the way down to the basement. When we got into the basement, she was dead."

Steve Davis shook his head and buried his face in his hands. Debra was his sister—strangled and dead in the basement. A young, beautiful woman with so much going for her. One of the jurors looked at Steve and cried. The courtroom turned eerily quiet, but for the soft sniffles from the jury box. Wyshak took a moment before he moved on.

Whitey did not display any emotion over Debra Davis. Was he capable of strangling a woman? He denied it later in a letter to us.

BEHIND THE SCENES

Theresa Stanley, Whitey's longtime live-in girlfriend, told us in one of her last interviews before she died about Whitey's violent behavior toward women: "He would hit me . . . he would get rough with me."[1]

Flemmi continued testifying about how he wrapped Debra's dead body in a tarp, while Whitey went back upstairs to take a nap. There was no furniture in the house, so he lay down on the floor. Jack Curran and Pat Nee removed Debra's clothes, tied the tarp up, and drove to Neponset with her corpse.

"I dug the hole," Flemmi said. "Then we buried the body."

"Why doesn't he do any of the work?" Wyshak pointed with his elbow at Whitey, who was taking notes at the defense table.

"That's what he does." Flemmi raised his voice, mocking Whitey.

"What, kill somebody and make everybody else do the work?" Wyshak rolled his eyes.

"Objection!" Brennan shot out of his seat.

"Sustained."

It was 1:05 and time to break for the weekend. Judge Casper reminded jurors not to discuss the case. At least two wiped tears from their eyes as they filed out of the courtroom. Steve Davis rushed out with his head lowered. We walked through the front doors of the

Debra Davis before Stephen Flemmi brought her to a home in South Boston to be strangled. Flemmi claims that Whitey strangled her because she knew about their corrupt relationship with FBI agent John Connolly. She was twenty-six when she died.

air-conditioned courthouse into a wall of stifling heat. The reporters and camera people wiped the sweat trickling from their brows.

Who wouldn't go home that weekend and think about a young beautiful woman with a man's hands wrapped around her throat? Blue and dead in the basement? The testimony was so real, so emotional.

Flemmi was a dramatic storyteller; no wonder he was a star witness. He remembered gory details and could rattle off names going back to the 1950s. He recalled who killed whom and why, how scores went down, and where they buried bodies. A good memory bolsters credibility.

Brennan and Carney walked past the long bank of microphones, carrying their boxy briefcases. They had to ignore the reporters' requests for interviews due to the gag order. We waved and they stopped to chat.

"It's going to be a long weekend." Brennan dropped his briefcase on the sidewalk. He looked drained.

We wished him luck. They'd spend the weekend cooped up in the office preparing for cross-examination. They had so much ground to cover.

The Red Sox beat the Yankees that night in the heat.

3|0

HE DID IT

We had killed together, we were partners . . . for penny and for pound.
—Stephen Flemmi, trial testimony

ON MONDAY MORNING, THE COURTROOM HEATED UP RIGHT AWAY with more drama. This time tempers flared in the spectators' gallery shortly after Flemmi assumed his position behind the witness stand.

"And during the course of your testimony," Wyshak said, "you had mentioned that one of the Davis brothers was, in your view, using drugs and might be an informant. Do you recall that testimony?"

Flemmi nodded. "Yes, sir."

"Which Davis brother were you referring to?"

"Steven Davis."

"Steven Davis?" Wyshak appeared puzzled.

"Yes, I was referring to him. But he wasn't the one I was actually referring to."

"Objection!" Brennan said.

"That's a lie!" Steve Davis leaped from his seat and pointed his finger at Flemmi. "That's a fucking lie!" he shouted.

Flemmi gazed into the gallery at Davis. "I said no—"

"There's no testimony on me being a rat, you piece of shit!" A red-faced Davis bolted toward the witness stand until two marshals grabbed him by the arms and dragged him back.

Judge Casper jumped up. "Mr. Davis!"

Flemmi ignored the judge and addressed Davis: "I just declined it. I just told you I inadvertently made a mistake. I said it wasn't you that I was referring to."

"Mr. Davis!" Judge Casper raised her voice again. "I need you to be respectful of these proceedings. Okay?"

Davis removed his bitter gaze from Flemmi and looked up at the judge. "Yes." There wasn't much he could do with the marshals holding him back.

"I need your promise that you can do that," the judge said. She seemed to be sympathizing with him. The jurors watched the exchange, and likely picked up on her softer tone.

"Yes," he said quietly. The marshals escorted Davis toward his seat in the front row.

Judge Casper addressed the jury. "Jurors, you'll disregard anything that was said from the gallery."

Who could simply forget that drama? They certainly wouldn't. They likely felt for Steve, especially after the gruesome details that had been discussed on Friday surrounding his sister's strangulation.

Flemmi leaned over the witness stand toward Davis. "I apologize for that remark."

"Thank you," Davis said, as he sat back down. His chest heaved in and out. He continued looking distraught. A few minutes later, his wife led him outside.

We were surprised to hear Flemmi apologize. Did he also sympathize with Davis? Was he feeling remorse in his old age? Whitey had perked up over the exchange; he seemed to enjoy the high drama.

Wyshak continued after the disruption. "Now, after you buried Debbie Davis on the banks of the Neponset River, did you attempt to obtain her dental records?"

Flemmi sighed. "Yes, I did."

"And how did you do that?"

"Had a friend of mine, George Kaufman, who knew the dentist . . . and he obtained the records."

"What did you do with them?" Wyshak asked.

HE DID IT • 231

"Destroyed them."

"Why?"

"A deterrent to identification, so there's no trace of her dental records."

Wyshak coughed and cleared his throat several times. It sounded like he had laryngitis. The stress of the trial must have been wearing him down. He checked his notes and moved on to the investigation into World Jai Alai and the Wheeler murder. Steve and his wife came back in; he appeared calmer than before.

Flemmi explained they'd heard a rumor that Halloran might be cooperating with the feds.

"As a result of hearing those street rumors, did you have a conversation with Mr. Connolly?" Wyshak cleared his throat again.

"Yes."

"And what did Mr. Connolly tell you?"

"He said that he was giving—he gave information on Jim Bulger and myself and John Martorano in connection with the Wheeler murder." Flemmi was referring to Halloran.

Wyshak nodded. "As a result of receiving information—that information—what, if anything, did you and Mr. Bulger decide to do?"

Flemmi rubbed his fingers together. "Put everything in motion to kill him."

He was not present for the Halloran and Donahue murders on the waterfront, as Weeks had confirmed. Later that night, Whitey told him all about it.

"And what did Mr. Bulger say to you?" Wyshak asked.

"He said, 'The balloon burst.'"

"What did it mean?"

"It means he got killed."

Flemmi described the car they used for the hit: "The boiler was the car that we had all souped-up with all the different features on it."

Wyshak cocked his head. "Like what?"

"Well, we had switches if the car was being chased, say at nighttime, you could switch the lights off. There was a feature on there that you could hit a switch, and it would release oil out of the manifold and would create a smoke screen in case you were chased." Flemmi rubbed his chin. "It had special tires on it that were souped-up . . . it was a hit car." Flemmi sounded like he was still proud of that car.

"Did it cost a lot to soup it up, so to speak?" Wyshak rubbed his thumb and two fingers together.

Flemmi smiled. "I think it cost thirty thousand dollars."

"So Mr. Bulger told you he got the boiler, and then what did he tell you?"

"They *used* the boiler." Flemmi spoke as if he still wished he hadn't missed it.

"Who's they?"

"Pat Nee, himself, Kevin Weeks. . . . He said he positioned themselves behind . . . so he got good firepower on the car."

"What, if anything, did Pat Nee say about the shooting?"

"He said the gun jammed."

"His gun jammed?" Wyshak asked.

"Yes."

We saw Tommy Donahue shaking his head in disbelief as he listened from the victims' benches. Weeks had said he didn't know who had the ski mask on in the backseat. Now, Flemmi had identified Nee, but said his gun had conveniently jammed.

Tommy whispered something to his brother Mike.

The marshal ran over. "Quiet in the courtroom!"

Wyshak displayed a report from Whitey's informant file on the screen. It read: "'The outfit' wanted to kill Halloran."

Flemmi explained that, "Jim Bulger said it to Connolly, I was present."

"Were you trying to trick or fool Mr. Connolly?" Wyshak asked.

"Yes."

"Why?"

"We didn't—" Flemmi paused and looked at Whitey. "We wanted to take the heat away from Jim Bulger."

Wyshak nodded and moved on to the meeting in New York City where Whitey, Martorano, and Flemmi discussed the necessity of killing John Callahan.

"What did John Martorano say after Mr. Bulger told him about John Callahan?"

"Well, he was a little reluctant . . . after we told him he'd be a threat . . . that Callahan wouldn't face the prospect of doing twenty years to life and that the FBI would be able to probably have him dis-

James Bulger and Stephen Flemmi taken by Boston FBI agents during the Roger Wheeler murder investigation. They were instructed to dress in business suits to throw off Oklahoma's investigation. The Boston FBI didn't want them looking like gangsters.

close what happened in the Wheeler murder . . . that he should kill John Callahan."

"Who said that?"

Flemmi motioned toward Whitey. "Jim Bulger," he proclaimed with zeal.

Later, Flemmi traveled to Florida for a meeting with Rico and Martorano. They asked if the Jai Alai deal was still viable. Rico told them, "There's no deal here."

When the heat came down on the Boston FBI to investigate the Wheeler murder, Agents Montanari and Brunnick asked Whitey and Flemmi to meet at the FBI office and "dress conservatively in business suits."

"Why?" Wyshak asked.

Flemmi smiled. "They were going to send those photos down to Oklahoma."

"Why dress in business suits?"

"Well—" Flemmi grinned again. "To show that we were probably legitimate business people."

"That's not the way you ordinarily looked?"

Flemmi chuckled. "No."

Wyshak displayed the photographs, and there they were: looking like a million bucks in those business suits.

Wyshak moved on to the Michael Solimando extortion. Flemmi and Whitey falsely claimed that Callahan owed them from a real estate deal, and demanded four hundred thousand dollars from Solimando.

"Jim Bulger had a pistol on the table and a machine gun on his lap. . . . Bulger was insistent," Flemmi explained.

"Did John Callahan owe you money?" Wyshak asked.

"No." Flemmi waved his hand in dismissal.

"So why were you—"

"It was extortion."

"It was fabricated?"

"Yes."

Weeks had said the same thing. We wondered how many more extortions went unreported.

"Whose idea was it to try to get money from Mike Solimando?" Wyshak asked.

"Jim Bulger." Flemmi leaned back and folded his arms. He added: "Jim Bulger did the talking. He said to him, 'Don't bother to go to the FBI because we'll hear about it.'"

"Was that true?" Wyshak shot Whitey a disgusted look.

"It would be true," Flemmi said. He added that they gave Solimando a script to use when he was later called to testify before the grand jury in Miami. They instructed him to blame the whole thing on Arthur "Bucky" Barrett, who was dead and buried without his teeth by then.

Wyshak transitioned to the Bucky Barrett murder.

"Jim Martorano brought him down," Flemmi said. "When Barrett arrived at the house, they chained him to a chair."

"Why are you chaining Mr. Barrett up?" Wyshak placed his hands on his hips.

"For effect." Flemmi wiggled his eyebrows.

"What kind of effect?"

"To kind of, you know, terrorize him."

Flemmi explained: "Jim Bulger wanted to find out anything he could find out." While Barrett was chained up, Whitey "asked him questions about Joe Murray's marijuana business, which Bucky answered because he was involved with Joe Murray."

"Why?" Wyshak asked.

Flemmi shrugged and regarded Whitey. "Maybe for a potential score down the road." Flemmi despised Whitey, and enjoyed throwing him under the bus whenever possible: "We had killed together, we were partners . . . for penny and for pound."

Wyshak asked Flemmi to explain how the Barrett murder went down.

"So, on the way down the stairs"—Flemmi made a rolling motion with his hands—"I was in front of him, a couple of steps down, he shoots him in the back of the head."

"Who shoots him in the back of the head?" Wyshak asked.

"Jim Bulger shoots Bucky Barrett in the back of the head."

Flemmi provided more detail: "I was right in front of him, I was in the line of fire, and when he shot him, the bullet could have went through him and hit me, but the gun happened to be on single shot. It was a fully automatic weapon. If it was on fully automatic weapon, it would have hit me also. But the body hit me, we both went down the stairs." He glared at Whitey for a moment as if he was still upset over the near-death experience.

"Were you angry about that?" Wyshak asked.

"I was. . . . I said, 'You know you could have shot me.'"

"What did he say?"

Flemmi huffed. "He made some asinine statement. I don't remember what it was."

After they got all Barrett's money, Flemmi felt that Whitey should have let him live: "He didn't have to kill him . . . because Bucky Barrett was never going to say anything. He would have taken his losses. He was a wise guy. He could have gone out and made money on the next score."

"Why did he lie down?" Wyshak asked. By now we knew that Whitey had a strange habit of taking a nap after a murder.

"I don't know." Flemmi looked at Whitey and considered the question. "Maybe he was mentally, physically exhausted. I don't know. Maybe he got a high on it."

Wyshak glanced back at the clock and then made eye contact with jurors. They appeared eager to hear more. Whitey kept his head down; he wouldn't give Flemmi the satisfaction.

Wyshak touched on the sale of the liquor store involving Rakes. Flemmi claimed Rakes wanted to sell, they had a meeting, and ultimately came to an agreement of one hundred thousand dollars. He wasn't present for the meeting that Weeks had testified about involving the gun on the table and extortion.

Steve Rakes was not present for this testimony. He would have been there, but he was dead now. We wondered if Flemmi had heard about the previous week's suspicious death of the government witness. The Rakes investigation appeared to be stalled. The Middlesex District Attorney had recently announced there were no apparent signs of trauma to his body. They were waiting for toxicology results, which could take weeks.

Wyshak moved on to the weapons shipment for the IRA aboard the *Valhalla*.

Flemmi testified: "We sent—we had a stash with a large amount of weapons, and we didn't need all those weapons, so—enough weapons to supply an army company."

Wyshak inquired how they obtained the arms.

"We collected them over the years . . . different sources, robberies, weapons that came off the boat that was going to send the weapons over during the war, the Vietnam War, from the docks."

Wyshak's eyes widened. "Somebody stole them?"

"We stole them." Flemmi looked at the prosecutor as if he'd asked a stupid question.

Flemmi explained how they became involved in shipping arms: "Pat Nee and Joe Murray were IRA sympathizers; we were partners so we went along with them." He corroborated what Weeks and Martorano had said about how the Irish authorities found the weapons, and the subsequent seizure of the drugs aboard the *Ramsland* by the coast guard and DEA. "The *Ramsland* was a ship that Joe Murray owned—forty-eight tons of marijuana," Flemmi said. McIntyre had been arrested for drunk driving, and they suspected him of snitching about the *Valhalla* and the *Ramsland*. According to Flemmi, Agent Connolly confirmed their suspicions, so Nee lured him to the murder house.

"And what did Mr. McIntyre say?" Wyshak asked.

"He admitted it. He apologized to Pat Nee." Flemmi had just placed Nee very close to the McIntyre torture and murder. Nee has never been held accountable for his role. We knew that Nee had brought McIntyre there using the ruse of a party. We wondered how long Nee had stayed?

"Where did Pat Nee go?" Wyshak asked.

"I think he left." Flemmi wrinkled his brow as if trying to remember his lines. "I'm not certain though."

Wyshak quickly changed the subject. "And what did Mr. McIntyre do when Mr. Bulger was trying to strangle him with the rope?"

"He was choking. He was gagging and choking."

"Was somebody holding Mr. Mc-Intyre?"

"I believe both of us. He was choking him, but I was holding him."

"And then what happened?"

"He shot him in the head," Flemmi said rapidly.

"Who shot who?" Wyshak asked.

Flemmi looked right at Whitey. "Jim Bulger shot McIntyre in the head."

Wyshak paused to make eye contact with the jurors. "Then what happened?"

"He was on the ground and I picked him up a little bit to see if he was still alive, and he was still pulsating and he shot him again." Flemmi's words sounded so matter-of-fact.

Murder victim John McIntyre's remains, recovered in 2000. Whitey tried strangling him at first, but the rope was too thick, so he shot him in the head. The gaping bullet wounds can be seen here on the skull.

Wyshak had a brief coughing spell before moving on to the next murder: Deborah Hussey, Flemmi's stepdaughter. He had to tread carefully. We watched him glance at the defense table, where both lawyers were poised with pen in hand, ready to jot down Flemmi's exact words. The defense would try to pin the murder on Flemmi. They'd likely argue that Flemmi had the motive to kill Deborah because she had told her mother that he had been sexually abusing her.

After a few introductory questions, Wyshak delved right into the bad stuff. "Did you have a sexual relationship with her?" he asked.

"Not intercourse, no." Flemmi lowered his gaze.

Wyshak moved on a bit too fast. "Did there come a time when you had a further discussion with Mr. Bulger about Ms. Hussey?"

"Yes."

"And what was that conversation?"

"He wanted me to—" Flemmi paused for a moment as if trying to remember his lines. "He wanted me to kill her, and I told him, I said . . .

'Well, why don't we just send her off, I'll send her off somewhere.' I kept sending her off and she kept coming back." Flemmi explained that Deborah had become a source of embarrassment for Whitey. She had been using his name around town. She was a loose cannon. "So it came to the point where he wanted to kill her," Flemmi said.

"And did you agree?" Wyshak asked.

"Reluctantly." Flemmi pursed his lips. "Yes."

"When you got there who was there?"

"Pat Nee, Kevin Weeks, and Jim Bulger."

"And when Deborah Hussey walked in the door, what happened to her?"

"Well, she was in front of me. She walked in . . . she walked into the kitchen area . . ." Flemmi rubbed his brow. "Jim Bulger stepped out from behind the basement stairs and grabbed her by the throat and started strangling her."

"What happened then?" Wyshak asked.

"Well, he lost his balance and they both fell on the floor. He continued strangling her."

Weeks had testified he saw Whitey and Deborah on the floor after hearing a thud. This was corroborating testimony.

"And how long did it take to strangle Deborah Hussey?"

"Didn't take long," Flemmi said. "She was a very fragile woman."

A juror wiped tears from her eyes. Flemmi must have seen her.

"What were you doing?" Wyshak asked.

"I was there." Flemmi glanced at the jury. "I wasn't doing anything."

Anything? He did not mention that he participated in the murder. Weeks had testified that Flemmi placed a rope around Deborah's neck and used a stick to pull it tight. Hank Brennan jotted notes in a legal pad. The cross-examination on this point was going to be riveting.

Next, Wyshak asked Flemmi to explain what happened during the hearings before Judge Wolf when he had presented his immunity defense. Flemmi admitted he was an FBI informant, and had argued that the FBI promised him immunity to commit crimes for many years in exchange for information. Flemmi had hoped that Agent Connolly would save him, but he didn't.

"Why were you protecting John Connolly?" Wyshak asked.

"Well, because, like I said, he assured me on several occasions he was going to come forward in my defense."

"Was that true?"

"No." Flemmi explained that he shielded Connolly at first by placing the blame for FBI leaks on John Morris.

"And why blame John Morris?"

"Because they had a little feud between them, and he didn't like John Morris anymore."

"Is it fair to say your claims at the hearing before Judge Wolf were false?" Wyshak knew the defense would get into it on cross, so he had to soften the blow.

"Yes, and I'd like to publicly apologize to Judge Wolf for purging myself in his courtroom." Flemmi probably meant to say he was sorry for *perjuring* himself.

Wyshak wrapped up his direct examination. His legal strategy for placing Flemmi near the end of his case-in-chief was to show how he and Whitey operated a closely held criminal enterprise which extorted people, earned boatloads of money through the drug trade, paid off law enforcement, laundered money, and committed many murders. The government had to hammer home on that fearsome reputation that Whitey and Flemmi instilled in others. Flemmi also pinned the two hands-on strangulation murders of Debra Davis and Deborah Hussey on Whitey.

Hank Brennan rose for cross-examination. He looked like he was about to dive into a thick-cut sirloin steak.

3|1

DADDY'S LITTLE GIRL

Is it hard for you to accept the fact that you strangled somebody who sat on your knee as a little girl?
—*Defense attorney Hank Brennan,*
cross-examination of Stephen Flemmi

BRENNAN BRANDISHED A LONG, RAZOR-SHARP BAYONET AS HE LED THE charge against Flemmi on cross. Court would break for the day in fifteen minutes. This was his chance to shine. He had to make an impression on the jury and the media.

He inflicted a bloody wound right away by attacking Flemmi's character. Flemmi was married with two young children when he cheated on his wife with Marion Hussey, who had a baby girl, Deborah (Debbie). The couple started living together.

"When you moved in and little Debbie was there—do you remember holding her as an infant?" Brennan asked.

"I wasn't a very domestic person as far as that was concerned."

"Did little Debbie sit on your knee?"

"I never let her sit on my knee. I didn't even do that with my own children."

Brennan widened his eyes, appearing shocked. He reminded Flemmi that he had testified differently under oath in a civil wrongful death trial brought by the Hussey family.

Flemmi knew where Brennan was going with it and admitted that the other lawyer's questions were boring and he simply answered yes, yes, yes.

Brennan pounced. "How many of Mr. Wyshak's questions over the last few days do you think were boring, Mr. Flemmi?"

Flemmi scowled. "Not many."

Wyshak sat very still at the government table, but his insides must have been churning.

"Tell this jury, sir, what questions you answered that were not accurate?" Brennan raised his voice.

"All of the questions Mr. Wyshak asked me were accurate to the best of my memory." He sounded defensive.

"When you testified under oath in *Hussey,* and you said that little Debbie Hussey would sit on your knee, and you'd read her stories, were you telling the truth?"

"Well, at the time . . ." Flemmi sighed. "It was just a general question, and I said yes when she asked me that."

"Do you sometimes say yes when it's not true?"

"I was telling the truth, but at that time it didn't mean much to me."

"So answers that don't mean that much to you . . . you're willing to lie about?"

Brennan jabbed the frustrated witness several more times with the previous conflicting testimony, and reminded him about his moral obligation to tell the truth while under oath. The jury got the point, so he jumped right back to the baby Deborah Hussey.

"Is there any reason why you would want to distance yourself from holding a little girl on your knee?" Brennan asked.

"It's just the way I responded."

"Is it hard for you to accept the fact that you strangled somebody who sat on your knee as a little girl? Is that hard for you to accept, Mr. Flemmi?"

"I didn't strangle her!" he shouted.

"She would call you Daddy, Mr. Flemmi, wouldn't she?" Brennan used a soft, mocking tone.

"Mr. Brennan, I didn't strangle her."

"Mr. Flemmi, did she call you Daddy?"

"That's besides the point, the fact of the matter is I didn't strangle her."

"Mr. Flemmi—what you need to do is answer the questions." Brennan spoke slowly as if this hardened criminal were a mere child. "There's a question pending." He was clearly baiting the witness, looking for an outburst.

"Go ahead." Flemmi knew what Brennan was trying to do and contained himself.

"Did little Debbie Hussey call you Daddy?" Brennan used his sweet, singsongy voice again.

"As a young girl . . . she thought I was her daddy." Flemmi answered in a monotone.

"Did she call you Daddy?"

"Probably did." He shrugged.

"Do you have any failure of memory about that, Mr. Flemmi?"

"No."

"Did she call you Daddy?"

"She probably did—she did."

Brennan finally got the answer he was looking for, but continued pressing, trying to create that courtroom drama that the media would embrace.

"Is it hard to accept strangling someone who sat on your lap as a little girl?"

"I didn't strangle her." Flemmi balled his hands into fists. "Mr. Brennan, I didn't strangle her." He clenched his teeth and his chin quivered.

Brennan looked into the jury box and raised his eyes in disbelief. He then questioned Flemmi about his relationship with Deborah as a young grammar school child and innocent middle school student.

"You were charged with protecting her?" Brennan asked.

"Nobody would hurt her."

"As a good father, were you charged with the responsibility of making sure nobody hurt her, Mr. Flemmi?"

"I just answered that. Nobody would hurt her."

Brennan stared at him. "Except *you*?" He let those words hover in the courtroom. Flemmi mumbled a denial.

"This little girl who would call you Daddy, it's the same little girl just a decade later that you started abusing sexually, wasn't it, Mr. Flemmi?"

Deborah Hussey, Stephen Flemmi's step daughter. Flemmi had been sexually abusing her from the time she was a teenager. He and Whitey murdered her in January of 1985 when she was 26 years old.

"When you say sexually abusing her, would you clarify that just a little, please?" Flemmi came across as cocky. "You're talking about intercourse?"

"Any kind of sex with your daughter?"

"Nothing, I didn't inflict any abuse on her—that was consensual," Flemmi said.

When Brennan refused to let it go, Flemmi admitted to some kind of sex: "On two occasions, two occasions." He raised two fingers. "Let's clarify that, two occasions, and I regret it, a moment of weakness, it happened, but it happened later on in life."

"You had a number of moments of weakness with her, didn't you?" Brennan asked.

"We all did." Flemmi nodded in Whitey's direction. "So did Bulger and myself. We all had moments of weaknesses."

Judge Casper pointed to the wall clock, and informed everyone that court was in recess. Most jurors gazed at Flemmi with disgust; one shook his head as they filed out of the courtroom.

Brennan had succeeded in vilifying Flemmi in just fifteen minutes. After a full morning of testimony by the government's star witness, Brennan's cross was what the crowds discussed outside the courthouse. The local and national media swarmed and chased him across the street and all the way to his car with their microphones. He wasn't allowed to speak with the press.

3|2

WHERE ARE ALL MY TEETH?

You had that stick and that rope around her neck and you continued to twist and twist and twist it. Isn't that right, Mr. Flemmi?
—Defense attorney Hank Brennan,
cross-examination of Stephen Flemmi

IT WAS POURING OUT TUESDAY MORNING; THERE WERE ACCIDENTS ALL over the place—Boston traffic at its worst. Whitey's caravan got stuck heading north on Route 3 behind a multiple-car pileup. Boston drivers refused to pull over to make room for Whitey. *No way.* He'd have to wait with the rest of them. There were reports of drivers giving Whitey the finger that day, too.

The lawyers battled with Judge Casper in open court while waiting for two tardy jurors. *More conflict and drama.* Carney argued that he should now be allowed to present Whitey's immunity defense to the jury because the government opened the door by asking Flemmi about his immunity claim before Judge Wolf. Whitey wanted to present evidence to the jury that Jeremiah O'Sullivan, who headed up the DOJ's Strike Force, had granted him free reign to commit crimes. Kelly argued that the judge had already ruled on the issue, and most of Carney's witnesses on his list were irrelevant because they related to the barred immunity defense. Judge Casper cut off the arguments and deferred her decision.

Marshals escorted Flemmi back to the stand. He had dressed in layers with the same windbreaker, another button-down dress shirt, and a white tee underneath. His gray hair was neatly combed back.

"All rise for the jury," the clerk said.

The jury took their seats, appearing anxious for Brennan's cross-examination showdown with Flemmi to begin again.

Brennan started right in: "At what point did you become attracted to your daughter?"

Flemmi tried to wriggle out of it by saying Deborah Hussey was not his biological daughter.

"Is there a difference between being a stepdaughter and biological daughter?" Brennan asked.

"She had a totally different lifestyle." Flemmi went on to explain that Deborah had started doing drugs, and was a different person. She was in debt and he had to give her money.

"Did the sexual relationship have anything to do with money?" Brennan widened his eyes.

"No, it wasn't." Flemmi reddened, appearing embarrassed.

"How did it get from a father relationship to an intimate relationship?"

"It wasn't a father relationship later on. It was the type of relationship that developed—she was a different person."

Brennan wouldn't let up: "At the time you started the sexual relationship with your stepdaughter, you were still involved in a sexual relationship with her mother, weren't you?"

Flemmi examined the back of his hands. "Probably."

"When she consented at eighteen, you were forty years old, Mr. Flemmi?"

"That's correct."

"Did you have any long-term plans to date or marry your stepdaughter?"

"No." Flemmi flinched; he appeared taken aback. "No, absolutely not."

"Young women who are molested turn to drugs to self-medicate, don't they?" Brennan asked.

"Objection!" Wyshak leaped up.

"Sustained."

"You knew that having this relationship with your stepdaughter was wrong, didn't you, Mr. Flemmi?"

"So did Mr. Bulger."

"I'm asking you—"

"Yes, yes, but we shared a lot of information, both of us, Jim Bulger and myself." Flemmi leaned over the witness stand and pointed at Whitey. "He had a young girlfriend, sixteen years old, that he took to Mexico. That's a violation of the Mann Act."

Brennan ignored the comment and accused Flemmi of blaming Whitey for the murder of his stepdaughter. He reminded him of his obligation to tell the truth in court, an essential part of the deal he had forged with the government. He pointed out that Flemmi had told multiple versions of "the truth" pertaining to the Hussey murder in the past while under oath. Sometimes Flemmi said Whitey strangled her with his hands while on other occasions he said it was done with a rope. Thus, the government's star witness had a major credibility flaw. It was Brennan's way of creating reasonable doubt.

"In *McIntyre versus United States,* when you were asked: 'How did he strangle her?'" Brennan paused. "What was your answer, Mr. Flemmi?"

"With a rope."

"Well, if you tell the truth, it's always the same, isn't it, Mr. Flemmi?"

"Well, it should be. Yes, I would say so . . . you can ask him when he takes the stand." He pointed at Whitey again.

Brennan repeatedly asked why Hussey was such an embarrassment that she had to be killed. He fired questions so fast that Judge Casper had to instruct him to slow down.

"I sent her on vacation and she kept coming back." Flemmi rubbed his eyes; he looked like he hadn't slept much the night before.

"You're talking about her like she's a stray dog?" Brennan raised his arms. "That was your stepdaughter, Mr. Flemmi."

"Objection!" Wyshak stood. The question was argumentative.

"Sustained."

"You said that when you agreed to kill your stepdaughter, you did it reluctantly?"

"I did it because I was coerced into it." Flemmi bristled. "And Mr. Brennan, I didn't kill her."

"You agreed to kill her?"

"I didn't kill her, but I agreed to it." He pursed his lips. "Yes, to go along with it."

Brennan had Flemmi on the defensive; his face appeared flushed, angry. He kept egging him on. "Did you lead her to her death, Mr. Flemmi?"

"I brought her there." He exhaled loudly into the microphone, blowing out the speakers. "Yes."

"Tell us about the drive?" Brennan raised his voice an octave, sounding sarcastic. "Did you have small talk?"

"I took her shopping."

Brennan gazed at him with his mouth wide open. "You took her *shopping*?"

"Yeah."

"Knowing you were going to kill her?"

"That's right, I took her shopping."

Brennan raised his eyebrows and made eye contact with jurors. "You didn't tell her she was going to be killed?"

"No."

"So, you *lied* to her?"

"Yes."

"Took her shopping . . . knowing you were going to kill her?" Brennan repeated. "Took her to a few stores?"

A juror in the back row shook his head. The concept of taking a woman shopping before killing her was absurd. Who could make stuff like this up?

"So, you thought the last moments of her life were best spent with *you*?" Brennan pointed at him.

"Objection," Wyshak said.

"Sustained."

"You never turned the car around? Did you walk with her up to the front door?" Brennan asked.

The line of questioning became so intense that Wyshak asked for a sidebar several times to save his witness, and interrupt the flow of Brennan's cross.

"Let me ask you again, Mr. Flemmi—no one forced you to walk her into that house? She wasn't aware she was going to be killed?"

Flemmi gestured with both hands toward Whitey. "All he had to do was say stop and we would've."

Brennan laced his fingers around his own neck. "He could have said *stop* when you had that stick and that rope around her neck, and you continued to twist and twist and twist it. Isn't that right, Mr. Flemmi?"

"Mr. Bulger . . ." Flemmi gestured toward Whitey. "He could have at any time prevented that. All he had to do was say 'pass.' Four words—four little letters: p-a-s-s. That would have been the end of it, and I would have been so happy."

"Did you defend her in that house?" Brennan pressed.

"All he had to do was say 'pass.'"

"Did you fight for her in that house?"

Flemmi rolled his eyes. "You're being very dramatic."

"She'd be alive today, and the same thing with Debra Davis!" Brennan raised his eyebrows, appearing incredulous.

"He was in control." Flemmi raised his voice, and pointed at Whitey again.

"*You* drove her there."

"I know."

"Did you take a stick and put a rope on it, and twist it around her neck?"

"No!" Flemmi was too close to the microphone again. It blasted everyone's ears in the courtroom and all the overflow rooms.

"No?" Brennan asked. "Weeks said you took a rope and a stick and twisted it around her neck." He made a twisting motion with his hands.

"I don't remember that version. Show me a document." Flemmi challenged him. There was nothing documenting what Weeks had just testified to. The official transcript had not been filed.

Brennan asked him about the sweater that he pulled around Deborah's neck. Flemmi mentioned that he took her sweater off after she was dead.

"Were you saying you pulled the sweater around her neck to deflect those accusations that you strangled her with a rope and a stick?" Brennan asked.

"No, I don't understand why I would."

Brennan reminded Flemmi about the timing of that testimony:

"The sweater around her neck made it look like you were strangling her? You used those words."

Flemmi denied it and Brennan moved on to more disturbing details making the gangster out to be a monster.

"You took a pair of pliers and put those in her mouth?" Brennan pointed to his own mouth.

A juror in the front row grimaced. Was she imagining the cold pliers? *The taste of stainless steel?*

"Yes," Flemmi replied. "I tried to pull a few teeth out. I tried . . . I was in a semi-traumatic state. Very difficult thing for me to do."

"Do you remember how many teeth you pulled out of your stepdaughter's mouth?"

"No."

Brennan grimaced, and gazed into the jury box.

"You dug a hole with Kevin Weeks?" he asked.

"We dug a hole. Kevin Weeks was there. It was a concerted effort. I dug the hole."

"At some point you took her body out and put it in an unmarked grave?"

Flemmi snickered. "It wouldn't make sense to mark the grave."

Brennan displayed a haunting photograph of Deborah Hussey's skull. "Is that a reminder of how many teeth you pulled?" The skull appeared stained and grotesque, with all the teeth missing. Flemmi was too much of a coward to look at it. Several jurors looked and turned away in disgust.

He left the photograph up for a moment. It felt like the young murder victim was right there in the courtroom, staring down at Flemmi and asking: *Where are all my teeth? Where are they?*

Brennan took the photograph down and addressed Flemmi. "Well, you know that having a reputation of a murderer, although some people would look at it negatively, you enjoyed that reputation, didn't you?"

"Mr. Brennan, when I was in the military, I killed a lot of Chinese. I never enjoyed that. I never enjoyed killing anyone my whole life. It was distasteful."

Brennan dug deeper. It was obvious that he wanted Flemmi to lose his mind and have the outburst of the century. He resorted to the "P" word.

"There's a word in jail that's worse than murderer—and that's *pedophile*, isn't it, Mr. Flemmi?"

"I wasn't a pedophile!" Flemmi's nostrils flared. "You want to talk about pedophile?" He pointed with his entire arm at Whitey. "Right over there at that table."

Whitey never looked up. His lawyers must have warned him about the line of questioning, and advised him to remain calm.

Brennan kept at it. "In jail they call pedophiles—"

Wyshak stood. "Objection!"

"Diddlers, or skinners, don't they?" Brennan finished the rest of the sentence before the judge cut him off.

"He's trying to goad the witness!" Wyshak shouted.

"Sustained." Judge Casper admonished Brennan and warned him against "ad-libbing and adding commentary."

Brennan paused before taking another swing at Flemmi. "You murdered your stepdaughter!"

"In the eyes of the law? Yes."

Brennan accused Flemmi of continuing relations with Deborah's mother, Marion, after they killed Deborah. He pointed out that poor Marion was waiting for the return of her daughter, but "she never showed up, she never came back."

It was time to switch gears; the jury had heard its fill of the Deborah Hussey murder. Brennan moved on to the murder of the next woman, Debra Davis. He would try to convince the jury that Flemmi's real motive for killing his girlfriend was jealousy over her plans to leave him for another man named Gustav from Mexico. Brennan started by attacking Flemmi's alleged motive behind the murder—that Whitey killed Davis because she knew about their relationship with FBI agent Connolly.

Brennan noted that Connolly had dinner at Flemmi's parents' home and his mother cooked. His parents must've known about Connolly. "Did anything happen to your parents?" he asked.

"You mean did I kill my parents?" Flemmi looked at the government's table in disbelief, hoping Wyshak would object. When the prosecutor didn't do anything, Flemmi said, "I don't even want to answer that question," he said. "It's such a ridiculous question!"

Next, Brennan focused on small inconsistencies in Flemmi's previous testimony pertaining to the exact chain of events leading to the murder of his girlfriend, Debra. Flemmi waffled on where Davis had been right before the murder, whether Whitey used a rope or his hands, and whether she was upstairs or downstairs when she died.

Steve Davis scowled out in the gallery as he listened. Several jurors gazed at him with expressions of pity.

"Was she dead upstairs or downstairs?" Brennan repeated.

"I don't know. She was dead." Flemmi crossed his arms. "I'm not a doctor."

"Did she scream?"

"She couldn't." Flemmi squinted at Brennan. "She was being strangled."

Brennan noted that Flemmi had made a statement, "Let her pray."

"I blurted it out—it was a reaction on my part," he said.

"If she was dead, what was the point of that?"

Steve Davis mumbled something from the gallery.

"Quiet in the courtroom!" the marshal said.

"Did you smash her teeth out?" Brennan asked.

"I didn't smash her teeth out with a hammer. Show me where I said that." Flemmi spread his arms. "You made the accusation."

"Now, this is the woman that you loved but weren't in love with?" Brennan asked, mocking him.

"I loved her but wasn't in love with her. . . . If I was a jealous person, I certainly wouldn't have sent her off, given her money to go off on vacations to meet people." He added, "I've had a guilt trip all these years, it was such a distasteful act."

Brennan hadn't even asked about his jealousy yet. Flemmi jumped the gun. Would the jurors pick up on that?

Suddenly, Flemmi blurted: "Correction. Jim Bulger murdered her, not me." He turned to the judge. "Your Honor, I'm sorry. Sometimes I just get a little emotional here." The elderly gangster sounded like he was getting tired and frustrated; it was almost time for the morning break. Brennan's goal was to take him "off script," he told us later.

Brennan brought up how Flemmi lied to Davis's mother by telling her he would try to find Debra.

"They asked me if I could find out," Flemmi said. "That was part of the cover-up scenario." He gazed toward Steve Davis in the gallery, and then back at Brennan. "When you commit a murder, you cover up on it; you don't admit it to people. I don't know if you're aware of that, you should be—you're an attorney."

"When you watched this woman, Ms. Davis, suffering, waiting for her daughter, you continued to mislead her over and over again, Mr. Flemmi, didn't you?"

"Mr. Brennan, I didn't meet her over and over again."

Brennan pushed his glasses up and wrinkled his nose. "Was she seventeen years old?"

"She was married. It's documented—check it out."

"I'm not disputing the fact she was married."

"I thought you were, the way—I'm looking at your facial expressions, you're looking like that, like, I'm lying."

Brennan had mastered the art of facial expressions. Sometimes he'd get away with making a face like a schoolboy does when the teacher isn't looking.

"Was she seventeen years old?" he asked again. Brennan wanted jurors to imagine a young, teenaged Debra Davis. Perhaps one of them had a daughter the same age?

"Seventeen," Flemmi admitted.

"And you were forty-two?"

"Thirty-nine when I met her, I believe." He sounded testy and short with his answers.

"Did you know she was dating somebody who ended up dead in New Hampshire or in the Blue Hills?"

"Not that I know of."

"When you were first dating her?"

"No."

Brennan noted that when Flemmi bought Davis a Porsche, her father took a bat and smashed it up. He'd been upset about the older wise guy dating his young, beautiful daughter.

"Shortly after he smashed up that car, he ended up dead, didn't he, Mr. Flemmi?" Brennan had heard that Debra's father had mysteriously drowned.

"That's what I heard." Flemmi kept his voice even.

Wyshak sprang from his seat, stretched his arms toward the ceiling, and demanded a sidebar. Judge Casper motioned them up to the bench.

Wyshak spoke first: "This is the second time that Mr. Brennan is insinuating that Mr. Flemmi killed, first, her boyfriend, and now her father. It's totally outrageous. Does he have a good-faith basis for this questioning?"

"I do," Brennan said.

"What is it?" Wyshak studied his opponent with his hands on his hips.

"The father smashed up her Porsche, and within weeks, he ended up drowned. And there's a pattern of conduct by Mr. Flemmi when people get in the way of his relationships, they end up dead. He has a history of being a murderer, he is violent. He has a possessive relationship with his women. Anybody who gets in the way—"

Judge Casper cut him off and warned him to stay away from that line of questioning. Brennan had no proof that Flemmi had killed Davis's boyfriend or father.

Wyshak also complained about "Mr. Brennan's incessant taunting of the witness . . . I think he's intentionally trying to get the witness to have an outburst." He was right about that.

Brennan came back from the sidebar with a smile, acting like he'd won. He always did that.

Brennan resumed questioning Flemmi like he hadn't missed a beat. "Were you living with her when you murdered her?"

"Yes," Flemmi said, without denying that he murdered her. Was he not listening to the question? Did he accidentally admit to killing Davis? It was evident that the aggressive cross had worn Flemmi down; perhaps he couldn't think straight, or he couldn't remember his lines.

"When you suspected that Debbie had a friend, a man other than you, could you tell us how you tapped the phones at your house to record the conversation?"

"Sure."

"Tell us." Brennan gestured toward the jury box.

"Jim Bulger insisted on it because he did it to his wife, his girl-friend Theresa, and found out that she was cheating on him."

"And when you listened to those phone conversations, Mr. Flemmi, you learned that she met a man by the name of Gustav, didn't you?" Brennan leaned forward.

"She told me prior to that."

"As it so happens, you brought this beautiful young woman to your parents' home that you just bought after you learned that she was see-ing somebody else, right?"

"The time frame—"

"And it so happens, Mr. Flemmi, that she ends up dead on the basement floor a month or two after you learn about this?" Brennan rubbed his chin.

"Objection!"

"Sustained."

"Do you remember telling her she was going to a better place?"

"No, I didn't." Flemmi glared at Brennan. "I never said that."

"When you spoke to John Martorano, why did you tell John Mar-torano that you choked her by accident?"

"I never said that."

Brennan opened his mouth wide and cocked his head.

After that, he accused Flemmi of having sexual relations with Da-vis's younger sister, Michelle. Flemmi blushed again and appeared insulted. He blurted: "Mr. Brennan, I'm an aggressive person. If some-body attacks me verbally or physically, I'm going to respond, and I'm responding now verbally."

Brennan accomplished several legal goals with his aggressive cross-examination of Flemmi pertaining to the murders of Hussey and Davis. Flemmi was the government's star, and Brennan did his best to turn jurors' stomachs when they looked at him. Flemmi was not only a mass murderer, but was sexually abusive to women, and, on top of that, a pe-dophile, when it came down to his stepdaughter, Deborah Hussey.

He also tripped him up on details pertaining to the murders of Hussey and Davis. How could someone forget if a woman was stran-gled with hands or a rope around the neck?

If the witness has a propensity to lie to serve his personal agenda, why should the jury believe him? The legal goal: poke as many holes as possible in the government's case by discrediting their witnesses. The government has the burden of proof. The bottom line for the de-fense is always reasonable doubt.

Next, Brennan changed course in his cross-examination, attacking a larger and, possibly, much more dangerous target than Flemmi.

chapter

$$3 | 3$$

A LICENSE TO KILL

Clearly you understood that the federal government and their agents knew that you were involved in murder, didn't you, Mr. Flemmi?

—*Defense attorney Hank Brennan,
cross-examination of Stephen Flemmi*

BRENNAN INFLICTED DEEP WOUNDS UPON FLEMMI WITH HIS BAYONET, but the gangster was not the only one. Through clever and at times sophisticated cross-examination, Brennan's attack on the federal government yielded a deadly result. The courtroom drama may not have been as intense when Brennan delved into the history of Boston's underworld, but it was an eye-opening lesson about the government's role in all of it.

"Punchy McLaughlin . . . was the first man you killed in the streets of Boston?" Brennan asked.

"Yeah, he got killed." Flemmi didn't seem to care. Perhaps it was easier than answering questions about pedophilia and the murder of women.

"Was he the first one you killed?"

"Yes, I think so." He scratched his cheek. "I don't recall. I'm not sure."

"You can't remember the first person you—"

"There was a gang war going on."

"You murdered a lot of people outside a lot of those barrooms before you met Mr. Bulger?"

"Yes." Flemmi sighed as if to say, *Here we go again.*

While Brennan critiqued him for his countless affiliations with other gangsters and multiple murders, Flemmi slung an insult that only a gangster could: "You don't understand the underworld, nothing. You're an attorney."

Jurors who had been sitting on the edge of their seats earlier in the cross-examination seemed to lose interest when the questioning became too detailed about Flemmi's role in old gangland war before Bulger came upon the scene. Brennan rattled off too many names, too many scores, and too many dead bodies. Sometimes lawyers need to make their point and sit down.

BEHIND THE SCENES

We asked Hank Brennan why he dragged some of the cross-examinations out, and this was his response: "You can be critical, I won't take it personally. I knew Flemmi's history would drag the cross but there are three important reasons why I did it. One: To show Flemmi didn't need to have Bulger to direct him on how to murder. Flemmi was a more seasoned and established killer well before he met Bulger. Also, many techniques he developed were important to show his modus operandi to kill Davis and how Jim didn't. For example, before Bulger, he knew how to wiretap phones, bury bodies, and strangle people. Two: I am convinced the U.S. Attorney's Office intended a Rule 35 for Flemmi based on the Florida plea transcript." [A Rule 35 motion could reduce Flemmi's jail time.] "The worse I made him look, the more pressure against the DOJ for granting such a motion. Three: By establishing such an extensive history of killing and protection by Rico and the DOJ, the better basis of liability for victims' families against the DOJ in the future. Same reason I dragged on during parts of *Marra.* I knew the jury wouldn't quite get it but I was trying to do a number of things behind the scenes that could help beyond this trial."[1]

Brennan zeroed in on the theory of his case by focusing on the long history of government corruption deep inside the Department of Justice. The questions about Flemmi's role as a government informant and how the FBI chose sides in the gang war were right on point.

"You were valuable to the Department of Justice, weren't you?" Brennan stretched out the word "valuable."

"Yes," Flemmi said.

FBI Agent Paul Rico "gave you information to eliminate opponents on the other side, right?"

"Yes."

"In fact, you're excellent at misleading people, aren't you, Mr. Flemmi?" Brennan referred to his role as an informant that most of the underworld didn't know about at the time.

"Mr. Brennan, I did what I had to do because it was a survival thing, and if you didn't—if you didn't—if you weren't good at doing certain things, you weren't going to survive."

Brennan suggested that he needed Rico, his FBI handler, to survive.

Flemmi agreed: "He was a valuable asset to me and I was a valuable asset to him. It was a quid pro quo situation." He used his favorite expression again.

"So, you were both *assets* to each other?" Brennan looked at the jury.

"A symbiotic relationship."

"So, these two agents, or more particularly, Mr. Rico, was taking sides in the gang war, wasn't he?" Brennan slowed his pace, emphasizing the importance of the question.

Flemmi nodded. "I would think so."

Brennan now covered a subject area where he and Flemmi saw eye to eye. The Department of Justice controlled the puppet strings. A person's very survival depended on which side the government decided to take. It amounted to a deadly game of chess. The government had sanctioned murder during the gang wars, and had done it again throughout Whitey's reign of criminal activity.

When the jury was not present in the courtroom, the lawyers battled over the immunity issue and the defense strategy of exposing the long history of government corruption going back to the 1960s. Brennan argued to the judge that his questions focusing on government corruption going back to Barboza were relevant and went to the heart of the case.

Joe "the Animal" Barboza was the FBI's first top echelon informant. In 1965, Barboza lied on the witness stand to convict four men for the murder of Edward "Teddy" Deegan. The wrongfully convicted were: Peter Limone, Joseph Salvati, Enrico Tameleo, and Louis Greco. The government knew about the perjury, and stood by as these innocent men were framed and sentenced to death. Years later, it was proven that FBI agents, in particular, H. Paul Rico, withheld exculpatory evidence in order to protect FBI informants Vincent "Jimmy the Bear" Flemmi and Barboza. In 2007, a federal judge awarded damages of $101.7 million to the four men. Tameleo died in prison in 1985, but his estate received money.

"I'm showing to what extent the government will go to protect someone," Brennan said. "Just like they protected Joe Barboza and allowed four innocent people to be prosecuted and convicted. . . . I know it's a damning issue for the federal government, but it's one that exists."

Wyshak argued that the Limone case was not relevant to the Bulger case, and that the defense wanted to bring it up for the sole purpose of jury nullification. The strategy would be to get the jury so upset and inflamed over past government corruption that they'd come back with not guilty verdicts in favor of Whitey, simply to punish the government. Judge Casper ultimately ruled in favor of the prosecution by not allowing Brennan to go into great detail about the four men who were wrongly convicted back in 1965.

Brennan spiked up the drama after spending such a long time on the old gang war days. He had to wake the jury up, and calling a gangster a rat usually does the trick: "You didn't like the word 'rat,' did you?" he asked.

Flemmi glared. "I don't think anybody likes it. I don't think Mr. Bulger likes it either."

"Because in jail, a rat is somebody who is considered to be parasitic, isn't it true, Mr. Flemmi?"

"Objection!" Wyshak stood. "Relevance."

"Sustained."

"A rat is someone who scurries around in corners and feeds off of other people?" Brennan wiggled his fingers and zigzagged his hands, imitating a rat running around.

"Objection!"

"Sustained."

"So when you use the word 'quid pro quo' that's Latin for the term 'rat,' isn't that fair to say?"

"The situation was that he was giving me information. I was giving him information—survival situation." Flemmi raised his voice. "The Mafia is doing the same thing."

Brennan pinched his lower lip. "There's always a justification for what you do. Isn't there, Mr. Flemmi?"

He leaned forward, making eye contact with Brennan. "That's the real world."

Brennan reminded Flemmi how he and Whitey happened to be on the government's "good" side when the race-fixing indictment came down: "Unlike Howie Winter, by taking you out of the indictment, it allowed you to continue your criminal activity on the streets of Boston over the next decade, didn't it?" Law enforcement looked the other way when it came to them.

Flemmi nodded. "We were taken out of the indictment, Jim Bulger and I . . ."

"You committed many crimes over the next decade, didn't you?"

"Yes."

"And over the next decade, you committed crimes, including *murder*, didn't you?"

"Yes."

"Extortion?"

"Yes."

"Threats?"

"Threats."

"Violence?"

"Whatever is in that indictment." Flemmi glanced at the government's table. "Yes."

"You thought that John Connolly would come forward to help because over these years you had given so much valuable information to the federal government, you thought that John Connolly and the federal government owed you back, didn't you?" Brennan's question went right to the heart of the immunity issue for Flemmi—that the government had granted him special immunity to commit crimes and he should never have been prosecuted.

"That's correct," Flemmi said.

"Because they were aware that you were committing these crimes on many occasions, and they did nothing to charge you whatsoever, did they, Mr. Flemmi?"

Wyshak practically knocked his chair over jumping up. "Objection! Objection!" he yelled.

"Sustained."

"And your relationship with Rico . . . you're giving him a gun and he's giving you directions to murder somebody. Clearly you understood that the federal government and their agents knew that you were involved in murder, didn't you, Mr. Flemmi?" Brennan was suggesting a special government license to kill.

Wyshak slapped his hands on the table as he stood. "I object to this broad-brush federal government—"

"Sustained." Judge Casper eyed Brennan. She sounded very firm. She apparently didn't like the suggestion that the government had granted Flemmi a license to kill—it was Brennan's backdoor attempt to raise Whitey's forbidden immunity deal.

Brennan gazed in astonishment at the judge and then Wyshak, as if they were both desperately trying to suppress the truth like partners in crime. He shook his head and made eye contact with the jury. He knew he had to back off the immunity argument, but he hoped the jury would read between the lines. If the government had granted Flemmi a license to kill, had they issued a similar license to Whitey? And if they had, why should Whitey be prosecuted at all?

"You have great conditions, don't you?" Brennan referred to the atmosphere in Flemmi's special Witness Security prison. He wanted to show the jury that even in prison the government had given this mass murderer special treatment.

"I wouldn't say *nice*." Flemmi raised his eyebrows.

"It's like the Club Med of federal facilities?"

Flemmi grimaced. "You really think so?"

"Can you get rib steak?"

"If I gave some of that food to my dog, he'd bite me."

Everyone laughed.

"Can you get salmon?"

"No, we can't get salmon." Flemmi smirked. "It's not on the commissary list, no."

"Smoked oysters?"

"Smoked *what*? Oysters?"

"Yes, Mr. Flemmi."

"You probably could get some of those items at Christmas time."

"On Memorial Day and the Fourth of July, they celebrate with hamburgers and hot dogs and watermelon, don't they, Mr. Flemmi?"

"You know something?" Flemmi wrinkled his nose. "The hot dogs were burnt. The hamburgers were burnt."

People laughed again.

Brennan paused and then regarded Flemmi for a long moment. "Did anyone ever raise the issue of *perjury* with you after that testimony, Mr. Flemmi?"

"There was—No one ever mentioned anything."

Brennan nodded and gazed at the government's table as if they had turned a blind eye.

"I have no further questions for this witness." Brennan turned away with a look of satisfaction.

Wyshak's redirect of Flemmi pointed out that Bulger was his partner; they were always together making decisions to kill and shaking people down. In addition, Flemmi's testimony corroborated that of prior witnesses, specifically Martorano and Weeks. The strategy behind redirect examination is to rehabilitate the witness who was beaten up during cross.

Overall, Brennan scored points with his aggressive style of cross-examination. He showed how Flemmi had a propensity to lie, and an incentive to please the government with different versions of testimony. Most jurors appeared to like Brennan. They chuckled when he raised his eyebrows in an expression of disbelief or when he made a funny face. They seem to be rooting for him, especially when he took on stone-cold killers like Flemmi and Martorano. Brennan was the underdog who attacked like a pit bull.

We wondered if the cross-examination of Flemmi, no matter how good, would make the jury discount his testimony. The bottom line for the defense is reasonable doubt. They have to poke holes in the government's case. That's why defense lawyers must go after star government witnesses hard. Jurors may not like Flemmi, but he corroborated the testimony of other witnesses.

While the lawyers huddled around the bench for a sidebar, Whitey sat by himself, while several jurors gazed at him . . . contemplating . . . wondering . . . deciding his fate.

3|4

THE BUSINESS OF BEING WHITEY

He takes a shotgun off the table and sticks it in my mouth.
—Richard Buccheri, trial testimony

THE PROSECUTION TEAM HAD FOUR WITNESSES TO GO. FOLLOWING the intensity of Flemmi, they chose three shorter witnesses first. The jury needed to decompress. The final witness would share the exciting story of Whitey's capture in California, and there would be more guns. It's always good to go out with a bang.

Zach Hafer called Kevin O'Neil, a former owner of the infamous Triple O's bar in South Boston. His testimony provided insight into the money laundering and extortion counts. He was a very large man, with a pockmarked bulbous nose and a full head of thick white hair. He spoke in a loud monotone with a thick Boston accent. He'd hired Kevin Weeks as a bouncer and knew all the characters of the day, including Flemmi.

"Were you involved in criminal activity?" Hafer asked.

"Maybe bookmakin'." O'Neil kept his answers short.

O'Neil claimed that Whitey asked to be on the Triple O's payroll but didn't work.

"Why not say no?" Hafer glanced at Whitey.

"I didn't think that was smart." O'Neil answered. Several people laughed at his matter-of-fact intonation. Who could say no to Whitey back then?

In 1999 O'Neil was indicted for money laundering and extortion, and entered into an agreement to cooperate with the government. He was sentenced to a year and a day. He added: "I had to wear a bracelet for quite a while." The bracelet was akin to house arrest—the government would monitor where you went. He also had to forfeit the South Boston Liquor Mart and pay real estate agent Ray Slinger twenty-five thousand dollars in restitution for extortion. Slinger had been shaken down by Whitey, and O'Neil was the middleman. When Slinger handed the extortion money to O'Neil to give to Whitey, O'Neil complained to Whitey that he could lose his liquor license. Whitey replied, "You could lose your life."

O'Neil collected rent from bookmakers such as Dick O'Brien, and "gave the money to Whitey or Stevie." He commented that O'Brien was afraid and didn't want to come over.

He helped Weeks, Whitey, and Stevie Flemmi run the liquor business, and then purchased it in 1986 for three hundred thousand dollars. O'Neil thought they were getting the building with the purchase, but it was not included and he and his partner had to pay rent to Whitey, Weeks, and Mary Flemmi (Stevie's mother). He also purchased the Rotary Variety Store with Bulger, Flemmi, and Weeks.

Whitey and Flemmi asked to be on the payroll at the liquor store, which amounted to about five hundred dollars a week. These were obviously no-show jobs, and part of a scheme to show that the gangsters earned a legitimate income. O'Neil couldn't say no to them because "that would be stupid," he said, flatly.

The answer produced more laughter in the courtroom, but it sounded truthful.

O'Neil and his partner finally purchased the property for the liquor store for four hundred thousand dollars and made mortgage payments to Whitey even after he went on the lam in January of 1995. He kept paying because he believed Whitey was coming back.

On cross-examination, Carney focused on how the government accused O'Neil of being involved in sixty-eight slayings, which wasn't true, and wanted him held without bail. They strong-armed him into cooperating by holding a long sentence over his head. When he finally agreed, they treated him favorably.

"So, you never went back to jail after you agreed to be a prosecution witness?" Carney asked.

"That's right."

Extortion victim Richard Buccheri took the stand after O'Neil. He was a real estate developer who built the screen house at the back of Stephen Flemmi's mother's house. He made the mistake of providing an opinion on the positioning of a fence on a property line of a piece of land that Kevin Weeks wanted to buy. His advice about the fence was not favorable to Weeks. Thus, Flemmi called and told him that Whitey wanted to meet him in South Boston at the screen house. He was so afraid that he told his daughter about it in case he didn't make it back from South Boston that day.

Buccheri walked into the screen house with Flemmi and observed Whitey sitting there. He testified that Whitey banged on the table. Buccheri demonstrated by slamming his fist on the witness stand, and startled everyone. Whitey told Buccheri, "You know, Rich, sometimes you should just keep your mouth shut. You know Kevin Weeks is like a surrogate son."

Buccheri testified: "He takes a shotgun off the table and sticks it in my mouth. Then he took it out, punched me in the shoulder, and said, 'Richard, you're a stand-up guy. I'm not going to kill you.'"

After that, Whitey "puts a .45 to my head" and demanded two hundred thousand dollars in thirty days, "threatening to kill me and my family."

Buccheri cut a check for two hundred grand, which Flemmi cashed days later. The Braintree bank teller called him for permission to cash the check, which he gave. He felt lucky to get out of the screen house alive.

After he got the money, Whitey called Buccheri a friend. He never saw Whitey again.

On cross-examination, Brennan questioned him about his friendship with John Martorano, which continued while Martorano was on the lam in Florida. In 1995, Brennan emphasized that Buccheri lied to a grand jury by saying that the two hundred thousand dollars was for a real estate transaction, not a shakedown.

"I was in fear for my life," Buccheri explained. *Who wouldn't be?*

Overall, Buccheri presented jurors with a clear picture of Whitey as a brazen extortionist. His harrowing story was similar to Mike Solimando's testimony. Brennan did not accomplish much on cross. It is understandable why Buccheri and Solimando had to lie to the grand jury. Whitey Bulger was a man of power who could get away with shaking people down for large sums of money. Who would dare go to the police? The government was smart to call Buccheri toward the end; he made a very credible witness. There is no doubt the extortion went down just as he said it did.

Next, the government called IRS agent Sandra Lemanski. She testified about seizing $2.3 million in assets from Flemmi, including his expensive Back Bay properties. She also explained the money laundering aspect of the case to jurors, with charts detailing various real estate transactions along with the South Boston Liquor Mart and Rotary Variety Store deals. The businesses and property were purchased with illegal proceeds, which made them tainted. Through Lemanski, the government introduced a number of checks to help the jury follow the money trail for the multiple allegations of money laundering against Whitey.

On cross-examination, Brennan highlighted the fact that the government allowed Flemmi's family to keep properties purchased with illegal proceeds. He suggested that the government may someday use

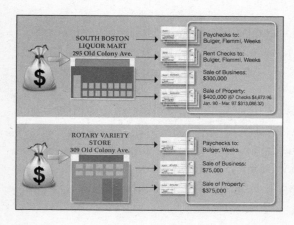

These charts were used at trial to show how Whitey Bulger laundered money through two businesses that he controlled.

a loophole under Federal Rule 35, which could pave the way for Flemmi's release from prison early without having to serve a life sentence. This would provide Flemmi with a significant incentive to follow the government's script. In addition, Brennan pointed out that Lemanski was not asked to investigate Martorano's real estate purchases for money laundering. That played right into the defense theme that the government favors cooperating witnesses.

chapter

3|5

CAPTURED

You know who I am; I'm Whitey Bulger.
—Scott Garriola, trial testimony

SPECIAL AGENT SCOTT GARRIOLA FINALLY TOOK THE STAND AS THE government's last witness. He looked clean-cut and tough; the perfect G-man to capture Whitey. He worked for the FBI's fugitive squad in Los Angeles. On June 22, 2011, he had been on vacation when he received a tip about the location of Whitey and his girlfriend, Catherine Greig.

"The first thing I did was get a babysitter," he said. Garriola knew he had to think it through and make all the right moves. After all, Whitey had been on the lam for more than sixteen years. He had been at the top of the FBI's Most Wanted list. This would make national news.

BEHIND THE SCENES

The FBI received many Whitey Bulger tips because of the television show *America's Most Wanted*. John Walsh, the host, told us, "I constantly believed we were going to smoke him out. The first time he was in Lafayette, Louisiana, hiding with his girlfriend. We got tips that he liked Cajun food. He probably thought, *Who would look for a Boston Irishman in Lafayette?* It's swampland. Then he allegedly fled to Europe, and we went to London. You went with me, Jon. The Boston FBI wanted me to keep doing the story. Whitey was a challenge for me, and a challenge for *America's Most Wanted*. They found a safe deposit box in Dublin—Whitey had five passports, krugerrands, and euros. He certainly had prepared for his run!"[1]

Garriola testified that Whitey and Greig had been living in a rent-controlled apartment at 1012 Third Street, apartment 303, in Santa Monica, California. The manager of the apartment complex identified the renters as Charles and Carol Gasko, a couple who kept mostly to themselves. When the manager saw the mug shots, he buried his face in his hands, and couldn't believe the fugitives had been his neighbors for five years.

BEHIND THE SCENES

FBI Agent Richard Teahan told us that the reward for Whitey's capture was higher than for anyone in history except Osama bin Laden: "He's so important—such a brutal killer—we sought out the highest reward for him, of $2 million."[2]

Garriola and his team set up surveillance, and tried to look in the windows. They saw Greig on the balcony, and had to figure out how to lure Whitey out. They came up with a plan for the manager to call the apartment, and inform the couple that their storage locker had been broken into, and he was going to call the police. He called the couple and left a message. He was nervous. Would the plan work?

Greig called back within five minutes saying that she'd send her husband down. They could hear the elevator. When the door opened, out stepped a bearded man in a white fedora, dressed in soft white colors.

Whitey Bulger and his longtime girlfriend Catherine Greig. They had been living together in Santa Monica, California, until arrested in June of 2011.

Guns recovered from Whitey's Santa Monica, California, apartment.

Garriola and his team surrounded him: "We asked him to get down on his knees. . . . He swore at us a few times, told us he was not going to get down on the ground . . . there was grease on the ground." They finally handcuffed him.

"Who are you?" Garriola asked him.

"Charles Gasko."

Garriola called his bluff: "We'll ask Cathy."

The man paused. "You know who I am; I'm Whitey Bulger."

Whitey's demeanor changed when they asked if a SWAT team had to be called in to get Greig out. He told them it wasn't necessary, and signed a consent form for a search of the apartment. According to Garriola, as he signed his true name, Whitey said, "This is the first time I've signed this name in a long time." He informed agents he had loaded weapons in his bedroom, but Greig had never held any of the guns. She was not allowed in the room.

Upstairs, agents rushed to the door, Greig opened it, and identified herself. She realized what was happening and asked to change clothes. Whitey told her he was cooperating in exchange for the government's future consideration on her behalf.

Garriola displayed all of the evidence he recovered in hiding places, including in a shaving kit, behind a mirror, and under the bed. There were multiple loaded guns, ammunition, knives, pepper spray, fake IDs, and $822,000 in cash.

Cash recovered from Whitey's Santa Monica, California, apartment.

Garriola also revealed that Whitey liked reading mob books, and recorded episodes of himself on *America's Most Wanted*.

On cross-examination Carney pointed out how cooperative Bulger had been during his capture. Garriola admitted that when he asked Whitey if he planned to have a shootout with police, "He paused and said, 'No, because a stray bullet may hit someone.'"

Carney emphasized that Whitey gave the agents a tour of his living space, and pointed out all the weapons and money, and told them the guns were loaded.

Carney said, "All he was looking for was that this cooperation would be brought to the prosecutor's attention so that consideration would be given to Catherine. Are you aware that Catherine is serving an eight-year sentence?"

"Objection."

"Sustained."

Carney suggested that the government couldn't be trusted; they turned their backs on Catherine even after Whitey cooperated.

BEHIND THE SCENES

Whitey remains bitter about Catherine's sentence of eight years in federal prison for harboring a fugitive. In a letter he wrote to us, Whitey complained about "seeing a helpless woman treated worse than mass murderers ... a woman you love ... kept in a cell twenty-three hours a day." He lamented that the government "could do this to Catherine!"

"No further questions," Carney said, and all eyes focused on Wyshak. Was Garriola really the last government witness?

Wyshak rose and addressed the judge. "At this time the United States would rest its case against James Bulger." He sounded relieved.

From a legal standpoint, the final week is pivotal, and the government nailed it with dramatic testimony and more guns. They presented a compelling case against Whitey. Jurors seemed engaged and emotionally attached, some cried.

How would the defense try to undo the government's sixty-three witnesses who painted Whitey as a cold-blooded, hands-on killer?

We were about to find out.

chapter

3|6

STONEWALLED

I wanted Halloran in the witness protection program. . . . I thought
he might get whacked—it was very serious. I was getting the impression people were stonewalling our action.
—*Robert Fitzpatrick, trial testimony*

WHEN THE DEFENSE LAUNCHED ITS CASE IN CHIEF, THEY HAD ALREADY
managed to poke holes in the government's case through vigorous
cross-examination of star witnesses. The defense could have rested
right then; Whitey didn't have to present witnesses or prove a thing.
The government had the burden of proof. What would the defense
consider a win? Were they hoping for a hung jury, or simply to expose
evidence of far-reaching government corruption and suppression of
the truth in this already muddy case?

We knew they wanted to persuade jurors to think outside the box.
Carney made a promise in his opening statement that the FBI and the
Department of Justice had a mandate to do everything possible to go
after the Mafia, which created tremendous pressure on agents to develop top echelon informants.

They had to make sure the lead-off witness was a heavy hitter who
could drive home their theories. Jurors appeared alert and interested
in what they were going to do.

Brennan marched to the podium. "The defense calls Robert Fitzpatrick."

Fitzpatrick walked to the witness stand with arms swinging and a story to tell. He was a big man, heavyset with a pockmarked face and a mustache that showed the wear and tear of twenty-one years in the bureau. His cheeks were flushed red.

As the Assistant Agent in Charge (ASAC) from 1981 through 1986, Fitzpatrick had been embroiled in a cauldron of corruption in Boston's FBI office. He didn't quite look the part of a former FBI ASAC. He wore a gray jacket with a gray-and-black-striped dress shirt underneath. No tie. Fitzpatrick was raised in a Catholic orphanage; a no-nonsense fighter, who achieved success through hard work. The FBI hired him in 1965.

He possessed expertise in developing informants; thus, the bureau sent him to Boston. There was a territorial battle going on at the time between the state and local police, and the FBI. Fitzpatrick was brought in to figure out what was going on and fix it. We wondered if they had set him up for a fall?

"What was your objective when you came to Boston?" Brennan asked.

"My objectives were to stop the leaking, which was occurring in Boston. Apparently, there were people inside the FBI and outside the FBI that were leaking information, causing a lot of the investigations to go south—in other words, to get corrupted."

The FBI placed him in charge of organized crime, which included the Mafia and the Irish gangs. One of the first things he did when he arrived in Boston was to have John Morris, his underling, take him to meet their most secret top echelon informant: a man named Whitey Bulger.

BEHIND THE SCENES

Fitzpatrick told us "everyone was telling me how great he [Whitey] was. . . . I was going over there with the idea of learning how much he was helping the FBI . . . that he is a great informant, and lo and behold I found just the opposite!"[1]

Fitzpatrick described his first encounter with Whitey: "So, I exited the car, went, knocked on Bulger's door, and Mr. Bulger came to the door, and I put out my hand to shake his hand, and he didn't take it. And I said, 'That's not a nice way to start the conversation,' but that's the way it was. I pulled my hand back."

He had his doubts about Whitey from the beginning: "I sized him up right there. He's a guy who was wearing a baseball cap, Boston, of course; he's got sunglasses on; he's got a body shirt on. . . . I used to teach profiling . . . one thing about a person is their eyes, and we used to say their eyes are the windows to the soul, and of course, he had sunglasses on, so I couldn't see his soul."

Fitzpatrick paused and regarded Whitey before describing the rest of their meeting: "I didn't sit. We didn't pull up a chair and sit down. It was kind of a very formal situation. I was looking at him, obviously trying to assess him, but the room was dark, the shades were drawn, he's got sunglasses on. I don't know how the heck he saw me, but I'm looking at him and trying to assess."

He added, "I wouldn't call him stone-faced but he wasn't smiling."

Fitzpatrick described how Whitey mentioned right away that he was the guy from Alcatraz; he had his Alcatraz belt on. They spoke for a half hour, and Fitzpatrick tried to get answers about what Whitey was doing for the FBI as an informant. Whitey kept changing the subject and acting evasive. When he tried to get more answers, "out popped John Connolly, one of the agents. And I was just shocked."

"You didn't expect him to be there?" Brennan asked.

"He wasn't supposed to be there." Fitzpatrick shook his head. "He wasn't allowed to be there. This was supposed to be a one-on-one talk with the informant. We get down to grassroots, you know. I wanted to find out who is this guy and what is he doing."

Fitzpatrick had the impression that Whitey controlled the relationship with Morris and Connolly. He testified: "Bulger said he was not paid. Most informants are paid. He made a point of the fact that he was not paid, that he, in fact, paid others. I didn't challenge this." Fitzpatrick sipped his water. "He also said that he was the leader of the gang, that he was the top guy with the Winter Hill Gang. And that resonated with me, because, you know, in the FBI, you can't have the head of a gang as an informant because then you're validating the gang, you're actually part of the management process, if you will."

BEHIND THE SCENES

We asked Colonel Foley of the Massachusetts State Police whether he would have had second thoughts about using Whitey as an informant. He said, "I never would have used a Bulger and a Flemmi as informants. Even if they came in to try and make a deal, I wouldn't have participated in that. It's like making a deal with Hitler, and him giving you his field marshals and commanders below. It doesn't make any sense. He's the target. He's the one responsible, not some minor low-level individual he throws to you to make you happy, which goes in the books, and it looks like you're doing your job. In this business, you start at the lowest levels possible and work your way up. This case proves my point. We started at the bookmaker level with low-level informants, and worked for years going up the chain."[2]

"I thought, *What am I doing here?*" Fitzpatrick testified. At one point, Whitey told him he wasn't an informant. He went back to the office, and questioned why Morris would be telling him what a great guy Whitey was.

"I turned to John Morris and said, 'Well, I am going to close him,' and he said, 'No you're not.'" Fitzpatrick frowned as he recalled the conversation. "And I got more angry."

"Why did you get more angry when Mr. Morris told you that you weren't going to do that?" Brennan asked.

"Well, first of all, Morris is my subordinate, and secondly, he doesn't make the decision about what I'm going to do. So I took that as a personal offense, if you will, that he was challenging, if you will, my authority."

Brennan cocked his head. "You thought you were in charge of Morris?"

"I *was* in charge of Morris. And I didn't like what he was—how he was challenging me."

Fitzpatrick tapped the witness stand with his index finger. "Never in my entire bureau career did I have a situation where I didn't trust another agent. You trust the people you're with, who have your back. I wanted Morris to talk to Connolly because the reports were not good."

Fitzpatrick's face reddened even more; he clearly took offense that Morris had challenged his decision and authority. Within days of that meeting in 1981, he dictated a two-page report recommending that Whitey be "closed" as an informant. He gave it to Special Agent in Charge Lawrence Sarhatt, who put it in the safe in his office. Only Sarhatt could close an informant.

"And what happened?" Brennan asked.

"Nothing."

Whitey wasn't closed. Fitzpatrick testified that FBI Headquarters wanted to keep Whitey open, for they considered him to be capable of taking down the Mafia.

Brennan asked about the bureau's focus back in the early 1980s: "Is Boston involved in investigating the LCN [Mafia]?"

"Oh, yes."

"Is that the most important case in Boston?"

Fitzpatrick raised his finger. "Priority one."

"Was it a priority for Boston or a priority for headquarters?"

"National priority and priority for Boston," Fitzpatrick said.

BEHIND THE SCENES

Fitzpatrick told us: "Bulger destroyed the criminal justice system in Boston and New England. I am saddened by the fact there were corrupt agents. As I said before it was beyond something I could grasp. Once the information became available I reported it to the director of the FBI, and the legal section of the FBI, and they did nothing about it. They do in fact kill the messenger and I don't like that. The corruption on the part of Connolly and Morris . . . and then they get all the commendations? Everybody was getting on the wagon back then, and now everyone is getting off the wagon."[3]

Another problem became apparent: Brian Halloran. He came forward as an informant willing to cooperate against Whitey in the Wheeler murder investigation.

"I wanted Halloran in the witness protection program," Fitzpatrick said. "I thought he might get whacked—it was very serious. I was getting the impression people were stonewalling our action."

According to Fitzpatrick, the obstruction came from the U.S. Attorney's Office. Jeremiah O'Sullivan, a federal prosecutor, was in charge of the New England Organized Crime Strike Force, so Fitzpatrick met with him regarding Halloran's safety. He warned the prosecutor that "killing could be imminent." However, Halloran was not placed in the Witness Security Program (WITSEC) because O'Sullivan opposed it.

Fitzpatrick, who referred to himself as a bulldog, went to see U.S. Attorney William Weld, who was in charge of the Boston office. "My objective was to complain that we're not doing enough to put Halloran in the witness protection program, and get him out of harm's way," Fitzpatrick said.

"When you spoke to William Weld about your complaints, was Brian Halloran put into the witness protection program?" Brennan asked.

Fitzpatrick leaned over the witness stand. "No."

"How many days after you spoke to William Weld was it that Mr. Halloran and Mr. Donahue were murdered?"

"Two days."

Brennan glanced at the jury with surprise. "What were your concerns?"

"My concerns were that we didn't act fast enough—I say we, and that's the Department of Justice and the FBI. We didn't act fast enough to get Halloran in the witness protection program so that we could pursue our case." Fitzpatrick gazed sadly into the spectator's gallery, where the Donahue family sat. "Halloran and Mr. Donahue are deceased, they're gone, and so that case that we had is more or less blown. We lost our witness, we lost the guy who was going to give us the perpetrators."

After the Halloran and Donahue murder, Fitzpatrick wrote a memorandum about what had happened. "I'm a scribe with this," he said.

Pat Donahue bristled when Fitzpatrick described himself as a "scribe" during his testimony. She said to us: "Are you kidding me? He was second in charge over there; he was much more than a scribe. He had the responsibility to do more than just be a scribe. Fitzpatrick should have come forward after the murder of my husband. He's not innocent in all of this."[4]

Fitzpatrick testified that FBI Headquarters instructed him to coordinate with Special Agent Connolly. He was upset because he had "received a report that Connolly was rifling through the files. . . . I got it loud and clear. I went down, talked to Morris and said that if I catch that happening again, he's going to be brought up on charges."

Ultimately, Fitzpatrick claims the FBI retaliated against him for being outspoken, and siding against Morris and Connolly. He received downgrades and tendered his resignation and never received the benefit of his pension. He wrote the book *Betrayal,* which documents his sordid history with the FBI.

Brennan made eye contact with the jury before walking back to his table. He had used Fitzpatrick to reveal the deep layers of lies and cover-ups within the Boston office in the early 1980s. They would bend over backward to protect informants like Whitey and Flemmi at the expense of others, including innocent victims.

Kelly paraded toward the podium with Fitzpatrick's book in hand. Brennan and Carney would soon wish he had waited until after the trial to publish it.

chapter

3|7

RING THE BELL!

That's a total bald-face lie!
—Assistant U.S. Attorney Brian Kelly,
cross-examination of Robert Fitzpatrick

"SIR, IT'S FAIR TO SAY, ISN'T IT, YOU'RE A MAN WHO LIKES TO MAKE UP stories?" Kelly's voice echoed throughout the courtroom.

Fitzpatrick leaned over the witness stand, and cupped a hand behind his ear as if he couldn't hear well. "I beg your pardon?"

"You're a man who likes to make up stories, aren't you?"

"No."

"In fact, for years you've been trying to take credit for things you didn't do, isn't that right?" Kelly said.

"No."

"Well, in fact, at the beginning of your testimony didn't you gratuitously claim credit for arresting the mob boss Jerry Angiulo?" Kelly referred to Gennaro "Jerry" Angiulo, leader of the Italian Mafia in Boston in the mid-1980s.

"I wish I did arrest the—*I did.*"

"Not what you *wished you did.*" Kelly paused and raised his voice. "Did."

"I wish I did arrest the—I did arrest him." Fitzpatrick appeared confused.

"Not what you wished you did." Kelly gestured toward the jury box. "Didn't you tell this jury, 'I also arrested Angiulo'?"

"I did arrest Angiulo."

"Okay." Kelly exaggerated a nod. "That's your testimony *under oath,* sir?"

"Yes."

"Sir, isn't it a fact that the case agent against Angiulo was Ed Quinn?"

"Yeah, he was ride-along with me. I was the ASAC in charge. I went to the table and put the arrest right on Angiulo."

Kelly's jaw dropped. "That's a total bald-face lie!"

"No, it's not!"

"In fact, Ed Quinn, who is still alive, sir, can testify he's the one who arrested Gennaro Angiulo at Francesca's."

"Ed Quinn was my subordinate." Fitzpatrick's words came out garbled. "He could say he was there, but the arrest was made by me."

Kelly smirked. "You had nothing to do with the arrest, did you?"

"Were you there?" Fitzpatrick huffed.

Kelly was prepared—he whipped out the report for the Angiulo arrest and showed it to him. "You did not handcuff Gennaro Angiulo, did you?"

"Did I?" Fitzpatrick asked.

Kelly waved the book *Betrayal.* "You claimed in your book, and you appear to be claiming now, that you put handcuffs on Jerry Angiulo?"

Fitzpatrick regarded the book. "No, if I read the book, I didn't put the handcuffs on him."

"Woah, woah, woah!" Kelly yelled. "Do you have a copy of your book in front of you?"

Kelly proceeded to show Fitzpatrick and the jury how much he had exaggerated his role in the Angiulo arrest for his book. He pointed to other sections of puffery. Fitzpatrick claimed he found the rifle that the gunman used to shoot Martin Luther King, but the truth was he had only transported it. Kelly called him out on that, too.

Fitzpatrick also had a picture in his book with him standing next to the pit where they unearthed McIntyre's body in the year 2000. He wasn't working for the Boston FBI at that point.

Kelly quoted a passage from the book: "'I stood watching the remains of a body being lifted from the ground.'" That never happened. It looked like he had Photoshopped himself next to the pit. It was embarrassing.

As cross continued, Kelly maintained an accusatory tone, ridiculing Fitzpatrick. He reproached the former agent for taking credit for things he didn't do. After a while, it felt like Kelly kicked Fitzpatrick over and over while he lay on the floor bleeding.

"There's no question in your mind that the FBI had Mr. Bulger as an informant, is there?" Kelly pointed at Whitey.

"He was an informant." Fitzpatrick nodded. "I went out to interview him as an informant."

"You wouldn't go to close a window if it wasn't open, right?" Kelly asked. He received several smiles from the jury box. It was a good line.

"What are you trying to say?" Fitzpatrick asked.

"You went to see—you thought he should be closed, that means he was open as an informant, right?" Kelly cocked his head sideways toward Whitey.

"I determined this closure after interviewing Mr. Bulger, not before."

Kelly harped on the point that this key defense witness confirmed Whitey was an informant. It would have been better off for the defense if Whitey had conceded that point. But it wasn't happening.

"Isn't it a fact you were demoted for fabricating FBI documents?" Kelly asked.

"No."

"Isn't it a fact you took a fifteen-thousand-dollar pay cut, and got sent down to Rhode Island?"

"I don't recall that."

Kelly attacked his employment record. Brennan had raised these issues on direct when Fitzpatrick claimed the FBI demoted him due to retaliation as if he was being punished for being a noble whistleblower.

"Well, when you went from ASAC to line agent, that's a fifteen-thousand-dollar pay cut, right?" Kelly asked.

"Well, first of all it wasn't a demotion. Secondly, I don't recall the amounts of money," he replied.

We found that hard to believe; it felt like Fitzpatrick was digging himself into a hole.

Kelly shot the jury a look of incredulity. "It's not a demotion to go from being an ASAC to a line agent?"

"Not the connotation," Fitzpatrick said. "It was a voluntary takedown, that's not a demotion."

That sounded like semantics to us. At this point it would probably be best if Fitzpatrick conceded. Whenever he tried arguing with Kelly, he lost.

"Didn't the director of the FBI refer to your deplorable conduct, your reprehensible judgment, and concluded you had in fact falsified bureau documents?" Kelly jabbed him again.

"Right." Fitzpatrick examined his fingers.

Brennan stood. "Your Honor, I object." He had to do something to save his witness.

"Sustained as to the form of the question," Judge Casper said. "You can put another question to him about what happened."

"Didn't the FBI director conclude that you had deplorable conduct?" Kelly asked.

"Objection!"

"Overruled."

"No, that's not fair to say." Fitzpatrick's face turned crimson.

"Isn't that why you got in trouble with the FBI?"

"No."

Kelly stared at him for a moment. "Are you on any medication that affects your memory?"

"Not that I recall."

We cringed with that answer. Others laughed. The press loved it, and would report on it later. It felt like we were sitting ringside in a boxing match, waiting for the referee to ring the bell and call the fight. Fitzpatrick was getting pummeled.

BEHIND THE SCENES

Fitzpatrick was flustered. He told us: "I don't care what happens to Bulger any more than I care about what happens to the justice system in Boston. You can't just go out and do what you want to do, and claim you shouldn't have. I am not talking about one incident when I am the second guy in charge. I got a real problem, and then no one is listening. I got a real problem."[1]

Brennan attempted to rehabilitate his witness on redirect, but there wasn't much he could do. Fitzpatrick repeated that he had been retaliated against, and claimed that the book was merely a "memoir."

Kelly jumped up for recross. "Do you think writing a memoir gives you the right to make things up?" he asked.

"No."

"Does the settlement with the FBI give you the right to lie under oath?"

Kelly had made his point, *many points*. If Fitzpatrick had exaggerated in his book, was he doing the same when testifying about the irresponsibility and level of corruption at the FBI and Department of Justice? It was an effective cross-examination, yet he may have taken it too far. Would jurors perceive Kelly as a bully?

3|8

TOP ECHELON INFORMANT

I intend to ask him a question concerning whether he is a top echelon informant.... It reflects again the extent the government will
go to make deals with people.
　　　　　—*Defense attorney Jay Carney, sidebar conference*

THE DEFENSE HAD SUBPOENAED PAT NEE, BUT HE DIDN'T WANT TO
participate in the show trial. *Not at all.* His name had been mentioned
dozens of times throughout the trial. He was here, he was there. According to witnesses, he brought victims to his brother's house to be
killed, and transported and buried bodies. Testimony also placed him
in the backseat of the "tow truck," Whitey's hit car in the Halloran and
Donahue murders. According to Flemmi, his gun conveniently jammed.
Nee has never been charged in any of the Bulger-related murders.
Would he have to finally testify in open court about what he knew?
Nee sat with arms crossed in the back of the courtroom, hoping to
hightail it out of there.

　　Most of the sensitive arguments over Nee's potential testimony
happened out of the spectators' and the jury's earshot. This sidebar
conversation at the bench provided us with an inside glimpse into how
badly the government wanted to keep Nee from testifying. We knew
there was more to it, and spent hours poring through court transcripts
later on. We finally found it. The content of this conference was never

made public by the press and never discussed. Why? It dealt with Nee's alleged current status as a top echelon government informant.

Steven Boozang, Nee's attorney, joined Whitey's lawyers and the government at the hushed bench conference. Boozang said: "I think it's clear that Mr. Nee is going to assert his Fifth Amendment privilege in each and every question other than his name and where he lives. I think Mr. Bulger has ensnared him in some very serious allegations. I think not only questions from Mr. Carney, whatever circus he wants to perform today."

The defense knew they couldn't question Nee about his criminal activity, but they wanted to focus on Nee's reality TV show called *Saint Hoods* on the Discovery Channel. The show featured Nee in his glamorous job as a bookmaker.

We shook our heads in disbelief. That was a first—*only in the Whitey trial*.

Carney whispered to the judge: "The show describes him as the largest bookmaker in South Boston and the show will describe how he does these activities. And he has the confidence to not only put this in a video but publicize it, and I suggest that it supports the fact, the argument, we've made that he is receiving special protection from the government given that he can do this, and that's a logical inference that can be drawn from this." He stepped toward the judge.

"Secondly," Carney said, "I intend to ask him a question concerning whether he is a top echelon informant. That is not a question to which he could assert a privilege, because if the person is a top echelon informant he isn't committing a crime by answering that."

Wyshak vehemently opposed: "How are either of those relevant to the charges in this case against Mr. Bulger?"

"Because it will present evidence to the jury of how they pick and choose who they want to have be prosecuted, and they make deals and sometimes those deals involve not even charging anyone with a crime. And that would explain why Nee is mentioned so much during this trial being involved with murder, attempted murder, accessory after the fact to murder, and nobody has charged him for any of those actions."

Wyshak countered: "Again, that's not relevant to proof of the charges or defense of the charges in this case. It's going to jury nullification, Your Honor, which is actually what this whole defense is about—presentation of totally irrelevant evidence to seek some kind of jury nullification." Wyshak anticipated that the defense would suggest in its closing that the jury should somehow punish the government with its verdict despite the overwelming evidence against Whitey.

"What does that have to do with whether or not Bulger killed any of the nineteen victims is beyond me," Wyshak continued. "And it's just putting irrelevant information into the record so he can make speeches during summation that have nothing to do with the case."

Carney argued, "The way the government is treating percipient witnesses to murder is a reflection on what the government's approach is in this case, and undermines the credibility of the other witnesses with whom they've made deals. The jury has heard Patrick Nee throughout this case. If they learn that he is a top echelon informant then that will be significant to them as to why he is not brought in here, and it reflects again the extent the government will go to make deals with people."

Carney was right. The FBI's willingness to protect its top-level informants was a central issue at the trial. They protected Whitey and Stevie at the expense of Halloran and Donahue. Castucci took the fall, so did Wheeler and Callahan.

BEHIND THE SCENES

We asked retired Massachusetts State Police Colonel Thomas Foley if he thought Pat Nee could be a top echelon informant. He hesitated: "I don't . . . no, I don't . . . I hope not . . . I don't see it right now." Foley added: "I'd love to see Martorano, Nee, and Winter—all those guys get caught up in something, and go to jail the rest of their lives."[1]

Judge Casper sided with the government, and Nee walked out of the courtroom. Just like that. *Poof and he's gone.* He didn't even have to take the stand and assert his Fifth Amendment privilege. That rarely happens. We had never seen it before.

Judge Casper may have recognized the need to protect an informant.

What was Whitey thinking about Nee's status? He hated rats, and even if it hurt his immunity argument, Whitey insisted he was never an informant—it was all fabricated by the FBI.

BEHIND THE SCENES

Donald K. Stern, former United States Attorney for the District of Massachusetts, discussed Whitey's insistence that he was never an informant: "It doesn't really matter, it had nothing to do with the criminal charges. But, it made his claim that he had immunity to commit murder sound absurd. Informants don't always get charged with the crimes they commit, sometimes they do get deals. Being an informant doesn't give you the right to commit crimes. The government needs informants to convict people—it's not a corrupt practice if managed properly."[2]

As Pat Nee left the courtroom, we wondered, who is being protected and why?

3|9

REASONABLE DOUBT

She said, "Ma I'm not lying," and I said . . . "I believe you."
—transcript of Marion Hussey

JOSEPH KELLY WAS THE SECOND WITNESS CALLED BY THE DEFENSE. HE
spent over twenty years in the Boston FBI's organized crime unit.
Kelly testified that John Connolly became the informant coordinator,
and he had unfettered access to all informant files. Connolly was responsible for meting out informant intelligence to agents who could
use it.

"Isn't it fair to say that John Connolly had access to every informant?" Carney asked.

"Yes," Kelly said.

"Did John Connolly have unfettered access compared to other
agents in the office?"

"Yes."

Kelly's time on the stand was short, but it advanced the defense argument that Connolly had access to other investigations and information was being leaked from the office onto the streets. The FBI should
have been doing more to protect top secret files, especially when informants and cooperating witnesses were getting killed.

The defense continued with its assault against the government.
Retired FBI Agent James Crawford testified that ten days before the

Halloran and Donahue murders, a confidential informant told him "'Flemmi was going to kill Halloran for being a snitch.'"

He said that his bosses at the bureau requested that he put that information in a memo, but he pledged to his informant that he wouldn't put anything in writing. He glanced at Whitey. "That's because she was scared, deadly scared."

"I refused." Crawford grimaced. "I had given my word that that person would not be ID'd, and my word meant everything to me." Crawford later spoke with a supervisor who said the information should be "put on a back burner."

The Donahue family whispered to each other in the gallery. Several people knew that Halloran's life was in jeopardy, and did nothing about it.

BEHIND THE SCENES

Colonel Thomas Foley told us: "The goal was to put Bulger away. It would be great right now if we could reconvene a case against the FBI so we could get all the information out there. I think the expectations were too much on the families and public that all wrongdoing could be exposed."[1]

The parade of retired FBI agents continued when Matthew Cronin took the stand. The defense clearly wanted to expose the dysfunctional nature of Boston's FBI office.

According to Cronin, it was a "watch yourself" atmosphere in the office when he arrived in Boston in 1978.

Brennan asked: "At any time when you needed to petition the C-3 squad and John Morris for their assistance, did you ever have any reluctance sharing confidential information with that unit or Mr. Morris?"

Cronin nodded. "I did."

"Was that from the beginning of your tenure on the C-7 unit or did that develop over some time, this caution you had?" Brennan asked.

"It was probably my belief on day one." Cronin raised a finger.

"Having just arrived in Boston on day one and knowing very little about the office, how did you quickly develop that caution or concern?"

"When I worked in New York . . . other people weren't that interested. When I was here, everybody seemed to be interested in everybody else's business. So you learned very quickly to keep your cards pretty close to your vest."

Cronin also investigated allegations from Olga Davis (Debra's mother) that she believed Flemmi killed her daughter. They followed leads, but came up empty-handed.

Retired FBI supervisor Fred Davis testified next. He wore a red, white, and blue tie that looked very patriotic. Davis testified about a lot of "paranoia in the bureau . . . they were nervous other agents in the office were leaking information."

According to Davis, John Connolly had been a suspected leaker back then. He said, "He would show up in my squad all too often. . . . A lot of my agents began to say he was up to no good."

Davis never alerted his superiors: "I didn't have enough specific information . . . so I handled it man-to-man, so to speak." He recalled he was out with Connolly and other agents one night, and he didn't have enough cash for tolls on his drive home. Connolly gave him twenty dollars with the message, "Agents in Boston should never want for money."

When Davis questioned the quality of Whitey's information, John Morris moved the top echelon files closer to his organized crime squad.

Before trial, Davis reviewed Whitey's FBI informant file, and found the quality of information "worthless." He formed the opinion that Whitey should have been terminated as an informant. "This file represents a lot more than what I saw," he testified, suggesting that the file had been tampered with or padded over the years.

Wyshak took offense at the suggestion: "Is it your testimony that this is *not* Mr. Bulger's file?"

During redirect, Brennan asked: "Do you remember your opinion of the quality of information in that file?"

"My opinion was that it was worthless," Davis repeated.

Brennan smiled. "Thank you for your time today."

"The defense calls Steve Johnson," Brennan said.

Lieutenant Steve Johnson had been employed with the Massachusetts State Police for more than two decades, and had worked on Whitey's case with Colonel Foley since 1993. The defense called him to the stand to demonstrate how the government's key witnesses had changed their testimony over the course of time. Johnson was the investigator who interviewed Weeks, Flemmi, and Martorano.

Brennan compared various versions: "I'd like to talk about what John Martorano told you about the stabbing death of Jack Banno. . . . In this trial he said he stabbed Banno, put him in a car, then stabbed him to death. . . ."

Johnson nodded. "Yes, sir."

"But in the police report that you wrote, the details are different. Martorano told you he stabbed him right away, and he placed his body behind the Diplomat [Hotel]?" Brennan said.

"Yes, sir."

Johnson acknowledged discrepancies over the years, but he downplayed them. When pressed on inconsistent statements from Flemmi, Johnson claimed it was more a function of how he took the report than what Flemmi actually said. Johnson smiled at the jury. "I would say it's more of a flaw of my writing."

He also pointed out that when he first interviewed Flemmi, "It was much more important to find out who killed who than where people stood."

The witness fell flat for the defense. Johnson came across as sincere, and jurors had seen him sitting in the back of the courtroom since day one. The inconsistencies seemed minor.

On cross-examination, Hafer drove the point home: "Who shot Bucky Barrett in the back of the head with a MAC-10?"

"Mr. Bulger." Johnson nodded toward Whitey.

Hafer reminded jurors of the central issue: this trial was about Whitey Bulger, not the government, and they had mountains of solid evidence against him.

Next, Carney mixed it up for the jury. He took a breather from law enforcement to read emotional prior testimony from Marion Hussey into the record. He wanted to produce as much evidence as possible against Flemmi for the Deborah Hussey murder. Deborah was Marion's daughter, who Flemmi had sexually abused.

Marion was too sick to testify in person. However, she had been adamant that Stevie Flemmi (her long-term live-in boyfriend) had a motive to kill Deborah.

Carney read prior recorded testimony to the jury that Flemmi had called his stepdaughter a "slut, a whore, a prostitute . . . doing drugs."

In October of 1982, Marion said she argued with Flemmi and then went upstairs to find him beating Deborah. At that point, Deborah blurted out that Flemmi had been forcing her to perform oral sex on him.

Carney read Marion's prior words. "'Debbie said something about sucking his . . . I've been doing it for years. I just couldn't believe what I had heard.'" Carney paused to make eye contact with jurors. He seemed genuinely upset by the disturbing testimony. He continued, "'She said, Ma I'm not lying, and I said . . . I believe you.'"

Marion was shocked and distraught at the revelation. She kicked Flemmi out of the house after that. Carney read from her transcript again: "'When I come home from work tomorrow, I want everything you own out of the house.'"

Flemmi escorted Deborah out of the house after that, and it was the last time Marion ever saw her daughter again. Thus, the defense would stress in closing arguments that Flemmi had the motive to kill his stepdaughter for revealing too much information to her mother about the sexual abuse. Deborah had become an embarrassment and a liability.

Jurors appeared mesmerized by Marion Hussey's prior testimony. Some studied Whitey with intensity. Flemmi certainly had the motive to kill his stepdaughter, but did that diminish Whitey's motive? Perhaps they both had different reasons for wanting to get rid of Deborah. Jurors would have to consider whether Weeks had told the truth when he testified about hearing a thud and then seeing Whitey on the floor strangling Deborah. It boiled down to witness credibility.

chapter

MAGIC PAPER

He told me to destroy it or we'd all get fired.
—Desi Sideropolous, trial testimony

"THE DEFENSE CALLS DESI SIDEROPOLOUS." A COIFED, WELL-DRESSED woman in her eighties walked to the stand with a confident stride.

"Could you please introduce yourself to the members of the jury, and make sure that the microphone is close enough so they can hear you?" Carney said.

"Okay." She spoke loudly. "My name is Desi Sideropolous, and I'm secretary to the Special Agent in Charge of the FBI in Boston."

Carney smiled. "Are you over the age of fifty?"

"Yeah—Yes."

People laughed.

"And you're currently the chief assistant to the Special Agent in Charge, is that correct?

"Yes."

"Please tell the members of the jury how long you have worked for the FBI in Boston?"

"Sixty-two and a half years."

A collective murmur rose up from the gallery. Over the years, Desi had worked for eighteen Special Agents in Charge (SACs), covering six decades. One of the FBI agents later told us that she essentially ran that office. Everyone knew Desi. A real firecracker.

Desi explained that her job entailed doing whatever the big boss wanted her to do. She often took dictation and transcriptions. Some documents were considered "for eyes only," meaning personal, confidential, and available only to the SAC.

"Does that phrase have meaning to you, 'strictly eyes only'?" Carney asked.

"Yes," she said.

"Would you tell the jurors what that phrase 'strictly eyes only' means, please?"

"Personal and confidential to the SAC."

Desi had been called to describe a document the defense had uncovered dating back to November 25, 1980, pertaining to Whitey. Desi testified that SAC Larry Sarhatt dictated words to her that she would remember to this day. Carney displayed it on the monitor.

"Ms. Sideropolous, can you explain, please, for the jurors what the writing on that document says?"

She nodded. "It says, strictly eyes only per SAC Sarhatt."

"And when it says per SAC Sarhatt, what does that mean?"

"I put that on there because he gave it to me. So I put 'per SAC Sarhatt' and that was his instruction."

"This was the material that was dictated to you by Larry Sarhatt?" Carney asked.

"Yes, it was."

"And could you read that paragraph for us, please?"

Desi read the document: "Informant was asked whether he would divulge the identity of the state police source that has been furnishing information to him, and he stated that he would not because this source is not doing it for monetary benefit but as a favor to him because of his close association with him. I asked him would I normally talk to this individual during liaison of MSP rank officers of my level. Source indicated that I would not normally talk to this individual as he is not of different rank within the MSP."

"Could you please read the paragraph labeled Observations?" Carney pointed to the section on the screen.

Desi read: "I am not certain that I am convinced that informant is telling the full story of his involvement. As . . . much as we no longer need his information . . . concerning another sensitive matter—consideration should be given to closing him and not making him a target."

Carney flinched. "I'd ask you to read the bottom line one more time, please. . . ."

"Okay. Consideration should be given to closing him and not—"

"Does that word say 'not'?" Carney asked.

Desi examined the document again. "Oh, wait a second," she squinted.

"Consideration should be given to closing him and on *making* him a target," she said. She nodded a few times, seeing how she had read it wrong the first time.

We looked at each other. This was a bombshell; it had never come out before. Desi had revealed that a document existed that suggested the government either wanted to shut Whitey down as an informant, and make him a target of an investigation, or more cynically, make him a target to be killed. *A bull's-eye.*

"Did he give you instructions about where to keep the original of this document?" Carney asked.

"He told me to keep it in the safe . . . to keep it in an envelope, a sealed envelope."

"And did he tell you to put it in the safe?"

"Yes."

Desi testified that Sarhatt kept it hidden in the safe, and when Jim Ahearn, the new SAC, came in to replace him, he instructed her to show it to him. She did and Ahearn read it.

"He told me to destroy it or we'd all get fired," Desi said.

Carney paused and regarded the jury with wide eyes. "That version was destroyed by you?"

"Yes."

We looked at Carney. How on earth did he happen to get it if the original had been destroyed? Did it suddenly materialize out of thin air? Like magic?

"Were you able to re-create the document that had been destroyed?" he asked.

"Yes."

We exchanged glances again. This nice older woman and career public servant had been instructed to destroy a government document. *Unbelievable.*

Kelly began his cross-examination by asking the judge to instruct Carney to get out of his way. "If he could sit down so I could see the witness, Your Honor?" He sounded annoyed, as if he wasn't happy with Carney, the witness, and the document.

Kelly was no match for Desi. The document spoke for itself. If Whitey had been shut down, lives may have been saved. What were jurors thinking when Carney projected that "destroyed document" on the screen? How would they interpret the phrase "making him a target"? Did the FBI want Whitey set up to be killed? Did he know too much? Would the FBI stoop so low? Carney knew all it would take was one holdout for a mistrial, which would be a win for the defense.

chapter

4|1

DRUM ROLL

He's prepped. Ready to go. It's just—It's probably the biggest decision in his life so I've told him I will respect his decision.
—*Defense attorney Jay Carney, trial hearing*

THE BIG QUESTION REMAINED: WOULD WHITEY TESTIFY?

He had been feverishly scribbling notes on a legal pad since the
beginning of the trial. Would he take the stand in his own defense?
We knew he had a story to tell, and people to embarrass. Would he
give up names? Who else did he bribe? Was he seeking revenge? We
also knew the moment Whitey took the stand, Wyshak would tear into
him. Did Whitey want to protect his family from embarrassment? Did
he trust the Boston media to report what he said fairly?

It's all we talked about in the hallways, the cafeteria, on the streets,
and in the bars. We took bets. Some thought he would, others thought he
wouldn't. After all, this was Whitey's show. What did he really have to lose?

Wyshak had been pulling his hair out for at least two weeks. He
demanded to know; he felt entitled. He was slated to handle the cross-
examination, and didn't want to do all that work preparing for nothing. He also knew that a criminal defendant has the constitutional
right to remain silent.

Whitey didn't have to decide to exercise his rights until the very last
minute. He also knew the suspense was killing Wyshak. There were ru-

Whitey Bulger with NHL champion Chris Nilan, and the Stanley Cup. Nilan was Theresa Stanley's son-in-law. Stanley was Whitey's longtime girlfriend.

mors coming out of the Plymouth jail that Whitey told a guard he would testify. U.S. Marshals had heard the same thing. Was Whitey bluffing? We speculated it could be a possibility. Everyone debated—ad nauseum.

Wyshak repeatedly demanded an answer. Judge Casper sympathized with him, but had to uphold the Constitution.

Even Carney felt his pain. At a hearing outside the presence of the jury, he said: "I realize it's frustrating. I personally often would have the same frustration when I was a prosecutor, but this is how our Constitution is set up. I'm trying not to play any games; for example, saying he will testify and cause the government, you know, to prepare a cross, and then rest before he is called to the witness stand. If that happened, shame on me. I also don't want to tell the government he's made up his mind not to testify, and have him tell me, you know, I've decided to testify. He's prepped. Ready to go. It's just—It's probably the biggest decision in his life, so I've told him I will respect his decision. I'm not putting the thumb on the scale or twisting the arm behind the back."

The national media swarmed the courthouse just in case. No one wanted to miss the show. Luckily we had that parking spot in the middle of Seaport Boulevard on the median. Which Whitey would we see if he decided to take the stand? The defense had submitted pictures depicting his softer side, showing him and Catherine with a number of pets, and Whitey posing with a star athlete. One picture depicted him smiling with a priest. Carney hadn't realized that particular priest had been convicted as a pedophile. *Too late.* The press had fun with it.

After the last defense witness, it was time for the big announcement. We held our breaths. The courtroom and overflow rooms were eerily quiet. Our favorite marshals didn't have much work to do.

The wait had become excruciating.

chapter

4|2

HE BLINKED

*And my thing is, as far as I'm concerned, I didn't get a fair trial, and
this is a sham, and do what yous want with me. That's it. That's my
final word.*

          —*James Bulger, trial hearing*

THE TIME HAD COME. ALL EYES IN THAT COURTROOM ZOOMED IN ON
the defense table. The jury had not yet entered; they waited in the
conference room.

Carney rose. "Your Honor, when the jury returns, the defense will
rest."

The room fell silent for a moment, and then it filled with disappointed murmurs and sighs. "Rest" meant that the defense would not
be calling any more witnesses, including the defendant. They were
resting their case.

Judge Casper wanted to make sure the defendant understood his
rights, and asked him to rise.

Whitey stood. He had arguably been the most powerful gangster
in Boston at one time. At that point, he looked like an average senior
citizen armed with a legal pad.

Judge Casper regarded the old gangster. "Okay, Mr. Bulger," she
said. "I just want to address you directly. You understand that this is
the juncture of the case at which I ask for a decision about whether or

not you're going to testify. Mr. Carney has just represented on your behalf that you're choosing not to testify?"

Whitey nodded. "Correct."

"Is that correct?"

"That is correct," he confirmed.

"And have you done that after careful consideration, sir?" Casper asked.

"Yes, I have."

"Have you done it after consultation with your attorney?"

"Yes."

"And are you making this choice voluntarily and freely?"

"I'm making the choice *involuntarily* because I don't feel—I feel that I've been choked off from having an opportunity to give an adequate defense, and explain about my conversation and agreement with Jeremiah O'Sullivan. For my protection of his life, in return, he promised to give me immunity."

Judge Casper folded her hands. "I understand your position, sir, and certainly you're aware that I have considered that legal argument and made a ruling."

"I understand."

"I understand, sir, if you disagree with it, okay?" she said.

"I do disagree, and that's the way it is." Whitey sounded resigned, defeated. "And my thing is, as far as I'm concerned, I didn't get a fair trial, and this is a sham, and do what yous want with me. That's it. That's my final word."

"Okay, you've decided not to testify in this case?" she asked again.

"Correct."

"Thank you."

"Coward!" Pat Donahue yelled from the spectators' section, where she sat in the front row.

Judge Casper raised her gaze. "I need silence in the gallery!" After the outburst, she addressed Whitey again: "Mr. Bulger, I understand your position, but my question was a simple one about how you've decided not to testify in this case?"

"That's my answer," Whitey said.

BEHIND THE SCENES

Donald K. Stern, former United States Attorney for the District of Massachusetts told us: "This was a show trial for Whitey. He didn't take a deal because he had this perverse view that he wanted his day in court. His lawyers said that when he was arrested he knew he would die in prison. He wanted to present the image that he wasn't an informant, and that he didn't kill women. He also wanted to uncover corruption, and give the money to the victims' families. Whitey was probably trying to protect his reputation and honor amongst gangsters. I thought Whitey would take the stand, which went against my natural instincts when it comes to whether a criminal defendant will take the stand—they generally don't. But I think he witnessed the fierce cross-examination of other witnesses like Fitzpatrick and he blinked."[1]

chapter

4|3

GRAND SLAM

The evidence at this trial has convincingly proven that the defendant in this case, James Bulger, is one of the most vicious, violent, and calculating criminals ever to walk the streets of Boston.
—Assistant U.S. Attorney Fred Wyshak, closing arguments

THE TIME HAD COME. AFTER A LONG, HOT SUMMER OF TESTIMONY and boxes of evidence, lawyers would finally have the chance to argue their version of the facts to the jury.

Wyshak stood behind the podium, which faced the jury box like it had during opening statements. He opened a three-ring binder, and made eye contact with each juror.

"The evidence at this trial has convincingly proven that the defendant in this case, James Bulger, is one of the most vicious, violent, and calculating criminals ever to walk the streets of Boston."

Wyshak knew he had to rely on the hard evidence. That's what jurors would be looking at during deliberations. He had to wrap up the complex case in a way that wouldn't simplify it too much. Jurors hate to be talked down to. On the other hand, confusion breeds doubt. And doubt is something Wyshak did not want creeping into his case during the final stage of the game.

Legal strategy in delivering a closing argument is to anticipate what the other side will say. The defense spent time through cross-examination distancing their client from Flemmi. Thus, Wyshak had to illustrate how close they were.

"These two men, for twenty years, lived together day after day after day. They plotted, they schemed, they robbed, they murdered together, but they were also informants together, and if there's one thing you've heard during this trial, it's how secretive a relationship that is," he said.

"The last thing a criminal wants to be known as is an informant, and he certainly doesn't want any of his co-criminals to know about that." Wyshak gestured toward Whitey, who sat behind him and to the left. "Yet, these two men, Stephen Flemmi and James Bulger, shared that very sensitive and secret relationship together with the FBI. So now the defendant, James Bulger, wants to distance himself from Mr. Flemmi."

Wyshak wagged a finger. "He can't do it, ladies and gentlemen. This is his partner. They're two peas in a pod. They're the same. Everything you might say about Stephen Flemmi you might just as well say about James Bulger."

Wyshak also emphasized how Whitey had been partners in crime with Martorano for twenty-five years, rounding up bookmakers and planning murders. "Now the defendant wants to distance himself from John Martorano. He can't do it." He pointed out that, "It was James Bulger who chose these men to commit crimes with, to murder people with."

Next, Wyshak thanked jurors for their time, and expressed sympathy for any negative feelings they were having toward the government. He wanted to bring himself down to their level, as if he had heard about all the government corruption for the very first time that summer. In other words, he shared their pain.

"There's no doubt that the evidence that you've heard in this case is deeply disturbing. It's disturbing first and foremost because of the breadth and extent of the criminal activity in which the defendant and his coconspirators engaged. It's disturbing that it was happening while Mr. Bulger and Mr. Flemmi were informants for the FBI, and this criminal activity seemingly occurred right under the FBI's nose. It's disturbing that Mr. Bulger and Mr. Flemmi bribed FBI agents, bribed other local law enforcement, and in doing so, they enhanced their ability to commit crime and avoid prosecution for so many years.

It is disturbing that we are here in 2013, almost twenty years after the defendant was initially indicted, and we're here twenty years later because Mr. Bulger was tipped off by John Connolly, a corrupt FBI agent, and he fled Boston and remained a fugitive for all these years."

Wyshak had to acknowledge the negative parts of his case, state the obvious. It would be a bad idea to shy away from it. He had to admit that the corruption happened, but suggested that jurors shouldn't consider it an excuse for Whitey's behavior. He wanted them to focus on the crimes of Whitey Bulger.

"It doesn't matter whether or not Mr. Bulger was an FBI informant when he put a gun to the head of Arthur Barrett and pulled the trigger. Whether he's an FBI informant or not, he's guilty of murder. This trial is not whether or not John Morris and John Connolly were corrupt FBI agents. It's not about that. It's not about whether or not Gerry Montanari did a good job handling Brian Halloran. It's not about whether or not the FBI office in Boston was a mess. It's not a referendum on whether or not Kevin Weeks and John Martorano should be spending the rest of their lives in jail, just like Mr. Flemmi." Wyshak shook his head and pointed back toward Whitey. "It's about whether or not the defendant is guilty of the crimes charged in the indictment."

Well said. We noticed a juror nodding in the front row. Wyshak continued by shining the spotlight on the unique relationship between Special Agent Connolly and Whitey.

"Essentially . . . there are four people dead because of the relationship between John Connolly and James Bulger. That's why you heard about that relationship. That relationship also enhanced Mr. Bulger's ability to commit crime and avoid prosecution." Wyshak raised his voice and slowed the delivery. "The defense would have you think that the entire Department of Justice, the U.S. Attorney's Office, the Strike Force, is corrupt. Not so, ladies and gentlemen. Use your common sense. You know, there's an old saying, a few bad apples spoil the barrel."

Wyshak had gained an advantage when Carney essentially admitted Whitey's guilt on some of the charges during opening statements. He took the opportunity to pound away on that low-hanging fruit.

"He told you that his client, James Bulger, was involved in illegal gambling, loan sharking, drug dealing, extortion. We don't dispute that, we agree with that. The evidence, again, has proven it. He told you that

James Bulger made millions of dollars from engaging in this criminal activity. Again, we agree. The evidence has shown that as well. He told you, Mr. Carney, in his opening, that James Bulger paid money to other members of law enforcement other than John Connolly. And again, there's no dispute about that."

Wyshak pulled out his favorite chart for the Winter Hill Gang, circa 1975, and gave the jurors another history lesson.

"James Bulger cares more about his reputation as an FBI informant than as a murderous thug." Wyshak delivered the line with disdain. He also had to deal with another issue that the defense had been harping on: the credibility of his star witnesses.

"You may not like some of these witnesses, but it's about whether or not you *believe them*. John Martorano and Kevin Weeks are not on trial. Don't forget it's James Bulger on trial here today." He twisted and pointed at Whitey again.

"Does John Martorano deserve to spend the rest of his life in prison?" Wyshak raised his arms and wiggled his hands. "Absolutely. Absolutely. No question about that. Did the government have the evidence to put him there? Absolutely not. He would have been entitled to a trial, just like this one that you're sitting in here, and the government would have had to have proven that he engaged in those murders, and there was no evidence, none of those murders had ever been solved, there was no evidence to convict him of any of those murders," he said.

"The relationship between John Connolly, James Bulger, and Stephen Flemmi was a cancer eating away at law enforcement in Boston. Bodies had piled up, South Boston had been flooded with drugs, and the last insult of all was Mr. Bulger had been allowed to escape because he had been tipped off by a corrupt FBI agent."

Several more jurors nodded as they listened. That was a good sign for the prosecution.

Wyshak explained that they had met their burden of proof for each count in the indictment against Whitey. He explained the tricky parts of the law that Judge Casper would review in her charge to the jury. "The law provides that you are as guilty as the principal if you aided and abetted the commission of a crime . . . Aiding and abetting is the guy who's maybe sitting outside the bank in the getaway car." Wyshak paused and flipped a page in his notebook. He provided the jury with several examples. "If you're a member of a conspiracy, you are liable for all the acts of every other member of the conspiracy that is reasonably foreseeable." This concept was essential for jurors to grasp regarding Whitey's liability for some of the earlier murders where he wasn't the shooter, but drove one of the backup cars.

Wyshak explained that "RICO is racketeering." Further, "the case against Mr. Bulger is the type of case that the RICO statute was designed to address when it was passed, an organized crime group composed of many individuals engaged in different types of criminal activities."

Wyshak downplayed the inconsistencies in testimony: Remember, again, that we are here in 2013 because that man ran away." He pointed at Whitey. "So we're here twenty years later. . . . I suggest to you that the amount of inconsistencies that may exist in some of their testimony is de minimis compared to what's important in this case. Again, you need to use your common sense. Let's say we all went to a Red Sox game. There's thirty thousand other people in the stands, and Dustin Pedroia— it's the bottom of the ninth, the Red Sox are losing—Dustin Pedroia hits a grand slam home run, it's a walk-off home run and the Red Sox win the game." Wyshak smiled; it was Sox season, and they would win the World Series that year.

"Twenty years later, you're probably still going to remember that moment, because that's what's important. Are you going to remember who was on first, who was on second, who was on third, who was pitching, whether the ball went over the Green Monster or over the center field wall? That's how you have to bring your common sense to evaluating the evidence in this case. Do the witnesses remember the key points, what's important?"

At least half the jurors nodded. It was a simple, yet effective comparison.

"I suggest to you that regarding any of the significant information in evidence in this case, such as who shot who, why did it happen, who extorted who, who shook down who, there is no equivocation or inconsistency in any of the testimony that's before you."

Wyshak had anticipated everything the defense would hammer away on: sweetheart deals, witness credibility, and inconsistent statements. With that out of the way, Wyshak would knock off murder by the

316 • WHITEY ON TRIAL

numbers. He spent significant time reviewing evidence for the nineteen predicate acts of murder contained within racketeering Count Two.

The room was silent but for the random cough. Jurors paid close attention as he detailed more violent murders and extortions. Wyshak tore into the meat of his case, sparing none of the gruesome details. We could sense his passion, his longing for justice for the victims. He went through murders by number to correspond with the indictment. He highlighted details that he hoped would shock the conscience of jurors as they deliberated.

Wyshak paused and sipped his water to allow the images of violence to seep in. He described hit after hit starting with the hunt for Indian Al Notorangeli. He made us envision the violence: "Mr. Bulger is driving this time. . . . John Martorano is in the car with Howie Winter . . . they pull up alongside Mr. O'Brien's car and blow it apart with automatic-weapons fire." The brazen machine gun attacks: "James Bulger is in the backup car, and they find Mr. Plummer's car driving up Commercial Street. They pull up alongside of it again and let loose with a blast of automatic-weapons fire. . . ."

Wyshak touched on the McGonagle murder: "Paul McGonagle was one of the bodies that were recovered at Tenean Beach in 2000. . . . What did Bulger tell Flemmi? He told Flemmi that he lured McGonagle into the car with some counterfeit bills, again another scam, and when Mr. McGonagle got in the car, Mr. Bulger shot him . . . Mr. Bulger may as well have thrown his license into the hole when Mr. McGonagle's body was later recovered, because this is not a body on the street where it's found by the police and people can say, well, you know, anybody could have killed him. This is a body that's buried. It's secret."

Wyshak paused and made eye contact with each juror. "What else does Mr. Bulger go and do in his twisted way? He goes to young Paul McGonagle—and you heard young Paul McGonagle testify at this trial. And he tells young Paul McGonagle, as Paul described it, Bulger pulled up in his blue Malibu with his aviator glasses on, got out and told young Paul McGonagle, 'We got the guy who killed your father.'" He sighed.

"This is just the twisted mentality that we're dealing with in this case, but, again, that's another piece of independent evidence that links Mr. Bulger to this crime. He's now going to a family member, and you'll see this is not the first time he does it, and gives them a little zinger."

Wyshak made Whitey sound despicable. He continued on with the murder of Eddie Connors, and mentioned Whitey making the machine gun noise on the jailhouse tape.

He detailed the murders of Tommy King, Buddy Leonard, and Richard Castucci, commenting about "the cunning and arrogance of James Bulger."

He paused, glanced into the gallery at Steve Davis sitting in the front row, and launched into the murder of Debra (Debbie) Davis.

"Who is Debbie Davis?" Wyshak asked. "You heard she was Stephen Flemmi's girlfriend." He emphasized Whitey's motive to kill her: "Davis . . . doesn't like the fact that Mr. Flemmi keeps getting called away night after night to meet with Mr. Bulger, and finally Mr. Flemmi says, 'Hey, look, you know, we've got a connection in the FBI. It's John Connolly. I have to go to these meetings. I don't have a choice.'"

Overall, Davis knew too much and had to go. Whitey lobbied for her murder and strangled her. Steve Davis sat with his arms crossed, looking angry. He wanted justice for his sister.

"Now, again, this is where you need to focus," Wyshak said. "You don't have to decide who strangled Debbie Davis. That's been an issue that's been contested in this case. What you need to decide is whether Mr. Bulger has any criminal liability for this murder. He doesn't have to have been the one who strangled her to be criminally liable. If he aids and abets or is a coconspirator in that murder, he's as criminally liable as if he's the one who put the hands around her neck and strangled the life out of her."

Wyshak had to drive the coconspirator theory home for the Davis murder. The defense would argue that Flemmi had the motive of a jealous lover. We anticipated a battle in the deliberation room.

"Now, what do you know about James Bulger? You do know that he's the one who strangled Deborah Hussey to death, and you know that because it's not only Mr. Flemmi who's there, but it's also Kevin Weeks. So in determining who has the capacity to strangle a young woman like that, in deciding who is the perpetrator of the Davis murder, consider the evidence on Hussey. Consider what Mr. Flemmi said: He didn't have it in him."

The jury looked pensive. The killing of women was hard to stomach.

Wyshak went through the World Jai Alai murders: Wheeler, Halloran, Donahue, and Callahan. He made sure to make eye contact with the Donahue family.

He looked at the Barrett family as he once again highlighted the torture, murder, and basement burial of Bucky Barrett. Wyshak connected the dots: "Mr. Barrett's body was found in the same grave as John McIntyre and Deborah Hussey, and, again, that's another piece of forensic evidence that tells you that the person who committed that murder is the same person who committed the murders of Deborah Hussey and John McIntyre, to be found in an unmarked grave with two other bodies. They're not there by coincidence."

Wyshak highlighted Whitey's brutal extortions of drug dealers, bookmakers, and business people, including the gun thrust into Buccheri's mouth and the machine gun in Solimando's groin.

Wyshak showed jurors the weapons: The "tools of the trade," as he called them. "Like a carpenter has a hammer and nails, Mr. Bulger has guns and knives."

He apologized for taking over three hours, and looked up from his three-ring binder. Some jurors had glazed looks in their eyes, while others appeared alert.

"Finally, ladies and gentlemen, the evidence in this case is overwhelming." Wyshak slowed his delivery. "The government has proven beyond a reasonable doubt that the defendant was one of the leaders of the most ruthless criminal organizations ever in Boston. It wreaked havoc on this city for decades. The defendant is personally responsible for much of the criminal activity committed by this group, including murder, extortion, money laundering, firearms offenses, and drug trafficking. In his capacity as the leader, he is legally responsible for it all.

"He's either a principal aider and abettor or a coconspirator. I submit to you that after you've reviewed all the evidence in this case and deliberated, there's only one verdict that you can truly return, and that is a verdict of guilty on each and every count of the indictment."

Wyshak looked at each juror. "Thank you."

Most jurors studied Whitey. Wyshak had nailed his closing, and they appeared ready to convict.

4|4

DAVID VERSUS GOLIATH

They want the accolades, they want the glory, and they're willing to make deals. They're willing to protect criminals, murderers because of pride, because when law enforcement puts pride in the equation and self-importance in the equation, something about it gets distorted, something gets perverted, and something gets corrupt.
—*Defense attorney Hank Brennan, closing argument*

BRENNAN CAME OUT OF THE GATE SWINGING AS WE KNEW HE WOULD. He was the underdog. He faced an uphill battle trying to convince this jury that Whitey was anything but a cold-hearted monster and killer. The clearest path to that objective: attack the government, expose the ugly underbelly.

"About an hour ago, Mr. Wyshak was telling you about the fact that some of the most dangerous murderers in the history of Boston were walking the streets. John Martorano admitted to killing over twenty people, shooting most of them in the back of the head. Kevin Weeks, Pat Nee, James Martorano. He talked about how vicious and violent they were on the streets of Boston. And you have to sit there and ask yourself: 'Why are they still walking the streets? If they're so vicious and violent and our government knows about it, why are they out there right now?'"

Brennan knew how to raise questions about the role of the federal government as protectors of its citizens: "What have they done? Have they taken these men off the streets?" He gazed at the jury. "Is this something we just don't know as citizens? Is there something we're not entitled to know about? Because when you hear this as a citizen is there something in your stomach that just resonates, saying there's got to be more . . . there's victim after victim and family after family that have dealt with death and pain and suffering at these men's hands. Why didn't our government do anything about it?"

Brennan caused jurors to engage in higher thinking: "When you think about justice, ladies and gentlemen, there has to be some fundamental fairness for everybody, and justice means that if somebody is accountable, if somebody is responsible, for what they did, there has to be an accounting that everybody who was responsible is held responsible for what they did. There has to be an accounting. . . . if there's an accounting, justice, the truth, the truth applies equally to everybody."

Brennan took jurors back to the 1960s when Flemmi was a top echelon informant, and being protected during the time when the government's priority was to wage war on the Mafia. "And you know what happens when you do something at all costs? People start to think that the ends justify the means."

Brennan had a knack for making people think about the past and future, the bigger picture. "These are the types of relationships that they had, that they accepted, but none of us knew that. None of you knew that. But that's what they did. And then Stephen Flemmi blows up a lawyer. Blows off his leg, kills his boss, "Wimpy" Bennett. He's charged with murder, he's charged with attempted murder of a lawyer. If they put him in jail and they prosecute him, guess what happens? The next twenty years, those people don't die. . . . When we near the late 1970s, we know the temperament of the Department of Justice. We know the Strike Force, headed by Jeremiah O'Sullivan. . . . They want everybody to look at Boston and say, 'This is the prototype. These guys are the best at what they do.' They want the accolades, they want the glory, and they're willing to make deals. They're willing to protect criminals, murderers, because of pride, because when law enforcement puts pride in the equation and self-importance in the equation, something about it gets distorted, something gets perverted, and something gets corrupt. . . . You'll notice a pattern, a routine . . . it compels you to the conclusion that this is the way they operated." Brennan pointed to all the state police investigations that were compromised by the FBI.

Brennan raised more questions about why certain criminals get passes from the federal government. "You heard the government give you their version of what happened, and what they told you is that John Martorano shot Mr. Milano with Howie Winter. They both shot him and killed him. Howie Winter and John Martorano shot and killed Mr. Plummer. They shot and killed Mr. O'Toole. They shot and killed so many of these men, Howie Winter and John Martorano, and John Martorano they send back on the street? What about Howie Winter? Was there ever a grand jury? Was there ever an indictment? Why?

"Remember I asked John Morris, 'Do the ends justify the means?' And remember what he told me? 'Not always. Not always.'"

Brennan narrowed his eyes. "Never, never do the ends justify the means when we're talking about law enforcement. Never. But that's not the way they think. It's not the way they thought. It's not how they operated."

We knew Brennan boiled inside. He didn't like what his government had done. He took it personally. Brennan wanted to convey to the jury that this kind of behavior is not okay, it's reprehensible.

Brennan commented on the absurd secret alliances the government had with gangsters. "They didn't think about the suffering and the carnage. They were gangsters killing gangsters, they wanted their crown jewel. And as this led through the '60s and the '70s, what did they do? They [the government] engaged in partnerships with known criminals. They engaged in partnerships with organized crime figures, murderers. They did it intentionally. They did it knowingly. They engaged in relationships so they could achieve their objective at whatever cost it took. That's what our government did."

The jury appeared stone-faced and focused. Brennan had them thinking.

"Stephen Flemmi is just one, but it's a shining example. Look at Stephen Flemmi's relationship with the federal government in the 1960s. Informant, top echelon informant, Special Agent Rico, Special Agent Condon, look what they did. He was at war with other criminals. He was at war with other gangsters, and when he needed help, all he needed to do was draw on his friends, the federal government. . . . You want to murder him, I'll give you the bus stop he's going to be at. They're in a partnership with him. And when they needed his help, they needed some information, they needed a gun, they needed their car fixed, they'd call on their friend."

Brennan pointed out that many were responsible for the federal corruption. "So this prosecutor's office has spent two months in front of you trying to convince you that everything that happened is the result of John Connolly, a rogue agent. . . . Is it a rogue agent, one person, or is it responsibility, is it that part of the ledger where the federal government has to line up and recognize their responsibility?" He gazed at the government's table with disdain.

"You know, it could be me just sitting up here being a conspiracy theorist saying, the federal government. But let's look at the second witness they called in this case, retired Colonel Foley. Do you remember him? It was a long time ago. What did he say? Did he say it was a rogue agent? Did he say it was John Connolly? Did he ascribe to what this prosecution has been trying to sell you for two months, or did he recognize maybe it was a little more than a rogue agent, maybe the federal government has some responsibility."

Brennan was smart to remind jurors about Foley, who had criticized the FBI.

"This continues on throughout the 1980s. One example that just rings with poignancy and sadness is that of Mr. Donahue and Mr. Halloran. Federal agents knew that Mr. Halloran was in danger. They knew. They went to Mr. Fitzpatrick, who went to Jeremiah O'Sullivan, but they did nothing to protect him; whether he was a criminal, he was alleged to be a murderer, he was a citizen. What did they do to protect him? He went to the U.S. Attorney's Office, he went to William Weld. They shunned him, and two days later, Mr. Halloran and Mr. Donahue were dead." Brennan turned and made eye contact with the Donahue family.

"John Morris gets information that they need to look into it. He gives it to John Connolly to look into.

"Washington comes in every year to do a review of what's going on in Boston. Did you ever hear that there was one comment from Washington that something was awry, that there was an intervention needed? Did you hear one comment from Washington that there was a responsibility? Oh, and Mr. Fitzpatrick called Washington, what did they tell him? *Shut up. . . .* It's a very strict structure, you don't circumvent it. What happens when you circumvent it? They'll crush you. You saw what they did to Mr. Fitzpatrick. Twenty-two years, he leaves three years before his pension. They bully him, they berate him, *they crush him.* That's what happens if you're not with them, you're either with them or you're against them." Brennan emphasized "crush" and made a fist.

"When you think about the government's evidence in this case, you need to be certain that you got objective evidence. Whether it helps or hurts the government's case, the obligation is that it needs to be objective, honest. Do you feel like you got honest evidence in this case? I stood up there for days and hours asking question after question, and I don't think most of them were trick questions. I was trying to ask simple questions, and I couldn't get an answer. Witness after witness. It was a game.

"Talk about partners. Every time they want to blame something on James Bulger to clean the slate, whether there's evidence or not, any time they want to blame something on him, there's a problem with the evidence, well, he's Stephen Flemmi's partner. Well, John Morris was John Connolly's partner. So by that rationale, why is he getting immunity? Why is he getting a pension? Why is he walking in through the front door and being walked out by Mr. Marra through the same front door when he's done?"

Brennan clasped his hands and made eye contact with every juror. "Did you get honesty? Did you get integrity? Did you get the truth?"

He continued, "There comes a time, and it's rare, but there comes a time when we can make a difference. Each and every one of you is our government. It's like every day we have David versus Goliath. The government does something we don't like, they're not accountable, we have to push through the next day. Well, you know what, each and every one of you is Goliath because you're our government and you have a voice. When you look at this case and the way the government presented it, you can let them know, 'This isn't your government, this is my government, this is our government and there's going to be accountability, but there has to be accountability for each and every person, and this government is equally accountable.' You tell them that."

Brennan empowered the jury by telling them they had a voice. If they didn't like what they heard throughout the trial, their verdict was their voice. They could make a powerful statement. They knew they held the national spotlight. When Brennan took his seat, the courtroom was eerily quiet.

After a ten-minute break, Carney assumed the podium for the rest of the argument. "I'm usually nervous doing any closing argument," he said, "but I have to be honest, today I'm particularly nervous, not because it's a big case or a lot of people are watching, but for the first time in my thirty-five years as a lawyer, my mother is in court watching me, and I'm going to try to not make that affect me too much."

Most jurors smiled. That was also his way of endearing himself, and connecting with the jury on a personal level.

"Now, the prosecutor, Mr. Wyshak, talked about the fact that there are three witnesses to the murders: Martorano, Weeks, Flemmi. . . . They were described as despicable, evil, terrifying, and that you probably won't like them. . . . Two of these three who the government says should be serving life sentences, they walked in the front door of this courthouse rather than being locked up where they should be." He pointed to the courtroom doors.

"Well, that skips what I submit to you is the critical issue in this case, whether you can believe Martorano, Weeks, and Flemmi beyond a reasonable doubt.

"What is really going on here? And you probably don't hear lawyers talking this bluntly, but this, I submit to you, is what goes on: the government is buying the testimony of these witnesses. Sounds pretty awful to put it that way, doesn't it?

"The currency is the power of the government to keep someone locked up in a cell surrounded by four concrete walls, topped by barbed wire. . . .

"There's a higher price that can be paid, which is an offer of immunity . . . from prosecution. That's a higher price to pay."

Wyshak jumped up. "Objection!"

"Overruled."

"Unbelievable." Carney shook his head and made eye contact with jurors. "Even getting speaking objections during my closing argument."

Carney reminded jurors of Martorano's reasons for cooperating: "'When I learned that Jim Bulger was an informant, it broke my heart.'" He placed a hand on his chest. "I think if you did a CAT scan, you'd have trouble finding a heart in this guy. . . . Do you think that he decided to become a government witness because he knew the price would be high enough that he could get out, or was it really because he had a broken heart?"

Carney continued. "What else do you know about Kevin Weeks? Most of all, what he actually brags about is what a great liar he is. . . . Look, when I catch him in a lie: 'I've lied all my life. I'm a criminal.'"

Whitey wanted the world to know that he didn't kill the two women. Carney pinned the blame on Flemmi for the Hussey murder: "He killed his stepdaughter so she wouldn't say what he had been doing to her. . . . Stephen Flemmi was the one with the motive, the ability, and the disgusting propensity. . . ."

Carney also focused on Flemmi's motive to murder Debbie Davis, his prized trophy, due to jealousy. "She went to Mexico on vacation and met somebody and liked the guy and decided she wanted to start dating him." He reminded jurors that Martorano claimed Flemmi admitted to strangling her accidentally.

Carney made his final plea: "Members of the jury, I ask you to find strength in the oath that you took. When you took that oath, you became our country. You have the power to stand up to governmental abuse, to return a verdict based on the strength of your oath, that when the government brings a case against somebody and relies primarily on the testimony of three people, the likes of which are Martorano, Weeks, and Flemmi, and paid them for their testimony a price that is obscene, you can have the strength and power and come back and say, 'No, we don't find that evidence to be proof beyond a reasonable doubt.' You can say it with courage that the prosecutors have not met their burden of proof, and then you will embody our constitutional protections."

Wyshak sprang from his seat for rebuttal, the last word: "Let's get back to reality here. As I suggested during my initial summation, the defense in this case wants you to take your eye off the ball."

He gestured toward the defense table. "Although Mr. Carney can't bring himself at the end of his summation to say 'Find my client not guilty,' he suggests that you should essentially violate your oath as jurors here and issue some referendum on government misconduct."

Wyshak frowned and cocked his head. "They're asking you to render some verdict that doesn't comply with the evidence but sends some message about how the big, bad government needs to learn a lesson from this case. Well, I suggest to you that that will be a violation of your oath, and that's exactly what those two speeches that we just heard are all about."

Wyshak reemphasized the importance of examining all the documents and corroborating witness testimony: "So, again, you know, please, go back and take a look at the evidence in this case. Take a look at your notes." He reminded jurors the case was about Whitey Bulger and his murderous reign of terror. The government was not on trial.

4|5

THE LAW

Members of the jury, it is now time for the case to be submitted to you.

—Judge Denise Casper, at the end of her charge

BOSTON'S INFAMOUS MOB TRIAL DREW THAT MUCH CLOSER TO A CON-clusion when Wyshak sat down. Judge Casper turned toward the jury, and instructed them on the law. The lawyers looked interested, but we had the feeling they were barely paying attention. They already knew what the long-winded instructions entailed; they had argued over them. Still, jurors paid attention to everything, including facial expressions, and lawyers couldn't appear bored or disinterested in the judge's charge. The acting had to continue.

Judge Casper reminded jurors of the government's steep burden of proof; every element of the criminal charges had to be proven beyond a reasonable doubt. She instructed them not to infer guilt by Whitey's decision not to testify in his own defense. Several jurors glanced at Whitey. Would they hold it against him?

Judge Casper spent a long time explaining the federal racketeering law (RICO). She specified that jurors must decide beyond a reasonable doubt that at least two predicate criminal acts occurred within a ten-year period to establish a pattern of racketeering. Jurors could choose from crimes of extortion, drug dealing, money laundering, and/or murder. Their decision had to be unanimous on each.

Count Two, entitled "Racketeering Substantive Offence," contained thirty-three predicate acts, nineteen of which were murders. For each act of murder, Judge Casper explained the elements as follows:

1. The defendant caused the death of the victim.
2. The defendant intended to kill the victim, that is, the defendant consciously and purposefully intended to cause the victim's death.
3. The defendant committed the killing with deliberate premeditation, that is, he decided to kill after a period of reflection.

Or, if the defendant did not himself perform the act that caused the victim's death, the defendant knowingly participated in the commission of the murder and did so with the intent to commit the crime; or aided in the commission of the crime or was accessory thereto before the fact by counseling, hiring, or otherwise procuring such felony to be committed.

Prosecutors presented jurors with the option of conspiracy to commit murder and/or murder for several victims where the evidence against Whitey was not as strong. This applied to members of the Notorangeli group, James Sousa, Thomas King, Roger Wheeler, and John Callahan.

Judge Casper explained that the elements of conspiracy were:

1. That the defendant joined in an agreement or plan with one or more other persons.
2. That the purpose of the agreement was to commit murder.
3. That the defendant joined the conspiracy knowing of the unlawful plan and intending to help carry it out.

Jurors would likely use the seven-page verdict slip as a guide, and decide whether each act had been "proved" or "not proved" by the prosecution.

At 10:57 A.M. on Tuesday, August 6, 2013, Judge Casper said, "Members of the jury, it is now time for the case to be submitted to you." They

UNITED STATES DISTRICT COURT
DISTRICT OF MASSACHUSETTS

_____
)
UNITED STATES   )
)
        v.   )   Crim. Action No. 99-10371-DJC
)
JAMES J. BULGER   )
)
_____)

WE, THE JURY, FIND the defendant JAMES J. BULGER,

As to COUNT ONE (Racketeering Conspiracy)

_____ Guilty   _____ Not Guilty

As to COUNT TWO (Racketeering Substantive Offense)

_____ Guilty   _____ Not Guilty

If you found JAMES J. BULGER guilty as to Count 2, please indicate below which alleged Racketeering Acts you unanimously find that the government has proven beyond a reasonable doubt:

RACKETEERING ACT NO. 1:
Conspiracy to Murder Members of the Notorangeli Group

___ Proved   ___ Not Proved

RACKETEERING ACT NO. 2:
Murder of Michael Milano

___ Proved   ___ Not Proved

RACKETEERING ACT NO. 3:
Murder of Al Plummer

___ Proved   ___ Not Proved

RACKETEERING ACT NO. 11:
Murder of Francis "Buddy" Leonard

___ Proved   ___ Not Proved

RACKETEERING ACT NO. 12:
Murder of Richard Castucci

___ Proved   ___ Not Proved

RACKETEERING ACT NO. 13A:
Conspiracy to Murder Roger Wheeler

___ Proved   ___ Not Proved

RACKETEERING ACT NO. 13B:
Murder of Roger Wheeler

___ Proved   ___ Not Proved

RACKETEERING ACT NO. 14:
Murder of Debra Davis

___ Proved   ___ Not Proved

RACKETEERING ACT NO. 15:
Murder of Brian Halloran

___ Proved   ___ Not Proved

RACKETEERING ACT NO. 16:
Murder of Michael Donahue

___ Proved   ___ Not Proved

RACKETEERING ACT NO. 17A:
Conspiracy to Murder John Callahan

___ Proved   ___ Not Proved

RACKETEERING ACT NO. 17B:
Murder of John Callahan

___ Proved   ___ Not Proved

RACKETEERING ACT NO. 4:
Murder of William O'Brien

___ Proved   ___ Not Proved

RACKETEERING ACT NO. 5:
Murder of James O'Toole

___ Proved   ___ Not Proved

RACKETEERING ACT NO. 6:
Murder of Al Notorangeli

___ Proved   ___ Not Proved

RACKETEERING ACT NO. 7A:
Conspiracy to Murder James Sousa

___ Proved   ___ Not Proved

RACKETEERING ACT NO. 7B:
Murder of James Sousa

___ Proved   ___ Not Proved

RACKETEERING ACT NO. 8:
Murder of Paul McGonagle

___ Proved   ___ Not Proved

RACKETEERING ACT NO. 9:
Murder of Edward Connors

___ Proved   ___ Not Proved

RACKETEERING ACT NO. 10A:
Conspiracy to Murder Thomas King

___ Proved   ___ Not Proved

RACKETEERING ACT NO. 10B:
Murder of Thomas King

___ Proved   ___ Not Proved

RACKETEERING ACT NO. 27:
Extortion of Richard Bucheri

___ Proved   ___ Not Proved

RACKETEERING ACT NO. 28:
Extortion of Raymond Slinger

___ Proved   ___ Not Proved

RACKETEERING ACT NO. 29:
Narcotics Distribution Conspiracy

___ Proved   ___ Not Proved

RACKETEERING ACT NO. 30:
(Concealment) Money Laundering Conspiracy

___ Proved   ___ Not Proved

RACKETEERING ACT NO. 31:
(Concealment) Money Laundering
(Sale of 295 Old Colony Ave., South Boston, Massachusetts)

___ Proved   ___ Not Proved

RACKETEERING ACT NO. 32(A):
(Concealment) Money Laundering
(Sale of 295 Old Colony Ave., South Boston, Massachusetts)

___ Proved   ___ Not Proved

RACKETEERING ACTS NO. 32(B) – 32(PPP):
(Concealment) Money Laundering (Mortgage Payments)

___ Proved   ___ Not Proved

RACKETEERING ACT NO. 33:
(Concealment or Promotion) Money Laundering (Transfer of $10,000 to John Martorano)

___ Proved   ___ Not Proved

THIS PAGE AND THE NEXT PAGE: This document is a copy of the verdict slip that jurors took into the deliberation room.

As to COUNT THREE (Extortion Conspiracy: Rent)

_____ Guilty   _____ Not Guilty

As to COUNT FOUR (Extortion of Kevin Hayes)

_____ Guilty   _____ Not Guilty

As to COUNT FIVE (Concealment Money Laundering Conspiracy)

_____ Guilty   _____ Not Guilty

As to COUNTS SIX through TWENTY-SIX
(Concealment Money Laundering (Mortgage Payments))

Count 6	_____ Guilty	_____ Not Guilty
Count 7	_____ Guilty	_____ Not Guilty
Count 8	_____ Guilty	_____ Not Guilty
Count 9	_____ Guilty	_____ Not Guilty
Count 10	_____ Guilty	_____ Not Guilty
Count 11	_____ Guilty	_____ Not Guilty
Count 12	_____ Guilty	_____ Not Guilty
Count 13	_____ Guilty	_____ Not Guilty
Count 14	_____ Guilty	_____ Not Guilty
Count 15	_____ Guilty	_____ Not Guilty
Count 16	_____ Guilty	_____ Not Guilty
Count 17	_____ Guilty	_____ Not Guilty
Count 18	_____ Guilty	_____ Not Guilty
Count 19	_____ Guilty	_____ Not Guilty
Count 20	_____ Guilty	_____ Not Guilty
Count 21	_____ Guilty	_____ Not Guilty
Count 22	_____ Guilty	_____ Not Guilty
Count 23	_____ Guilty	_____ Not Guilty
Count 24	_____ Guilty	_____ Not Guilty
Count 25	_____ Guilty	_____ Not Guilty
Count 26	_____ Guilty	_____ Not Guilty

As to COUNT TWENTY-SEVEN
(Concealment or Promotion Money Laundering (Transfer of $10,000 to John Martorano))

_____ Guilty   _____ Not Guilty

6

As to COUNT THIRTY-NINE (Possession of Firearms in Furtherance of Violent Crime)

_____ Guilty   _____ Not Guilty

As to COUNT FORTY (Possession of Machineguns in Furtherance of Violent Crime)

_____ Guilty   _____ Not Guilty

As to COUNT FORTY-TWO (Possession of Unregistered Machineguns)

_____ Guilty   _____ Not Guilty

As to COUNT FORTY-FIVE (Transfer and Possession of Machineguns)

_____ Guilty   _____ Not Guilty

As to COUNT FORTY-EIGHT (Possession of Firearms with Obliterated Serial Numbers)

_____ Guilty   _____ Not Guilty

_____   _____
FOREPERSON'S SIGNATURE   DATE

7

had their work cut out for them. There were so many victims and criminal elements to think about, and piles of evidence to go through. They had listened to testimony from seventy-two witnesses throughout two months of trial.

4|6

BEHIND CLOSED DOORS

When you get twelve people together, they don't all agree, and some people are easily swayed . . . sometimes it depends on where they're sitting around the table.
—Juror Gusina Tremblay

THE JURY OF EIGHT MEN AND FOUR WOMEN WALKED OUT A BACK DOOR in the courtroom, and vanished into the deliberation room with a copy of the verdict slip. Twelve divergent personalities had to decipher the complex racketeering case and come up with a unanimous verdict.

The prosecution team headed up to their offices. Carney and Brennan wandered the halls and sat on benches. They had to remain close by in case the jury had a question. We all waited. No one wanted to leave and miss something, especially the verdict. We played cards with the victims' relatives, continuously snacked, and later in the afternoon, most of us meandered across the street for drinks at the Barking Crab. We wondered what they were talking about? How long will it take?

In the meantime, the alternate jurors had to wait in a separate room. They were not allowed to discuss the case. If a deliberating juror became ill or had a death in the family, he or she would be dismissed, and then an alternate would be called in. The deliberation process would have to start all over again. As the jury deliberated,

Whitey waited too, but in a cell. Marshals transported him to the courthouse every morning as usual.

Juror Gusina Tremblay noticed the disappointed faces on the alternates. Some had listened diligently, and filled several notebooks. "I can't imagine sitting through the trial, and taking all that time, to end up as an alternate. We felt sorry for them."[1]

On that first day, Judge Casper dismissed the jury around four thirty in the afternoon. They looked exhausted . . . no one smiled.

On Wednesday morning, the jury went back to work. They asked for eleven copies of the judge's instructions, the law on conspiracy, clarification about the statute of limitations for murder, and whether their verdicts had to be unanimous on each predicate act. Casper instructed them that they didn't have to concern themselves with the statute of limitations. If that had been an issue, those counts would have been dismissed early on.

Juror Gusina Tremblay told us, "When you get twelve people together, they don't all agree, and some people are easily swayed . . . sometimes it depends on where they're sitting around the table. There were key players and those who simply bowed their heads."[2]

In the afternoon, Judge Casper called the lawyers into the courtroom for a secret sidebar conference. It dragged on and on; we strained to hear what they were discussing. They even pulled out law books. U.S. Attorney Carmen Ortiz joined in, which was a first. We wondered what was going on? They were so secretive. They never made it public, which gave us the impression there was a problem with one of the jurors.

Juror Gusina Tremblay told us later that they were having a problem with one juror in particular. The judge told them they'd have to do their best to work together. Emotions were raw.[3]

After the hours passed, we sat outside on the benches and watched the boats sail by. We told stories. People charged phones all over the place. We gossiped. We learned that Carney had painted his toenails purple—he took off his shoes and showed us.

Two FBI agents sat in the back, guarding a large black bag containing over eight hundred thousand dollars in cash. We tried to trick them and take it as a joke. *Didn't work.* We were all getting punchy . . . and anxious.

We had a big pool going on, with bets on when they'd come back with a verdict. Someone won, but we can't say who.

When the jury had questions, everyone rushed up to court, including Whitey. The jury filed in, and Judge Casper answered their questions after consulting with the lawyers.

When Friday rolled around, day forty-six, we were convinced they'd render a decision before the weekend. Nothing happened. No word, not even a question. The wait had become excruciating.

Finally on Monday, day five of deliberations, the news broke. Many of us will always remember where we were when we heard. We were sitting at one of the tables in the cafeteria with Pat Donahue.

"Verdict! Verdict! Verdict!" someone yelled from the balcony on the fifth floor. We left our food there and bolted for the elevators. Our friends at the Barking Crab who had just ordered another round left full drinks behind. Word of the verdict traveled throughout the streets of Boston. The media descended; helicopters hovered overhead in no time.

chapter

4|7

THE JURY SPEAKS

The trial was a victory for dedicated law enforcement and prosecutors, who worked for years to bring Whitey to justice.
—*Former U.S. Attorney Donald Stern*

THE JURORS ENTERED THE PACKED COURTROOM ONE BY ONE. MOST did not make eye contact with Whitey, who sat at the defense table with his lawyers. This was it.

"We have a verdict, ladies and gentleman," Judge Casper announced. The twelve jurors stood in the jury box, while the six alternates remained seated. The jury foreman had a look of concentration as he presented Lisa Hourihan, the clerk, with their seven-page verdict slip. She handed it to Judge Casper, who reviewed it.

Silence descended upon the courtroom. The process felt like it took hours, not minutes. We felt the tension as Hourihan stood to announce the verdict. She seemed to be moving in slow motion.

"Count One, racketeering conspiracy: guilty.

"Count Two, racketeering substantive offense: guilty."

Hourihan paused, and moved on to the thirty-three predicate acts contained within Count Two. The jury had found Whitey guilty on at least two acts within a ten-year period. Now we would find out exactly which ones were "proved." This was what we were all waiting for, since nineteen of those acts consisted of murders. Victims' families had been waiting decades for this moment.

Hourihan read: "Conspiracy to murder members of the Notorangeli group: not proved.

"Murder of Michael Milano: not proved.

"Murder of Al Plummer: not proved.

"Murder of William O'Brien: not proved.

"Murder of James O'Toole: not proved.

"Murder of Al Notorangeli: not proved.

"Conspiracy to murder James Sousa: not proved.

"Murder of James Sousa: not proved."

We were in shock. The jury had decided that the prosecution had not presented enough evidence to prove those earlier murders. Wyshak, Kelly, and Hafer looked dejected. Whitey sat still. The defense lawyers exchanged a glance with each other. They must have been pleased. Even though Whitey had been found guilty overall, it was a minor victory.

Hourihan continued reading the jury's verdict:

"Murder of Paul McGonagle: proved.

"Murder of Edward Connors: proved.

"Conspiracy to murder Thomas King: proved.

"Murder of Thomas King: proved.

"Murder of Francis 'Buddy' Leonard: not proved."

"You've got to be kidding me!" one of the relatives of Leonard shouted from the gallery. Jurors had found another murder where there wasn't enough evidence to convict beyond a reasonable doubt.

"Murder of Richard Castucci: proved.

"Conspiracy to murder Roger Wheeler: proved.

"Murder of Roger Wheeler: proved.

"Murder of Debra Davis—" Hourihan paused for a moment and turned to the judge. She asked what "NF" meant. Hourihan nodded and continued reading: "No finding."

Steve Davis moaned from the gallery. We couldn't believe it. They must have been undecided as to whether Flemmi or Whitey strangled Davis. Whitey was likely pleased with that result.

Hourihan continued reading the verdict: "Murder of Brian Halloran: proved.

"Murder of Michael Donahue: proved."

Pat Donahue placed her hands on her heart and cried. The family embraced each other.

"Conspiracy to murder John Callahan: proved.

"Murder of John Callahan: proved.

"Murder of Arthur 'Bucky' Barrett: proved.

"Murder of John McIntyre: proved.

"Murder of Deborah Hussey: proved."

Overall, the jury decided that the government had produced enough evidence to prove eleven of the nineteen murders.

The clerk moved on to the extortion acts, which were proven with regard to victims Richard "Dickie" O'Brien, Michael Solimando, Stephen and Julie Rakes, and Richard Buccheri. The extortions of Kevin Hayes and Raymond Slinger were "not proved." The money laundering and narcotics distribution acts were "proved."

Count Three charged Whitey with extortion conspiracy: rent, and the jury found him guilty. Count Four dealt again with the extortion of Kevin Hayes, and the jury checked off the box for "not guilty." Count Five alleged money laundering, which came back guilty. Counts Six through Twenty-six listed individual mortgage payments as money laundering, and the jury came back with guilty findings on each. Count Twenty-seven involved the illegal transfer of ten thousand dollars to John Martorano: "Guilty."

The jury returned guilty findings for all remaining counts, which consisted of possession of firearms, machine guns, and firearms with obliterated serial numbers. The foreperson signed and dated the verdict slip August 12, 2013.

Judge Casper thanked jurors for their service. When they left, Whitey gave his brother John a thumbs-up sign. As marshals escorted him away, Cheryl Connors yelled out: "Rat-a-tat-tat, Whitey!" Later she told us that she wanted to remind Whitey about his jailhouse tape where he mimicked a machine-gun sound when referring to victim Eddie Connors.

We walked through the front doors of the courthouse, and into the August heat. Throngs of media and onlookers surrounded the courthouse.

A shaky Pat Donahue felt relieved and happy with the verdict, but sorry for relatives affected by the acts of murder that were not found to be proved. Steve Davis was distraught. He had been waiting for so long to see justice come full circle for his sister, Debra. The "no finding" left him confused.

U.S. Attorney Carmen Ortiz, flanked by Fred Wyshak, Brian Kelly, Zack Hafer, and the lead investigators, congratulated the prosecution team: "This day of reckoning for Bulger has been a long time coming. . . . So many people's lives were so terribly harmed by the criminal acts of Bulger and his crew. . . . We hope they find some degree of comfort in the fact . . . that Bulger is being held accountable for his horrific crimes."

Donald Stern, former U.S. Attorney for the District of Massachusetts told us: "I'm pleased with the verdict and how it all came out at trial. It revealed the truth about Whitey, his violent crimes, drug dealing, his long reign of terror. He's not this grandfatherly old man. It was all part of Boston's painful past, and now it's time to move on. It's time for the healing to begin. The trial was a victory for dedicated law enforcement and prosecutors, who worked for years to bring Whitey to justice. The victims' families received some closure, their day in court."[1]

When the buzz of the press conferences and interviews died down later that evening, we joined many of the victims' relatives for dinner at the seaport. It was bittersweet. We couldn't celebrate the verdict in its entirety for some were disappointed with the final result. We toasted poor Steve "Stippo" Rakes, who should have been there with us. The toxicology report revealed he had been poisoned with potassium cyanide, and the Middlesex District Attorney claimed it was unrelated to the Whitey Bulger case. He had suffered for hours dying a slow, painful death.

That night, we celebrated our new friendships and toasted each other. It was time to move on.

chapter

4|8

WHITEY'S LETTER

The Stalinist trials were more humane.
—James Bulger

AFTER THE VERDICT, WE DECIDED TO WRITE A LETTER TO WHITEY AT the Plymouth jail to see if he wanted to comment about his trial, and perhaps explain why he didn't testify. Margaret drafted a letter explaining who we were, and that we were writing a book about the trial. Neither one of us thought he would write back, that's why we were so shocked to see the letter wedged in between a stack of bills and junk mail. We hadn't expected that Whitey would comment about his trial at all.

Whitey's letter to us discussed topics ranging from his love for longtime girlfriend Catherine Greig to government corruption going back to the 1960s with the mention of corrupt FBI Agent H. Paul Rico and Joe Barboza, the first top echelon informant who committed perjury so that four innocent men would be framed for murder. He mentions the unjust framing of the innocent men and the huge settlement that the government recently paid out for the wrongful imprisonment. Whitey noted that when Barboza was arrested for murder in California, FBI agents flew out from Boston to save him. He made no mention of former FBI Agent John Connolly.

Whitey was very upset that Catherine was sentenced to eight years in federal prison, and expresses his love for her. He noted that her sentence is higher than others who have committed murder.

Whitey is adamant that he was never an informant, instead, he paid law enforcement for information. He claimed he did not murder Deborah Hussey, Debra Davis, Roger Wheeler, or John Callahan. He commented on the ability of government witnesses to be making money through books and giving lectures. He referred to Weeks and Martorano. According to Whitey, the government prosecutors, especially U.S. Attorney Carmen Ortiz, abused their power. They were on a power trip—the government gang is "all powerful." He also believed that Judge Casper is arrogant and abused her power. Whitey is of the opinion that they are all in the Barboza camp, and the trial was a waste of taxpayers' money. Taxpayers will pay a defense bill of $2.6 million. This does not include the millions spent by the government.

He described his poor conditions, solitary confinement, sleep deprivation, and claimed the old Russian, Stalinist firing squads were more humane than what he had to go through. He described his trial as a show trial.

The beginning of the letter discussed stamps and envelopes because Margaret included a self-addressed stamped envelope and stationery with her letter, but Whitey warned her not to do that for the jail considers that illegal contraband and those often get returned. He mentioned Richard Sunday, his friend from the Alcatraz prison, who Margaret spoke with over the phone for background information.

We have transcribed the letter here:

Miss McLean:

Stamps and envelopes are considered contraband and cannot be sent in. I sign a form and they are supposed to be returned to sender. I have been here 2 years and 2 months and have received many letters too many to save and have no filing system. Have you wrote me in the past, were you in touch by phone with richard b sunday a friend of mine from prison years?

Prefer that you write me and let me know what your interest is, etc. Seems I have received a few things of stamps and envelopes and signed form. In the dark so if you care to write me a few lines and answer above questions.

LEFT: A young Whitey Bulger. RIGHT: Whitey Bulger and Catherine Grieg.

I'm in solitary cell 23 hours a day 5 days a week plus on Tues and Thurs 24 hours a day—little human contact and after long trial little sleep 3–4 hours a day at the most—kind of weary.

Being the main attraction at a "Stalinist show trial" seeing a helpless woman treated worse than mass murderers—a woman you love— kept in a cell 23 hours a day—no Bail—pleads guilty—compare her sentence to killers who have & been free for years.

Going to get off thats a waste of time and ink—I guess the streets are safer with her in prison and the gov witnesses free to write books, give lectures posture + pose and laugh—Pros + gov + judge abused their power Or Ortiz did and is in Barboza camp. What a joke and a waste of taxpayers $—a power trip—had to laugh at judge she enters courthouse and whispers and says quiet in the courtroom I am here BIG DEAL! ARROGANCE! gov gang all powerful.

[in left margin]—AND they make the rules! What a sideshow! They could do this to Catherine!

signing off going to read and escape for a while regret—yes—that disjointed letter—not in a good mood—all of the other women of the gov witnesses treated very well—free—kept property—never jailed or tried— Catherine + I not allowed to write. Goodnight—Jim Bulger

2

The Stalinist trials were more humane. Conducted at Lubyanka prison—when you left courtroom and returning to cell & a guard in the long corridor would step out as they marched you by and shoot you in the back of the head! Or out into courtyard to firing squad.

Not put you through this phony ritual—find you guilty and send down another part of the system—"machine that makes Hamburger out of their targets."

Another overpaid "Prob Dept worker to quiz and play God. Write a big report and decide your FATE—a big show—it was all determined years ago when they interviewed their witness gave the Deals Faustian deals—Barboza play book—2 ex Barboza gang members—Killer Joe killer Deegan—2 crooked FBI agents + him cook up story frame 4 innocent men. Joe says "I killed Deegan because they told me to! 4 men off to prison for leave—Joe B—you're FREE to kill a few more people. Making xxx "the animal" JB story—Barboza arrested for murder in California called Rico and Condon and Justice department to help him they are reluctant he said "get the fuck out of here or I will recant my confession and tell how we framed them" Rico and Condon flew out talked to judge—Joe walks free—32 years later 2 of 4 men dead other 2 proven innocent and freed govmt pays 111,000,000 dollar award for false imprisonment "FRAMED them" Agent Rico upon retirement became head of security for World Jai-Lai over Roger Wheeler is having him investigated for skimming $ Rico and John Callahan get John Matarano (fugitive for 14 years in Fla) to go to OK to kill Wheeler, he does. When caught years later like his mentor Joe Barbaoza he says, Whitey told me to kill him same when he kills Callahan—Rico ex FBI KILLER AGENT arrested dies in jail.

The envelope Whitey sent his letter in.

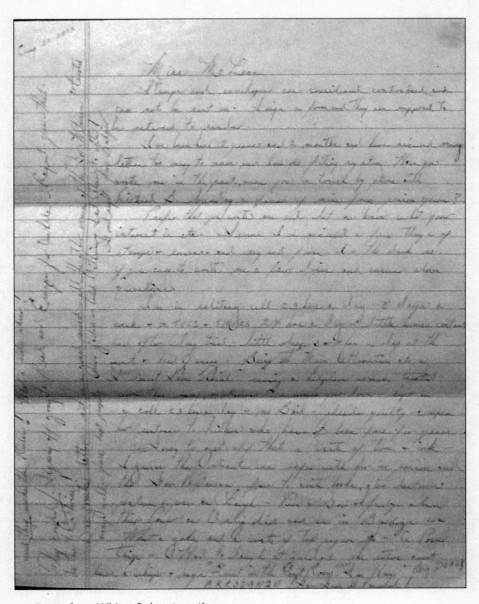

Letter from Whitey Bulger to author.

(cont.)

Letter from Whitey Bulger to author.

(cont.)

Letter from Whitey Bulger to author.

3

When asked about his role in framing 4 with Barboza and they are freed after 32 years in prison "What do you want tears? they can write a book! Rico answering got call from Ronnie Durmondy (Rico FBI agent then) asking for help gang is out to kill me"—Rico told him stay there in the shadows I'll drive over. Rico calls head of gang that's out to kill Ronnie—picks him up "Buddy Mclean" of Winter HIll Gang—they drive over and kill Ronnie Dermondy—Rico then drives Mclean home. Rico also gave Stevie a webley revolver and schedule of Punchy Mclaughlin he will be at W. Rox bus stop at 9am—kill him—Steve is there and kills P. Mclaughlin—Steve had been given info on Mafia since 1960—I never knew it until 2011-captured + attorney told me I got out of prison in 1965 met Steve years later—partners in WH gang!

I never killed any women or ever gave info to anyone—I bought info—everything I wrote has all been said in court by government witnesses. I have not recounted anything that has not been said before and confessed to by some

This I say I had nothing to with murder of Wheeler or Callahan— innocent—Period. And government knows it. Weary not up to going into it

Details I present—have probably wasted our time going on and on about this.

Again goodnight—James Bulger

chapter

4|9

THE MISSING WITNESS

Incalculable damage to the public's respect for the rule of law has been done by the actions of federal law enforcement personnel in Boston from 1965 until the present."
—*The Congressional Committee on Government Reform,*
"Everything Secret Degenerates: The FBI's Use of
Murderers As Informants," February 3, 2004

THROUGHOUT THE TRIAL, WE WONDERED WHY FORMER SPECIAL AGENT John Connolly Jr., Whitey's FBI handler for many years, was not called as a witness for the government or the defense. People continually asked us: Why isn't Connolly's name on the witness list? Can't they subpoena him? Would he take the Fifth and refuse to answer questions under oath? His name had been mentioned dozens of times by witnesses. In 2002, Connolly was convicted and sentenced to ten years in Boston for racketeering, obstruction of justice, and lying to an FBI agent. The charges stemmed from his long-term relationship with Whitey and Flemmi. The jury decided that prosecutors failed to prove the more serious charges that Connolly leaked information which resulted in three murders. Connolly is currently serving forty years in Florida for the second-degree murder with a firearm of John Callahan. The jury found that he leaked information which led to Callahan's murder in 1982. Connolly's case is pending an appeal in Florida based on his assertion that he had nothing to do with the murder of Callahan, and his conviction was unlawful. The University of Miami's School of Law's Innocence Project is representing him.

Both sides had the opportunity to call Connolly as a witness during Whitey's trial. We asked Wyshak why the government chose not to call him. "John Connolly wouldn't be a truthful witness," he replied. "We didn't want to provide him with a platform for his propaganda." The defense knew Connolly would testify about years of corruption within the Department of Justice, yet he'd likely also say that Whitey was an informant, and Whitey insisted he was not.

We wanted to know whether Connolly would have testified at Whitey's trial if he had been called as a witness. If his answer was yes, then we wanted to know what he would have said. People told us not to pursue Connolly for he had not granted any recent interviews. We learned that multiple media outlets had sought Connolly's opinion about Whitey's trial and were turned away. We relentlessly pursued this angle, and connected with Sharon Branco, a licensed private investigator and investigative journalist. We arranged for an interview with Connolly through Branco. It took several months to obtain this exclusive interview.

McLean: "Would you have testified at the Whitey Bulger trial?"

Connolly: "Yes. I would have testified to the truth of the Department of Justice's protection of Bulger and Flemmi."

McLean: "Were Whitey Bulger and Stephen Flemmi FBI informants?"

Connolly: "Yes, Bulger and Flemmi were FBI informants."

McLean: "How did the Department of Justice protect Bulger and Flemmi?"

Connolly: "Instead of prosecuting them for the Winter Hill 1979 race-fix case, they were protected from prosecution by the DOJ. The DOJ set out to frame me for protecting Bulger and Flemmi from prosecution for their authorized, nonviolent criminal activity when the FBI's ultra-secret Top Echelon Informant Program was exposed for the first time. I was scapegoated and falsely accused of doing exactly what the Boston U.S. Attorney's Office and the DOJ did as a matter of policy, procedure, and 'public authority.'"

McLean: "What exactly did the DOJ and the U.S. Attorney's Office do as a matter of policy? Are you saying they granted Bulger and Flemmi immunity to commit crimes in order to use them as informants against the Mafia?"

Connolly: "They protected Bulger and Flemmi from prosecution for nonviolent 'rent' collection from bookmakers and loansharking activities. They were authorized by former U.S. Attorney Jeremiah T. O'Sullivan to engage in gambling/loansharking, nonviolent ordinary criminal activity as cover for their informant activities. O'Sullivan and a colleague notified Assistant Attorney General Gerard McGuire that these 'reputed killers' were being protected from prosecution and being named as 'unindicted coconspirators' in the race-fix case. They protected Bulger and Flemmi to use them against the Mafia despite being aware that they were killers."

McLean: "John Morris testified that you and he approached O'Sullivan and requested that Bulger and Flemmi be omitted from the race-fix indictment. Did Morris lie?"

Connolly: "I never went to O'Sullivan about getting Bulger out of the indictment. In 1978, Whitey knew from his own sources that he and Flemmi could possibly be indicted in the race-fix case . . . his sources were telling him about the grand jury hearings. I reported this to my supervisor, Morris. I remember Morris then telling me that he was not going to lose Whitey Bulger as an informant. Morris told me that when the time was right, he would go to O'Sullivan and get Bulger and Flemmi out of the indictment. O'Sullivan also wanted Bulger and Flemmi to remain FBI informants in order to utilize them for the case against Mafia underboss Gennaro Angiulo. They were very crucial to him, so he used his 'prosecutorial discretion' and removed them from the race-fix indictment."

McLean: "Do you think that's one of the reasons the prosecution team did not call you to testify at Whitey's trial? Do you believe they did not want you attacking the credibility of their star witness, John Morris?"

Connolly: "John Morris was willing to say what I wasn't willing to say. The DOJ worried about what the press would report.

Morris was going to toe the party line and say what he needed to say in return for his freedom and never being charged with a crime. He was going to say that Bulger and Flemmi were never authorized to commit any crimes. Morris, as supervisor, could authorize it and he did. But it was formerly authorized when Bulger met O'Sullivan at the Meridian Hotel in Boston. This is when he told Whitey he could engage in criminal activities."

McLean: "When did the meeting between O'Sullivan and Bulger occur?"

Connolly: "That was about a month or so before the January 29, 1979, prosecution memo for the race-fix case authored by federal prosecutor O'Sullivan and another colleague. The prosecution memo pertained to the protection of informants Bulger and Flemmi. The DOJ had a problem: If the 1979 race-fix prosecution memo that was put under seal had been completely revealed to the public and the media, no matter what reason or justification the DOJ gave for protecting Bulger and Flemmi, all that the Boston papers would've cared about is that federal prosecutors protected Bulger and Flemmi from prosecution for their criminal activities. They could've put Bulger and Flemmi away for twenty to thirty years had O'Sullivan indicted them at that time. Many of their murder victims would still be alive today."

McLean: "Does the 1979 prosecution memo still exist?"

Connolly: "Yes. It is still under executive privilege. To conceal the truth about the DOJ's protection of Bulger and Flemmi, they needed to bury the memo to protect themselves. 'They' meaning the Justice Department, the Boston U.S. Attorney's Office, including O'Sullivan, McGuire, and others. I became the target—hang it all on John Connolly."

McLean: "How did this 1979 memo become privileged?"

Connolly: "Prosecutor John Durham implored Attorney General John Ashcroft and then–White House Counsel Alberto Gonzales, who convinced President George W. Bush to conceal it behind the assertion of executive privilege. They made sure the prosecution memo confirming the DOJ's protection of Bulger and Flemmi was kept hidden from ever seeing the light of day."

McLean: "Why is this document still privileged?"

Connolly: "The truth is being suppressed because the DOJ wants to avoid being blamed for protecting Bulger and Flemmi."

McLean: "Was this 1979 memo withheld from evidence at trial?"

Connolly: "This exculpatory memo was withheld recently at James 'Whitey' Bulger's trial, and at my Boston and Miami trials."

McLean: "Why would you consider the memo exculpatory, meaning evidence that could potentially clear you or Whitey of fault?"

Connolly: "It contains evidence that trial witnesses John Morris, Kevin Weeks, Stevie Flemmi, John Martorano, and Frank Salemme perjured themselves. It destroys the prosecutor's theory that I was a rogue agent acting without authority and that I gave Bulger and Flemmi protection. Salemme later plead guilty to perjury and obstruction of justice, and was not called as a witness in my Florida trial or Whitey's trial."

In our quest for the truth, we tried to obtain the memo, but Wyshak claimed it was still sealed under executive privilege, and noted "you'd be disappointed." We researched government documents, and Margaret, searching for answers, met with a former U.S. congressman. We discovered that the 1979 race-fix memo had been used during a congressional investigation and placed back under seal. We kept wondering what the DOJ wanted to hide for more than thirty years? In addition, why did they want the information hidden?

On February 3, 2004, the Congressional Committee on Government Reform submitted a report entitled "Everything Secret Degenerates: The FBI's Use of Murderers as Informants." They used the January 29, 1979, prosecution memo to question O'Sullivan about why he chose not to prosecute Whitey and Flemmi, known murderers, in the race-fixing case. Attorney James Wilson noted: "This memorandum, one of the ones the President claimed executive privilege over, states . . . that Bulger and Flemmi were part of the conspiracy to actually create the scheme." O'Sullivan admitted to the congressional committee that he knew Bulger and Flemmi were murderers and had tried to downplay their involvement. The 1979 memo proved that O'Sullivan had provided false testimony to the committee, and that he knew Whitey and Flemmi were key players. When presented by surprise with the 1979 memo, a smoking gun, O'Sullivan said, "You got me!"

O'Sullivan indicated there was little he could do at the time. If you go against the FBI, he testified, "they will try to get you. They will wage war on you." He blamed the FBI for Whitey's reign of terror: "because that would have precipitated World War III if I tried to get inside the FBI to deal with informants. That was the holy of holies, inner sanctum. They wouldn't have allowed me to do anything about that, Congressman."

The Committee concluded that "at least some law enforcement personnel, including officials in FBI Director Hoover's office, were well aware that federal informants were committing murders." The Committee warned that the "use of murderers as government informants created problems that were, and continue to be, extremely harmful to the administration of justice. Incalculable damage to the public's respect for the rule of law has been done by the actions of federal law enforcement personnel in Boston from 1965 until the present."

McLean: "Did O'Sullivan's testimony before Congress impact your trial?"

Connolly: "The DOJ sent a letter to the committee requesting that O'Sullivan testify *after* my trial, fearing 'the adverse effect of this hearing on our prosecution of Connolly.'"

We continued with our interview of Connolly, this time questioning him about the Halloran and Donahue murders.

McLean: "In the Whitey Bulger trial, John Morris testified that he passed information to you that Brian Halloran was cooperating with the FBI regarding the Roger Wheeler murder investigation. Thus he testified that you were responsible for the murders of Halloran and Michael Donahue, who were gunned down on May 11, 1982. Was Morris lying?"

Connolly: "Yes, Morris lied. I had nothing to do with the shooting of Halloran and Donahue, and I had nothing to do with causing their deaths. To the contrary, I provided information that, had it been heeded by Strike Force Attorney Jeremiah O'Sullivan, would have saved Halloran's and Donahue's lives."

McLean: "What were you doing at the time?"

Connolly: "I wasn't even assigned to the Boston FBI Office during the critical period of time. I was assigned full-time to the Kennedy School of Government at Harvard University, where I was working towards my Master's Degree in Public Administration. I was absent from the Boston FBI Office from September 6, 1981, to June 10, 1982. In addition, there were prior attempts on Halloran's life before he began his cooperation with the FBI."

McLean: "Can you tell me about those prior attempts on Halloran's life in more detail?"

Connolly: "Quincy and Boston police reports and the testimony of detectives show that Halloran was a target of three attempted shootings in 1981 before he cooperated with the FBI on January 3, 1982, which completely contradicts Weeks's and Morris's Boston 2002 trial testimony."

McLean: "Do you have any more specific information that Morris perjured himself when he testified?"

Connolly: "The false charge by Morris was that he told Connolly [me] of Halloran's cooperation sometime in late April of 1982 [while I was at Harvard], which supposedly led to Halloran's killing. However, the late Brian Halloran, himself, contradicts that story, having told FBI Agents when he began cooperating on January 3, 1982, that Flemmi had been setting up to kill him a few days earlier, when he emerged from a Boston hospital. He fled before Flemmi could kill him."

McLean: "When did Stephen Flemmi and Whitey Bulger first target Brian Halloran?"

Connolly: "According to investigative reports, Flemmi and Bulger were trying to kill Halloran since October of 1981, when Halloran murdered George Pappas in Chinatown, and the rumor was all over the street that he was cooperating with the Massachusetts State Police. The urgency to kill Halloran was necessitated by the fact that Halloran had stumbled upon Bulger and Flemmi meeting with John Callahan months prior to the May 27, 1981, murder of Roger Wheeler, which Callahan conspired to commit with John Martorano. Bulger and Flemmi feared Halloran knew too much and would give them up to the Massachusetts State Police, as Flemmi states in his DEA-6 report—not the FBI."

McLean: "Did you ever try to convince anyone at the FBI that

Brian Halloran's life could be in danger and that he should be placed in the witness protection program?"

Connolly: "Sometime in April 1982, Supervisor John Morris was assigned by ASAC Bob Fitzpatrick to complete a 'threat assessment' on Halloran to determine if he needed to be accepted into the federal witness protection program. This was a decision that only Strike Force attorney Jeremiah O'Sullivan could make, based on FBI intelligence and protocol. Morris's review and assessment was based on information I had provided in my informant reports. Morris concluded, 'There was a clear and present danger to Brian Halloran's life based on Connolly's information.'"

McLean: "What happened after Morris made that assessment?"

Connolly: "Strike Force attorney O'Sullivan summarily rejected Halloran's acceptance into the witness security program, citing his lack of credibility and drug use. Halloran was murdered shortly after O'Sullivan's rejection."

McLean: Were there any other FBI informants reporting that Halloran's life could be in danger?"

Connolly: "Yes. Contemporaneous to O'Sullivan's rejection of Fitzpatrick's 'Threat Assessment,' Special Agent Thomas Daly [in late April/early May 1982] authored two FD-209 TE informant reports reflecting that Halloran had been spotted meeting with FBI agents and that Whitey Bulger, Stevie Flemmi, Jimmy Martorano, and others were concerned. Daley's TE informant opined that if, in fact, Halloran is cooperating with the FBI, 'he should be reeled in before he meets an untimely demise.' The FBI had done what it could to protect Halloran, moving him and his family to a cape house eighty miles from Boston. However, Halloran was reckless and, despite warnings, continued to meet people in Boston. On May 11, 1982, Halloran was gunned down along with Michael Donahue on the South Boston waterfront. Former FBI supervisor Michael Hanigan and former agent Gerald Montanari testified that they had met Halloran on numerous occasions, confirming Daly's information."

McLean: "What else did John Morris know about Halloran's cooperation?"

Connolly: "John Morris was supervisor of the organized crime [OC] squad and was informed about ASAC Robert Fitzpatrick's plan to use Halloran to "flip" John Callahan on Bulger, Flemmi, and Martorano. Morris knew about Fitzpatrick's plan for 'wiring-up' Halloran to obtain incriminating statements from Callahan."

Mclean: "Thank you for your time."

Overall, we'll never know what impact Connolly's testimony would have had on the outcome of Whitey's trial. Both sides made a tactical decision not to call him. Perhaps Connolly's testimony would have clouded some of the relevant issues. Maybe it would have raised too many questions about government secrecy and hidden documents.

The Congressional Committee on Government Reform concluded its February 3, 2004, report as follows: "At a time when the United States is faced by threats from international terrorism, and a number of law enforcement tools are being justifiably strengthened, it is particularly important to remember that [English historian] Lord Acton's words are true: 'Everything secret degenerates, even the administration of justice.'"

5|0

THE CURTAIN CLOSES

This year, 2013, with all that's happened in this city, the City of Boston, both tragic and triumphant, you and the horrible things that were recounted by your cohorts during the course of this trial do not and should not represent this city.
—*Judge Denise Casper, sentencing*

THE COMMUNITY CAME OUT IN DROVES TO SUPPORT THE FAMILIES OF Whitey's victims and to hear how the loss of loved ones affected their lives forever at Whitey's sentencing hearing on November 12, 2013. Judge Casper allowed all victims' relatives who wanted to be heard a chance to speak, including those whose cases were not proven beyond a reasonable doubt.

Assistant U.S. Attorney Brian Kelly stood and addressed the packed courtroom for the last time. He began with Bulger's reign of terror. "It's hard to know where to start. . . . Bulger has been convicted of one heinous crime after another." He pointed out that the families of the victims had suffered most. "The carnage that he has caused is grotesque. . . . He helped flood his own neighborhood with drugs. . . . As long as he prospered, nothing else mattered." Kelly narrowed his eyes and glared at Whitey. "He desperately wants people to believe he wasn't an informant—that's the sham in this trial."

When it was time to hear from the victims' families, some became emotional and lashed out at Whitey, who refused to look up

and acknowledge them. Sean McGonagle raised his voice as he addressed Whitey: "You're a domestic terrorist fueled by greed. . . . My
father [Paul] was a better man than you could ever be."

Tom Angeli, the son of Al Notorangeli, regarded Whitey with disdain. "You lured him in and you executed him."

Marie Mahoney, daughter of William O'Brien, recalled her father
getting gunned down on his way back from Linda Mae's Bakery in
Dorchester with her birthday cake. They had planned a special father-
daughter weekend together. "How does a twelve-year-old come to grips
with a father not coming back?" she asked, as her voice cracked and her
eyes filled with tears.

Pat Donahue brought her husband to life by reminiscing about how
he was always on the floor playing with the kids, and on Christmas Eve
he would put the bikes together with the "handlebars on backward." Michael would wake up happy every morning. "Who does that?" she asked.

Theresa Barrett Bond, the daughter of Arthur "Bucky" Barrett,
asked: "Do you have remorse for taking my father's life? I think you do.
I forgive you." Her voice sounded resolute. Whitey changed his glasses
at that point. Did her words of forgiveness make an impact on him?

In an impassioned speech, David Wheeler blamed both Whitey
and the government. Roger Wheeler, his father, was shot between
the eyes by John Martorano at his country club, and the FBI stymied
the investigation. "Where was the Justice Department in all of this?" He
shook his head. "Was there no oversight at all?"

Whitey chose not to speak. "He believes that the trial was a sham,"
Brennan said. The defense made no desperate pleas for leniency.
They are appealing the conviction primarily on the issue that Whitey
was not allowed to present an immunity defense to the jury. Whitey
claims that the late federal prosecutor Jeremiah O'Sullivan gave him
immunity to commit crimes, and in the interest of justice, the jurors
should have been allowed to hear evidence about it.

The following day, Judge Casper presented Whitey with her findings in a dramatic and impassioned speech. "The scope, the callous-
ness, the depravity of your crimes, are almost unfathomable," she said,
after announcing the names of murder victims. She regarded Whitey
for a long moment and grimaced as if she were trying to rid herself of
a sour taste. "At times during the trial, I wished that we were watching

a movie, that what we were hearing was not real, but as the families of the victims here know too well, it was not a movie. At trial, we were hearing about the real inhumane things that human beings did to other human beings, seemingly without remorse and without regret." Casper highlighted the fear that Whitey instilled in others when he extorted them: "But make no mistake, it takes no business acumen to take money from folks at the end of a gun, no business acumen to shove a machine gun in the groin of Mr. Solimando or place a shotgun in Mr. Buccheri's mouth. It's not savvy, it's not being shrewd, it's not being resourceful, it's what anyone can get at the end of a gun." Whitey barely moved as he gazed up at the judge.

Casper concluded by alluding to the difficult year that the city had with the marathon bombing: "You have over time and in certain quarters become a face of this city. That is regrettable. You and others may be deluded into thinking that you represent this city, but you, sir, do not represent this city. This year, 2013, with all that's happened in this city, the City of Boston, both tragic and triumphant, you and the horrible things that were recounted by your cohorts during the course of this trial do not and should not represent this city."

Casper sentenced Whitey to two consecutive life sentences plus five years, and ordered him to pay fines and over nineteen million dollars in restitution to the victims' families. The money found in Whitey's California apartment will be divided and given to the families, and the search for the rest will continue.

The prosecution team and members of law enforcement received many accolades as they gathered for a well-attended press conference on the courthouse steps. Victims' families swarmed State Police Lieutenant Steve Johnson and DEA agent Dan Doherty, and expressed gratitude for their years of dedication.

Later, the prosecutors shared some of their thoughts with us.

"We're satisfied with the verdict after pursuing James Bulger for so many years," Fred Wyshak said. "It was a complicated case." He thought the most compelling part of the trial testimony came from Dr. Ann Marie Mires, who had testified about the recovery of several of the victims' bodies in 2000. "It was extremely disturbing evidence."

Wyshak had prepared for Whitey's cross-examination for a week. He thought Whitey would take the stand. Had he testified, Wyshak

said, "I would have walked him through all the charges in the indictment, all the murders and extortions. I would have asked about his relationships with John Connolly and John Morris, and other corrupt law
enforcement agents. It would have been about exposing people who
have been hiding in the shadows all these years. The statute of limitations may have run out on some, but we're all about exposing wrongdoing and achieving justice."

Assistant U.S. Attorney Brian Kelly is still embarrassed about drop-
ping one of the machine guns and having it break in several pieces in
open court.

"I still can't believe he did that." DEA agent Doherty laughed. "We
practiced that part with Brian a half-dozen times the day before."

Most relatives of Whitey's murder victims were satisfied with the
verdict and ready to move on. "I think today and yesterday were very
good days for the families," Tommy Donahue said. "They were able to
get a lot of emotions off their chest. It is the beginning of closure after
thirty years of waiting."

His brother Shawn felt differently. "I didn't get closure from this
trial," he said. "All it did was open more doors for me. Pat Nee walked
out the courtroom doors, and they didn't even put him on the stand to
take the Fifth for refusing to testify. Based on the testimony I heard, he
participated in many more murders, including the murder of my father."

Jury foreman Terry Fife attended the sentencing hearing. He volun-
teered for his role as the group's leader and the jurors voted him in. "I
realized I could trust myself to guide people through the deliberations.
It was the most difficult job I've ever had," he said. "At times I had to be
a bad person and influence people in ways that you might not want to."
In describing the evidence of Whitey's crimes, Fife recalled, "It was horrific." Throughout the trial, in an attempt to be fair and impartial, Fife
tried to detach himself from the defendant. "Today, he got what he deserved," he said.

Juror Gusina Tremblay noted that the most meaningful part of
Casper's speech was the following: "Your crimes, in my estimation,
are made all the more heinous because they were all about money."

The sun seemed brighter than usual, nearly blinding, for Whitey's
last day in South Boston. Most basked in the finality of the moment,
especially when Whitey's entourage raced with sirens blaring from

the courthouse for the last time. We watched him go, and the curtain closed on Whitey's final act. It is now time for the healing to begin.

The trial of James "Whitey" Bulger was dramatic and emotional; it impacted all of us in different ways. It brought a community of good people together.

Every day, we passed by a simple inscription etched on the wall in the main rotunda of the courthouse. It came from a speech delivered in 1914 by Louis D. Brandeis, one of the most renowned justices of the Supreme Court of the United States from Massachusetts. "Justice is but truth in action."

Those words from Brandeis made us think, and inspired us on our mission to accurately present the multiple layers and conflicts generated by this trial. As we listened to the testimony from certain witnesses, we wondered if truth was always in action in courtroom eleven. In the words of Lord Acton, "Official truth is not actual truth." What "official" truths pertaining to the history of law enforcement and organized crime in Boston had been passed down to us since the 1960s? Can we rely on those truths? If not, was justice achieved?

September, 2014

ON WEDNESDAY, SEPTEMBER 3, 2014, JAMES "WHITEY" BULGER TURNED eighty-five. Over a year has passed since Whitey left South Boston. He is now subject to the whims of the Federal Bureau of Prisons, where prisoners may be transferred to and from facilities throughout the country at any time. Whitey moved from the Plymouth County Correctional Facility, where he was held throughout the trial, to the Brooklyn Metropolitan Detention Center in New York, to the Federal Transfer Center in Oklahoma City, and on to the United States Penitentiary in Tucson, Arizona, where he lived for approximately nine months. Around the time of his eighty-fifth birthday, he traveled back through the Transfer Center in Oklahoma City, and now resides at the Coleman II Penitentiary in Sumterville, Florida. The prison houses 1,465 male inmates.

"As long as he stays in his orange jumpsuit, I don't care what happens to him," Tommy Donahue said, dismissively.[1] The Donahue family resumed their jobs and daily routines, yet memories from the trial, ranging from the most dramatic and gruesome to quiet, melancholy moments, will always be with them. They will never forget the senseless murder of Michael, who just happened to be in the wrong place at the wrong time.

Terry Fife, the jury foreperson, reflected on how the trial impacted his life: "I would be lying if I didn't say that I think about the trial every day. I can't really explain it, but it seems to be part of me now. When out with friends, if I meet someone new, it inevitably comes up from someone that I was the foreman of the Whitey Bulger jury. I don't mind this at all because I want to share my experience with people, and I'm happy to answer their questions. What is different about the whole experience is the amount of attention I get once people find out I was on the jury."[2]

Fife recalled how little he knew about Whitey and the victims' families when he took his seat for the first time in the jury box on that pristine morning in early June of 2013. "Throughout the trial, during sidebars and other short breaks in the action, I spent a lot of time observing all the people in the packed gallery," he recalled. "We didn't know who most people were. Those we did know were members of the media who sat in the same place every day. In time, we learned who those people were and how they were connected to the trial. The Donahue family, Theresa Barrett Bond, Stephen Davis, Michael Milano's brother, Sandra Castucci, Connie Leonard, and others were there nearly every day to support their loved ones. As a result of the trial, I've had the great pleasure to meet the Donahue family, Stephen Davis, Hank Brennan, and of course, you."[3]

Upon hearing the news of Whitey's transfer to prison in Florida, New Englanders perked up. Specifically, victims' relatives and members of the media questioned whether Florida prosecutors had arranged for the move. Were they finally going to try him for the 1982 murder of John Callahan in Miami? Many remembered the tough-talking Miami-Dade State Attorney Katherine Fernandez Rundle as she paraded before the press upon hearing news of Whitey's capture in June of 2011. She applauded the arrest and announced that Whitey's "criminal activities have been marked by the corpses his killers and associates have left behind in car trunks and alleyways." Rundle shot the audience a determined stare and peered into the cameras, "After a sixteen-year delay, I will be working to ensure that a Miami jury has the opportunity to look him in the eyes and determine his fate just as we did with his associate, ex-FBI agent John J. Connolly, Jr."[4]

Has a Florida jury looked Whitey in the eyes? Not yet. Over three years have slipped by. In fact, it has been over ten since the Miami-Dade grand jurors indicted him for the first-degree murder of Callahan in 2004 while Whitey was on the lam. It shouldn't be that difficult to land a conviction, since a jury in Boston decided that federal prosecutors had produced enough evidence to prove the underlying act of murder against Whitey for the ruthless massacre of Callahan, who was shot in the back of the head by John Martorano in the Fort Lauderdale airport. Jurors believed the words of the hit man when he described Whitey's role in planning the murder. Why not try him? It wouldn't take very long—it's only one murder as opposed to nineteen. Florida carries the death penalty. When pressed, Miami-Dade prosecutor Michael Von Zamft claimed they are waiting for Whitey's federal appeal to be resolved before making any decisions about pursuing the case in Florida.

Whitey still faces open first-degree murder charges in Tulsa, Oklahoma for the execution of businessman Roger Wheeler at the Southern Hills Country Club in May of 1981. Martorano shot him between the eyes with assistance from Joe McDonald. Oklahoma is a death penalty state. The federal jury found enough evidence against Whitey to convict him of the underlying act of murder. Tulsa County District Attorney Tim Harris is also awaiting the outcome of the appeal before he makes the decision whether to commence with a trial. He plans to consult with prosecutors in Florida and the Wheeler family.

Two capital murder cases are riding on Whitey's appeal before the United States Court of Appeals for the First Circuit, which was filed on August 14, 2014. Is it a delay tactic by state prosecutors or does Whitey have a chance at winning? If he wins, he wants a new trial in Boston at the taxpayers' expense. Documents filed on March 21, 2014 reveal that legal bills for defending Whitey at trial topped $2.7 million. The bill does not include countless hours the attorneys spent working on the appeal. If Whitey dies while the appeal is pending, his conviction will be vacated.

The primary issue presented in the appeal is unique, and deals with the defendant's constitutional right to take the stand and testify before a jury of his peers. Whitey claims he didn't get a fair trial, and called it "a sham." He wanted to tell the jury about the protection he gave federal prosecutor Jeremiah O'Sullivan in return for a promise of immunity. Prior to trial, the court conducted a pretrial hearing and ruled that Whitey could not testify about his special relationship with O'Sullivan, and how O'Sullivan had granted Whitey immunity for crimes he was later convicted of committing. By enforcing such a sweeping restriction, lawyers Hank Brennan and James Budreau argue that Judge Casper deprived Whitey of the most important constitutional right to testify in his own defense. Judge Casper also prevented Whitey from presenting evidence and witness testimony related to the immunity agreement. The memorandum of law filed by the defense specifies that "the defendant intended to show the systemic corruption that existed in the federal government during the 1970s through the 1990s and the political and institutional motivations that led Jeremiah O'Sullivan and the Strike Force to provide immunity to James Bulger. Jeremiah O'Sullivan's promise not to prosecute was part of Mr. Bulger's defense. Second, Judge Wolf's 'Salemme Hearings' exposed the DOJ's methods of prosecution and its systemic corruption, revealing that the DOJ made unprecedented deals with organized crime figures and murderers in an attempt to insulate themselves from civil liability and cover up their practices."[5] Brennan and Budreau argue that by not providing the jury with evidence and testimony related to this special immunity deal, their "theories of defense were compromised and infected by errors of constitutional import that violated the right to a fair trial."[6]

Would Whitey really testify if given another chance? Many don't believe it. Would he start spewing off names and pointing fingers? Pat Donahue called him a coward for not taking the stand. "I don't think we'll ever learn who else is responsible for all that government corruption," she said.[7]

"I'll tell you one thing," Tommy Donahue said. "When he dies, he's going to take a lot of secrets to the grave because he's the only one who knows how high up the FBI corruption goes." If Whitey had testified, Donahue had hoped to learn more concerning additional FBI leaks and cover-ups by insulated government officials within the Department of Justice.[8]

Terry Fife, along with many of his fellow jurors, had wondered whether Whitey would take the stand during the trial. Fife recalled, "One element to the immunity defense that would have been compelling is that Bulger would have taken the stand to testify on his own behalf. Imagine Bulger on the witness stand? And then, while under oath, saying, 'I killed him but Jeremiah O'Sullivan said it was okay.'" Fife reflected for a long moment imagining Whitey testifying and shook his head. "Now, that would have been something."

Federal prosecutors believe the law is on their side, and Whitey's lawyers will lose the appeal. They agree with Judge Casper's pretrial ruling that Whitey should not have been able to testify about the alleged immunity agreement with O'Sullivan. The immunity issue should be decided by a judge and not a jury. The prosecutors maintain there is no proof that an immunity agreement ever existed between O'Sullivan and Whitey, and if one did exist, it would amount to an illegal contract. A prosecutor cannot grant anyone carte blanche to commit crimes, and certainly not a license to kill.

The appeals court will likely base its decision on reviewing legal memorandums and hearing oral arguments from both sides. The decision may be appealed to the United States Supreme Court, where the justices would decide whether to grant certiorari and consider Whitey's appeal. If the Supreme Court does not take it up, the lower court's decision will stand. The entire process can take as long as two years.

If the defense wins the appeal and the case is tried again at the taxpayers' expense, would testimony pertaining to Whitey's immunity defense make a difference? Fife believes it would have made an impact during the last trial: "If Whitey had been able to present the immunity defense, things would be very different today. I honestly think the story would not be over. I am not certain if the verdicts would have been different, but I can assure you that all testimony and evidence would have been taken into account during deliberations. Acquitting someone of murder because they say they had permission is not something that would have come easily to me, but given enough reasonable doubt, who knows what may have happened? This would have exposed a level of corruption that would have been extremely difficult for the government to defend. One that they would probably still be defending today." Fife paused for reflection. "In my eyes, immunity defense or not, Mr. Bulger was a career criminal destined to spend the rest of his life in prison."[9]

The victims' relatives are still waiting to receive the money taken from Whitey's California apartment. Pat Donahue expressed frustration with the holdup: "Steve Davis and I keep going to court to ask for the money and they won't give us a straight answer. The defense isn't holding it up—once again, it's the government. We gave them papers from Hank Brennan saying that they don't want the appeal to delay the process. Bulger wants the money to go to the families. We're all very frustrated."[10]

Victims' relatives also expressed frustration with Suffolk County prosecutors and their indecision over whether to indict Whitey, Pat Nee, or Howie Winter on first-degree murder charges. Whitey was convicted of participating in eleven murders in federal court, yet never indicted for a single homicide in Massachusetts state court. Testimony revealed that Howie Winter was the shooter in multiple gangland slayings, and Pat Nee was identified as the third gunman in the backseat when Brian Halloran and Michael Donahue were gunned down in May of 1982. After the trial, representatives from Suffolk County District Attorney Daniel Conley's office informed victims' relatives that they would meet with federal prosecutors to decide what charges, if any, could be pursued. They expressed concern over plea agreements made by prior administrations that could prevent prosecutions.

"I'd be extremely pleased to see them indict Pat Nee for the murder of my father," Tommy Donahue said. "Sometimes it makes you wonder what goes on behind the scenes between Suffolk County and federal prosecutors."[11] Nothing has happened. Who are they still protecting and why?

Former FBI agent John Connolly had a surprise victory in the Florida appeals court. In a 2–1 decision, the court overturned his 2008 conviction for second-degree murder with a firearm. The justices ruled that Connolly never carried or fired the gun that was used to kill John Callahan in Florida. Connolly was 1,500 miles away when Martorano used his own gun to kill Callahan. The court criticized Florida prosecutors for adding the firearm offense to circumvent the four-year statute of limitations. This kind of clever lawyering violated Connolly's constitutional right to due process. Prosecutors disagree with the appeals court ruling and are seeking a rehearing. Connolly is pleased but remains behind bars as he awaits a final decision.

After Boston's big trial, the prosecutors and defense attorneys moved on to the next case, the media vans dispersed, yet many of us who had been consumed by the Whitey Bulger saga for decades couldn't believe it was finally over. The big event we all anticipated, and some thought would never happen, simply arrived and left us during that hot summer of 2013. Nevertheless, New Englanders will long remember the trial and the legend of Whitey Bulger. Many continue to share stories about encounters with Whitey and his gang. A new Whitey story emerges nearly once a week. Terry Fife agreed. "One of the things that surprised me the most after serving on the jury is the connection that people I know have with many who were intimately involved in the trial. After the trial, I learned that one of my golf buddies knows Tommy Donahue from childhood, several older friends from my town placed bets with Dickie O'Brien back in the day. I have friends and neighbors who are related to extortion victims who testified at the trial. Triple O's gets brought up a lot, and I even met someone who as a teenager was offered a job at Rotary Variety by Kevin Weeks. None of this would ever have been revealed if I wasn't on the jury."[12]

Several extortion victims and witnesses expressed relief that the trial was finally over after what felt like decades of waiting. Others have not received the closure they longed for. "We're still searching for answers from the government," Pat Donahue said. "They denied us money—wouldn't compensate us for wrongful death when they were to blame with their FBI leaks. They still won't give us answers. What are they hiding after all these years? I'd like to know."[13] Friends in law enforcement who investigated various angles of the Bulger case agree with Donahue that there's so much more to the story.

The government corruption and long, tangled tentacles of Whitey Bulger run deeper than we'll ever know.

Notes

2: ALL RISE

1. Interview with Patricia Donahue by Margaret McLean on June 7, 2013.
2. Interview with FBI Agent Richard Teahan by Jon Leiberman for *America's Most Wanted,* July 26, 2008.
3. Interview with Howard Winter by Jon Leiberman for *America's Most Wanted,* July 26, 2008.

4: THE PROSECUTOR'S KITCHEN

1. Interview with John Walsh by Jon Leiberman for Sirius XM Radio, August 12, 2013.

5: THE VOLCANO

1. Interview with retired State Police Lieutenant Robert Long by Margaret McLean on August 26, 2013.
2. Interview with Bulger juror Gusina Tremblay by Margaret McLean on September 6, 2013.
3. Interview with Assistant U.S. Attorney Fred Wyshak by Margaret McLean on September 10, 2013.
4. Interview with retired State Police Lieutenant Robert Long by Margaret McLean on August 26, 2013.
5. Interview with retired State Police Lieutenant Robert Long by Margaret McLean on August 26, 2013.
6. Interview with retired State Police Lieutenant Robert Long by Margaret McLean on August 26, 2013.
7. Interview with retired State Police Lieutenant Robert Long by Margaret McLean on August 26, 2013.
8. Interview with retired State Police Lieutenant Robert Long by Margaret McLean on August 26, 2013.
9. Interview with retired State Police Lieutenant Robert Long by Margaret McLean on August 26, 2013.

6: BIG GUNS

1. Interview with retired Massachusetts State Police Colonel Thomas Foley by Margaret McLean and Jon Leiberman on September 12, 2013.

2. Interview with retired Massachusetts State Police Colonel Thomas Foley by Margaret McLean and Jon Leiberman on September 12, 2013.
3. Interview with retired Massachusetts State Police Colonel Thomas Foley by Margaret McLean and Jon Leiberman on September 12, 2013.
4. Interview with Donald K. Stern, former United States Attorney for the District of Massachusetts by Margaret McLean and Jon Leiberman on September 4, 2013.

7: LAST MAN STANDING

1. Interview with retired Massachusetts State Police Colonel Thomas Foley by Margaret McLean and Jon Leiberman on September 12, 2013.

9: MURDER BY THE NUMBERS

1. Interview with Bulger juror Gusina Tremblay by Margaret McLean on September 6, 2013.

10: MORE MURDER BY THE NUMBERS

1. Interview with Bulger juror Gusina Tremblay by Margaret McLean on September 6, 2013.
2. Interview with Howard Winter by Jon Leiberman for *America's Most Wanted,* July 26, 2008.

11: BATMAN

1. Interview with Bulger attorney Hank Brennan by Margaret McLean on September 1, 2013.
2. Interview with Bulger attorney Hank Brennan by Margaret McLean on October 4, 2013.

12: REMEMBER US

1. Interview with Diane Sussman by Margaret McLean and Jon Leiberman in August, 2013.
2. Interview with Diane Sussman by Margaret McLean and Jon Leiberman in August, 2013.
3. Interview with Diane Sussman by Margaret McLean and Jon Leiberman in August, 2013.
4. Interview with Bulger juror Gusina Tremblay by Margaret McLean on September 6, 2013.

14: THE THROAT OF THE DRAGON

1. Interview with Bulger attorney Hank Brennan by Margaret McLean on September 27, 2013.

15: A RAT'S FILE

1. Interview with Assistant U.S. Attorney Fred Wyshak by Margaret McLean, November 14, 2013.
2. Interview with Patricia Donahue by Margaret McLean, September 18, 2013.
3. Interview with retired Massachusetts State Police Colonel Thomas Foley by Margaret McLean and Jon Leiberman, September 12, 2013.

18: DOUBLE LIE

1. Interview with Patricia Donahue by Margaret McLean on September 18, 2013.

19: THE GREAT PROTECTOR

1. Interview with Assistant U.S. Attorney Zachary Hafer by Margaret McLean, on November 14, 2013.
2. Interview with Bulger attorney Hank Brennan by Margaret McLean on November 24, 2013.

21: ON THE WATERFRONT

1. Interview with Patricia Donahue by Margaret McLean on September 18, 2013.

22: WARM BLOOD, COLD WATER

1. Interview with Stephen "Stippo" Rakes by Margaret McLean on July 8, 2013.
2. Interview with Theresa Stanley by Jon Leiberman for *America's Most Wanted* on July 26, 2008.

23: TWO RATS

1. Interview with Bulger juror Gusina Tremblay by Margaret McLean on September 6, 2013.
2. Interview with J. W. Carney Jr. by Margaret McLean on July 9, 2013.

25: WHY?

1. Interview with Bulger juror Gusina Tremblay by Margaret McLean on September 6, 2013.

28: SILENCED

1. Interview with Brian Burke by Margaret McLean on November 12, 2013.

29: BURNT BLOOD

1. Interview with Theresa Stanley by Jon Leiberman for *America's Most Wanted*, July 26, 2008.

33: A LICENSE TO KILL

1. Interview with Hank Brennan by Margaret McLean, September 27, 2013.

35: CAPTURED

1. Interview with John Walsh by Jon Leiberman on Sirius XM radio, August 12, 2013.
2. Interview with FBI Agent Richard Teahan by Jon Leiberman for *America's Most Wanted,* July 26, 2008.

36: STONEWALLED

1. Interview with Robert Fitzpatrick by Margaret McLean for *It's A Crime Radio* on June 15, 2013.
2. Interview with retired Massachusetts State Police Colonel Thomas Foley by Margaret McLean and Jon Leiberman on September 12, 2013.
3. Interview with Robert Fitzpatrick by Margaret McLean for *It's A Crime Radio* on June 15, 2013.
4. Interview with Patricia Donahue by Margaret McLean on September 18, 2013.

37: RING THE BELL!

1. Interview with Robert Fitzpatrick by Margaret McLean for *It's A Crime Radio* on June 15, 2013.

38: TOP ECHELON INFORMANT

1. Interview with retired Massachusetts State Police Colonel Thomas Foley by Margaret McLean and Jon Leiberman on September 12, 2013.
2. Interview with Donald K. Stern, former United States Attorney for the District of Massachusetts by Margaret McLean and Jon Leiberman on September 4, 2013.

39: REASONABLE DOUBT

1. Interview with retired Massachusetts State Police Colonel Thomas Foley by Margaret McLean and Jon Leiberman on September 12, 2013.

42: HE BLINKED

1. Interview with Donald K. Stern, former United States Attorney for the District of Massachusetts by Margaret McLean and Jon Leiberman on September 4, 2013.

46: BEHIND CLOSED DOORS

1. Interview with Bulger juror Gusina Tremblay by Margaret McLean on September 6, 2013.

2. Interview with Bulger juror Gusina Tremblay by Margaret McLean on September 6, 2013.
3. Interview with Bulger juror Gusina Tremblay by Margaret McLean on September 6, 2013.

47: THE JURY SPEAKS

1. Interview with Donald K. Stern, former United States Attorney for the District of Massachusetts by Margaret McLean and Jon Leiberman on September 4, 2013.

EPILOGUE

1. Interview with Tommy Donahue by Margaret McLean on November 14, 2013.
2. Interview with Terry Fife by Margaret McLean on September 14, 2014.
3. Interview with Terry Fife by Margaret McLean on September 14, 2014.
4. Statement of Miami-Dade State Attorney Katherine Fernandez Rundle on June 23, 2011.
5. United States of America v. James Bulger, Brief of Appellant, pp.18–19, filed August 14, 2014.
6. United States of America v. James Bulger, Brief of Appellant, pp.18–19, filed August 14, 2014.
7. Interview with Patricia Donahue by Margaret McLean on August 25, 2013.
8. Interview with Tommy Donahue by Margaret McLean on November 14, 2013.
9. Interview with Terry Fife by Margaret McLean on September 14, 2014.
10. Interview with Patricia Donahue by Margaret McLean on September 9, 2014.
11. Interview with Tommy Donahue by Margaret McLean on November 14, 2013.
12. Interview with Terry Fife by Margaret McLean on September 14, 2014.
13. Interview with Patricia Donahue by Margaret McLean on September 9, 2014.

About the Authors

MARGARET MCLEAN practiced law as a criminal prosecutor and civil litigation attorney. She is a legal analyst on numerous national television and radio shows, and has a nationally syndicated weekly radio show called *It's a Crime Radio.*

JON LEIBERMAN is an award-winning investigative correspondent, host, producer, and victim advocate. Jon hosts *Leiberman Live* on Sirius XM and is a crime contributor for CNN, HLN, and *WildAboutTrial.com,* and a crime blogger for *The Huffington Post.*